Modernizing England's Past

English Historiography in the Age of Modernism, 1870–1970

Michael Bentley

The Wiles Lectures for 2003

CAMBRIDGE
UNIVERSITY PRESS

CAMBRIDGE UNIVERSITY PRESS

Cambridge, New York, Melbourne, Madrid, Cape Town, Singapore, São Paulo

Cambridge University Press
The Edinburgh Building, Cambridge CB2 2RU, UK

Published in the United States of America by Cambridge University Press,
New York

www.cambridge.org
Information on this title: www.cambridge.org/9780521602662

First published 2005

Printed in the United Kingdom at the University Press, Cambridge

A catalogue record for this publication is available from the British Library

ISBN-13 978-0-521-84178-8 hardback
ISBN-10 0-521-84178-X hardback
ISBN-13 978-0-521-60266-2 paperback
ISBN-10 0-521-60266-1 paperback

Contents

Acknowledgements

An invitation from the Wiles Trust to deliver the annual series of Wiles Lectures in Queen's University, Belfast would brighten any historian's year and my overriding indebtedness is to the Trust for that very welcome opportunity. In my own case the invitation perhaps carried an unusual responsibility. For in 2003, when the lectures were delivered, we were approaching the fiftieth anniversary of the publication of Herbert Butterfield's first Wiles Lectures as *Man on his Past* in 1955; and because I was known to be working on the life and work of Butterfield, it was thought appropriate that the lectures and subsequent book could mark that anniversary. This context licensed me to talk a good deal about Butterfield, but it also implied that the printed version of the lectures should appear in 2005 and I have made every effort, with the collaboration of Cambridge University Press, to make that happen, despite inevitable frustrations in limiting the scope of the volume. As well as thanking the Trust collectively, I should express particular gratitude to Professor Peter Jupp and Professor Sir Ian Kershaw for their support throughout, and to the 'home team' at Queen's for their hospitality and enthusiasm, most especially to Professor David Hayton and Professor Jonathan Gorman. One of the extra delights associated with the Wiles is the chance to invite a panel of distinguished guests to discuss the lectures. I am enormously grateful to all those who came and would want to mention, invidiously, Professor Reba Soffer who made the trip from California and Professor John Burrow who was and continues to be a fount of encouragement. The comments, criticisms and affirmations of all these people have greatly strengthened the book, which none of them has seen and for which none is responsible.

The text rests preponderantly on archival sources and all working historians know how difficult it is to carry out scholarship of this kind when tied to professional duties in one's own institution, not to mention the writing of lectures against the clock for a fixed deadline. I was helped to navigate this problem in three ways and each has left me with an obvious debt that I wish to acknowledge. First, the Leverhulme Trust appointed me to a Research Fellowship in 2002–3 which freed me from teaching obligations. Second, the college in Cambridge with which I have a long association, Peterhouse, elected me to a Visiting Fellowship during that year. I am overwhelmingly grateful to the Master and Fellows for that delightful period of residence during which much of the writing was done. Third, my own University of St Andrews showed great generosity and flexibility in granting me leave of absence in order to prepare the lectures.

My greatest debt remains that owed to my wife, Professor Sarah Foot.

MB
University of St Andrews

Note on the text

All books referred to in the footnotes were published in London unless otherwise cited. All quotations retain their original form and punctuation except where an authorial intervention has been marked by square brackets.

The following abbreviations have been used in referring to periodicals:

A	*Albion*
AHR	*American Historical Review*
BIHR	*Bulletin of the Institute of Historical Research*
CHJ	*Cambridge Historical Journal*
CR	*Cambridge Review*
EcHR	*Economic History Review*
Econ.	*Economica*
EHR	*English Historical Review*
H	*History*
H&T	*History and Theory*
HJ	*Historical Journal*
HR	*Historical Research*
HT	*History Today*
HZ	*Historische Zeitschrift*
JBS	*Journal of British Studies*
JMH	*Journal of Modern History*
P&P	*Past and Present*
PBA	*Proceedings of the British Academy*
RH	*Revue historique*
SdS	*Storia della storiographia*
Spec.	*Speculum*
TLS	*Times Literary Supplement*
TRHS	*Transactions of the Royal Historical Society*
YAJ	*Yorkshire Archaeological Journal*

Introduction

In deciding what to offer the Wiles Trust for their annual series of lectures in 2003, I hit on the title 'English Historiography in the Age of Butterfield and Namier'. Traces of that concentration still exist in this published version, especially in chapters 4, 6, 7 and 8 which are revised versions of the original lectures. But what I had in mind to attempt in the series was not a simple description of what Butterfield and Namier had written, nor even an analysis of their arguments and eventual antagonism. Instead I set out to use these two historians as icons or symbols of opposed modes of thought that I recognized in the inter-war period and through into the 1950s and 1960s. One of them, epitomized for this purpose in Lewis Namier, saw the task before historians as one resting on the destruction of what had gone before, especially the so-called whig theory of history, and the substitution of an aggressive new methodology and ambition designed to make twentieth-century historiography more modern and sophisticated. The other epitome, for all his well-known criticisms of the 'whig interpretation', reacted against the process of modernization that Namier and others embodied and sought to reinstate an idea of history as a narrative art concerned with the lives and souls of humanity. The small scale of the Wiles series and the distinction of the invited panel that accompanies it made this focus conceivable: I was addressing an audience who knew the historical material well and had even been personally involved with the lives and work of my protagonists. For the book, however, it was clear that this would not do. Many readers will have only the haziest sense of who Butterfield and Namier were and lack any helpful context in which to situate them, while the argument between them itself draws on terms and assumptions that only those close to the period will find intelligible. So I sought a path that would widen into a more general discussion of the issues raised and take the argument far beyond the two historians with whom I had started.

This thinking took me towards stipulating 'modernism' as an organizing idea within English historiography in the century or so after 1870 and deciding to provide a fuller account of what it involved. The term

1

has never been defined or explained: indeed it is rarely used at all. Tutors in the universities who find themselves teaching classes on the impact of 'postmodernism' on historical writing know all too well the student who says, in effect: 'If this is postmodernism, does that mean there was something called modernism that it's supposed to be "post"?' This book says that there was, or at least that it may be helpful to conceptualize the period under some such rubric; but before we can make any sense of it we have to think about the language in which English historiography tends more commonly to be conceived.

Every historian, at whatever level, who takes an interest in the development of the subject will have heard of the 'whig interpretation of history' and appreciate that this way of thinking about the English past held great sway in the nineteenth century at the hands of famous narrative historians such as Macaulay, Freeman and the inevitable Bishop Stubbs. Most historians, at least at the higher levels, will have heard of 'postmodernism' as a comparatively recent mode of thought that has preoccupied some people working in the humanities for the past thirty years or so and which they associate with the masters of Parisian obscurity: Roland Barthes, Michel Foucault, Jacques Derrida, Julia Kristeva. In between the epochs in which these formations became dominant – the whig and the postmodern – stands the history that dare not speak its name, not least because it does not have one. Some would describe the years between (say) 1890 and 1970 as a period of 'positivism'. Others might reach for the more sneering 'empiricism'. Defenders of the achievements of these years would prefer to talk about a period of growing 'professionalism'; or they look back with some nostalgia on post-war times when history came to be thought of as a form of 'social science'. Each of these ways of characterizing the period offers a glimpse of something important about a facet of its nature. I prefer to talk about an *age of modernism* because I want to introduce the reader to a broader and more sympathetic conception of these important years than any reduction of them to a single way of organizing the past or to a sideswipe against an outmoded style of historical writing seems likely to do. The essential nature of that modernism – its origins, distinctive characteristics, achievements, weaknesses and consequences – is what this book sets out to identify.

Constraints of time and space have made the definition less articulate than it might have been if set in a still wider frame of comparative study. It would have been a valuable and challenging task to place the developments discussed here in a European and American context to a greater degree than has been possible: this must await its own authors. But at least we have an opportunity here to think across a significant era of development within a highly significant state and try to chart the transitions and repercussions that surrounded the modernist project in England.

'Modernism' encourages one form of primitive understanding if only by telling us that it came before 'postmodernism'. But it also encourages a misconception that postmodernists tend to share because of their confidence – sometimes plausible, sometimes absurd – that the onset of a postmodern era should be seen as some authors now see the Enlightenment of the eighteenth century – as a fundamental threshold across which all serious thought must pass if it is to acquire intellectual respectablity. This mood consigns some of the greatest historians of the twentieth century to a purely local interest as embodiments of a discredited genre. The modernists themselves made matters worse, moreover, by going out of their way to imply that they did not constitute a genre of any kind. They saw themselves as intelligent, critical historians approaching the technical work of history in a systematic, increasingly professional, way and thinking about the task of historical enquiry, when they turned their mind to it, as the application of a higher common sense. Individualists to a man (and woman after 1918), they saw their common work as no more than a random mosaic of writing with no connecting tissue beyond the intentions and interests that make people write about the past. They would have disliked and probably resented any attempt to see English historiography between 1890 and 1970 within a common frame. Although this book has been written partly in their defence, therefore, they would have hated it because it probes assumptions and connexions whose existence they would have denied and it brings onto the page private reflections never intended for sharing. That is the price of writing critically about historiography: the subject does not want to tell you what you want to know.

There is another misconception which helps explain why this book is arranged in a particular form. All talk of 'ages' asks for trouble, in one sense, by asserting beginnings and endings that prove notoriously hard to ground in documentary evidence. In the case of English historiography over the past two centuries we face a pre-cast list of 'ages' that this book wishes to challenge. The familiar story is that whig historiography flourished until it became undermined by a new breed of historian before the First World War and then was crushed by the cultural collapse of the conflict itself. What followed – the subject of this book – is then seen as a featureless period of professionalization and inward-looking technical history until the new Enlightenment dawned sometime after 1970 and we slid into the postmodern condition. In fact the 'Prelude' that begins this study argues that whig history survived *alongside* modernism in

England as a continuing critique of its tendencies. The first part of the book then explores some of the categories that had been central to the whig understanding – constitutional history, the place of religion, imperial history – in order to demonstrate how bifocal the age of modernism often was and the degree to which this complexity is deepened when we think about the relation between past and future in the minds of our historians, which is the point of chapter 4. It shows the sense of dislocation in the historical community in a period that is often thought of as dedicated to a particular series of purposes and projects. Indeed, by the end of the first part of this book the reader may be forgiven for wondering whether there is anything distinctive about 'modernism' at all.

The second half of the book suggests that there is. Having reviewed some of the preoccupations of the whig interpretation and examined their persistence in the twentieth century, the text focuses on what is new within the work of historians in these years and discovers important new territory among their projects – especially in the fields of economic and social history – but also reports a widespread commitment to the idea of modernization as a value, a sense that history needs somehow to be brought up to date. It demonstrates, too, that political history also found new breath, not least in its obsession with the English parliament: a whig subject treated now in a modernist style. Chapter 6 selects a case study in the relationship between the new approach and its critics by examining how the eighteenth century underwent transformation at the hands of the modernists, Lewis Namier pre-eminent among them, but only by stirring latent resentments among its critics, among whom Herbert Butterfield deserves pride of place. In effect we watch the conflict between the modernizing tendency and a reviving whig mood working itself out within discussions of eighteenth-century politics. Topics and case studies are important to the case being made here and a longer book would have far more to say about them. But still more urgent is the issue of methodology because if topics are plural, method suggests commonality across the diverse enquiries made by historians. Chapter 8 in many ways is the most important of the book in revealing how modernist historical method was envisaged and with what results. The final word, like the first, is about transition. The whigs were not 'superseded' by the modernists and modernism did not simply disappear in the face of postmodernity. Neither, however, did their modernist projects survive in the form in which they had recommended them during their years of dominance. Complicated currents in the culture between 1960 and 1980 turned English historiography away from the world they had complemented and called a different one into being, an age that we think of as our own.

Prelude: after the whigs

The whig history of England was a Bad Thing, most modern historians would agree. It worked, they might say, simply as a form of English literature and supplied uplift and emotional satisfaction rather than a careful and scholarly account of evidence. It sought too wide an audience for its own good and reduced the difficulties of real historical 'research' to swirling narratives of progress, improvement and derring-do. It rested on an implicit idea of the superiority of English culture in which the constitution continued to represent the most beautiful combination ever framed, in which the empire seemed no more than a natural outcome of character and enterprise, in which God was tolerant of Nonconformists but remained Himself a moderate Anglican. If it were triumphalist, it announced no triumph of the will, for that would suggest the intentions of the braggart. Rather, the whig historians told the story of a disposition bred into the national stock over a thousand years, one whose crucial adjectives – 'manly', 'frank', 'decent', 'staunch' – bonded naturally to the favourite collective nouns of England – 'people', 'nation', 'state', 'race'. And in accomplishing its stories the whig tendency fostered purposes and directions within the time-line of English development: always looking over its shoulder from a particular present that it sought to defend and evangelize. Constantly digging in the past for roots and seeds that would one day flower in national life, the whigs fertilized their creations with a special form of genius which made mere historical phenomena look like today's cherished institutions and conventions. Or their plants would come up instead as heroes, for whigs saw them as symbols of the grand narrative that was the English past, rather in the way that saints embody theology and bring its lessons down to the level of the common man. Through the nineteenth century, this mode of history that came to be called 'whig' acquired great strength: it so dominated the way in which the Victorians' past became framed that it becomes hard to think of anybody writing then who did not in some sense reflect its preoccupations. Even raging reactionaries such as Thomas Carlyle or Sir William Alison embedded their anti-Whig

5

proposals in a whig-historical form. Narratives varied in their force but narrative itself never did: it held a monopoly on how to write about the past and did not even begin to weaken before 1890.

Who, then, were 'the whigs'? Often they did not belong or subscribe to the group of progressive politicians known as capital-W Whigs, in the sense of people committed to a moderate reformism in politics with a particular relationship to what later became known as the Liberal party, though many of them replicated the recommendations of that political outlook in their historical writings. (It may help emphasize this distinction to indicate the political formation known as the Whigs with their capital letter and to render the historical whigs with a lower case one: that will in any case be the practice followed here.) The historical whigs formed an interlocking dynasty of authors with perhaps Henry Hallam and Thomas Babington Macaulay at one end of their period of dominance and William Stubbs, J. R. Green and E. A. Freeman at the other end.[1] In the early years – say from 1820 to 1850 – the tendency reflected an eighteenth-century heritage that celebrated the Glorious Revolution in which William III of the Netherlands had replaced – almost bloodlessly – the despicable Catholicism and tyranny of James II and substituted, via his successors, a new age of Protestant stability and prosperity with its constitution that supposedly secured through its checks and balances ways of guarding against interest-groups or democratic enthusiasms. It recognized, too, an historiographical enemy in David Hume whose *History of England*, written polemically to attract readers and backwards chronologically to guarantee speedy sales, had appalled right-thinking men for its sympathies with Charles I and therefore the cause of absolutism.[2] Having given the years after Charles's execution their due and extolled the eighteenth-century system of governance for which it had been the precondition, the nineteenth-century whigs instead allowed their minds to wander further back into the mists and to construct an ingenious and persistent account of English origins in Saxon forests, with a series of roles for the Norman Conquest, the tyranny of King John, Magna Carta, the first parliament of the realm and a crescendo of constitutional success, interrupted only by the malign Tudors, that culminated in the Bill of Rights of 1689. The other end of the nineteenth century became messier. The simple-mindedness of early whigs disturbed the later ones who wanted to mix a whig temperament with an awareness of science that their century had made *de rigueur*. In

---

[1] The reader will meet all these people again, and their biographies, in the pages that follow. Detail need not detain us now.
[2] David Hume, *History of England* (6 vols., 1762).

the hands of the Tory William Stubbs, Bishop of Oxford, for the medieval period and S. R. Gardiner and C. H. Firth for the seventeenth century, whiggery acquired an intellectual pedigree that its forebears neither possessed nor wanted. The overwhelming narrative supplied by Thomas Babington Macaulay, possibly the most widely owned and read history of England in the nineteenth century, now raised not only eyebrows but the flicker of a smile among those who believed that they had moved to higher ground. Accelerated by the sceptical power of a new breed of historian epitomized in the brilliance of F. W. Maitland, whiggery had begun its turn downwards (we are told) and met its Waterloo on the Somme.

It is a plausible and suggestive story: rise of the whigs in the age of Romanticism; annealing of the whigs in the age of science; annihilation of the whigs in a total war their world-view could not countenance. But it amounted to a way of thinking about the history of modern English historiography that betrayed two strange characteristics. First, it dealt in stark sequences divided from one another by a single threshold. Before the First World War a prevailing whig disposition supposedly suffered corrosion from a style of forensic enquiry that turned out to be more critical, more searching, more intelligent than its predecessor. The war then brought not only death, pain and loss but also futility; and, though whiggery could face the obvious consequences with a brave face, it had no stomach for – more importantly, it could give no account of – pointlessness. Always a doctrine of encouragement towards a progressive future that was contained in the past, whig history had nothing to say, the argument runs, when faced with a future-towards-death. So the very conditions that would give rise to the bleak recommendations of existentialism in the twentieth century were the same ones that suppressed the possibility of a whig cosmology after 1918. A second characteristic of this cast of mind lay in its having no vocabulary in which to talk about what came after the whigs. Quite simply, there had been a period of whig attrition before the war, after which the disposition had disappeared under the weight of tragedy. The historians who survived then built on the foundations of anti-whig historical writing and did something else, something altogether better but nameless, and they are the basis on which our historical profession now rests. The whigs died and left behind as the new voice of history . . . , well, *us*.

This book is going to worry about both of these assumptions. To begin with, the whigs did not die: they survived science, they survived Maitland; they found ways to survive the First World War and by keeping their heads either down, or at least out of the universities, they survived the twentieth century. True, their approach to history became unfashionable even as their celebrated avatar (and Macaulay's great-nephew), G. M. Trevelyan, rose to his peak of popularity with a general reading public. They lost the commanding heights of the academic economy to hard-nosed professionals and found themselves the butt of insufferable condescension from scholarship boys, even scholarship *girls*, from schools they had never heard of, located in towns far from Oxford and Cambridge and the British Museum. But they did not die. Their own stream of tendency, an idea precious to all whigs, took them away from glorious pronouncement and towards a form of distressed criticism, as though trying to remind the new culture that it owed something to the past's legacies. Modern people should think about what kind of society would result, whigs seemed to be saying, if history became a row of small-minded monographs written by authors calling themselves 'doctor', whose life-experience and sense of English culture extended no further than taking cups of tea in the Institute of Historical Research. The view that historians needed to write about Life and ought to get one of their own in order to do so has survived into the era of the tele-don, as has the notion that books are for reading by a wide audience rather than for reference purposes among a self-sealing elite. Indeed, in what we nowadays call the postmodern condition, whig presupposition has revived to a surprising degree, and it is the successors of the whigs who now look outmoded as the defenders of a narrow and unrewarding mindset, over-impressed by scientific method, under-impressed by the need to communicate their thinking to a wider audience, more responsible for killing history in its best sense than preserving it.[3]

'Postmodern' fashions have contributed to throwing doubt on the second assumption, that whig romanticism was succeeded by 'proper' history that we all now practise. The whigs themselves did not know that they were whigs, at least not until Herbert Butterfield told them that they were in 1931.[4] The post-whigs, similarly, had no sense of identity with their own era until a phase of thought came along that enabled posterity to shape it for them. After the whigs came the modernists, as we shall call them,[5] but no one could *see* 'modernism' until it became a contested or superseded entity itself, and only now is it becoming apparent that we lack a definition, even an understanding, of what preceded our own age. Just as we leave the earth in an aeroplane and, looking down,

---

[3] This line of thought is taken further in Peter Mandler, *History and National Life* (2002).
[4] Herbert Butterfield, *The Whig Interpretation of History* (1931).
[5] It will be obvious that by 'modernists' I mean not historians of the modern period but historians of all periods who share the thought-world of a persuasion called 'modernism'.

assimilate the entire landscape in a glance available to no one on the ground, so modernism remained a comprehensive, unremarked environment for historians in England for a century after 1870 until observers could leave it behind, conscious that they had moved somewhere else. Anyone who grew up during the later phases of modernism, absorbing its teaching as a form of practical common sense, recognizes this lack of definition instinctively. For modernists, history – very often mixed up with 'the past': it didn't seem to matter much – was dominated by 'the evidence' which had to be 'analysed'. 'The evidence' was mixed up with 'the sources' and both were taken to be finite and constricting. The whigs and all other forms of apprentice-historical scholarship had 'distorted' the 'truth' of the matter by becoming emotionally involved with their story and by insisting that history had to be a story in the first place. Modernized history did not do this or, if it did, that was because it had fallen into the hands of a bad historian whose 'interpretation' of 'the facts' was 'biased'. So in the universities – rarely in the schools until later – we were made to study 'documents' because these were the bedrock on which all our 'interpretations' would be built; and important as these various views might be, the point of it all lay in transcending the partialities of viewpoint in order to 'get at the truth'. The task of writing history, therefore, had an investigative aspect aimed at 'the sources': one began with 'research' in order to acquire 'the facts' and having retrieved or 'discovered' them, the project involved writing a text that gave a fair, accurate and balanced account of what had been found. Ideally, the historian wore the white coat of the laboratory and brought to the art of writing about the past a dispassionate objectivity. History might be difficult but its objectives as a truth-claiming 'discipline' demanded the same dedication to method and clear-thinking as biology or physics which it resembled far more than the fictional literature beloved of the whigs. The post-whig historian might make the past sound dull or implausible or befuddling in its detail. (S)he would never make it sound 'picturesque' or 'quaint'.

I have inflected the last paragraph with quotation marks in a way that no modernist would feel is helpful or necessary. Teachers of history at any level who taught classes in England in 1920 or 1945 or 1960 would tend to read these words and phrases transparently as part of a conventional wisdom about the subject and rarely see the need to go beyond them or to reverse some of the assumptions on which this entire fabric rests. For one of our postmodern critics, on the other hand, looking down from the skies over Paris, the language of modernist history should be read simply as a hegemonic discourse that operated through internal, and essentially arbitrary, codes. Here we shall picture it differently, for modernism was never as hegemonic as it believed and it was always more than a discourse or system of language-games. I shall speak of it instead as a *persuasion* (a modernist word, if not an English one[6]), by which I intend to suggest an open cosmology which contained a particular view of history as a learned discipline at its centre, but which also surrounded itself with supple, unspoken consensus and changing forms of legitimation that enabled it constantly to reinvent itself until new and unwelcome versions of counter-argument began to make themselves felt after 1970. Dates pose difficulties in thinking about the modernists and it is not productive to obsess about them. Speaking broadly, we might say that Stubbs, a Tory with a whig historical understanding, may stand as bench-mark for a sophisticated version of whiggery. We shall constantly refer back to his *Constitutional History of England* (1873–8) for guidance about the assumptions of that tradition. For a modernist exemplar at the end of the period of dominance of this strand of thought, one could not do better than cite G. R. Elton who committed himself passionately to modernist methods and objectives and dismissed those who failed to follow him as naive, dim or (worse) untrained. His most important statements outlining his attitude appeared in the 1950s and 1960s and, though he died only in 1991, raging against a very different world, it will do little violence to him and others to suggest that 1970 marks the onset of a challenge to the modernist outlook in English history. In thinking about English history between 1870 and 1970 we shall study a century dominated by some celebrated historians, then, but neither the century nor the historians are the subject of the book. The focus is on modernism as a persuasion: a set of attributes, a collection of presuppositions and enthusiasms, a cast of mind.

How to resolve that persuasion into focused language poses major problems of approach and organization. It would be possible to present a theoretical critique of the modernists by deploying the deconstructionist tools of a later generation in order to invigilate their texts and show them wanting. But the point of doing so seems unclear since it would merely show that the historians under consideration were unaware of some postmodern themes such as textuality and representation and that they remained untutored, a mixed damnation, by Foucault and Derrida. They would be blamed as modernists for not having been postmodernists. More intelligent might be an attempt to portray these historians in their own terms and allow their attitudes and assumptions to drift through the book as a cumulative impression, and this is what I have

---

[6] One thinks at once of Marvin Meyers's marvellous book *The Jacksonian Persuasion: Politics and Belief* (Stanford, CA, 1957), but there are other examples.

tried to do here by paying attention to their thought-world (public and private) and the kinds of history that they wrote. There are many historians to talk about, literally hundreds of them, and the book cannot refer to them all or present a précis of their books; nor would it be sensible to try, since the objective here is to produce, not a multi-biography, but rather what Thomas Carlyle wanted all history books to be, the essence of innumerable biographies. On the other hand, many readers will never have heard of, let alone read, the people who fly across the page in quotations or allusions, and I have thought it helpful to supply biographical notes on leading or recurrent figures so that the outline of a career can be followed or a rogue book tracked down if curiosity be caught. The more elusive elements of this history will emerge through quotation because only the contemporary language 'fixes' the image and it is in the atmospherics produced by *obiter dicta* as well as formal histories that a sense emerges of what made these historians tick. That is why stress has been placed on letters and unpublished material, for here one comes upon the subject in unguarded pose, especially when the letter is composed for a close friend, and wisps of assumption and unspokenness rise from the paper when they would surely have been dowsed in a formal manuscript.

Of course, the job of finding any statement of a theoretical position among modernists is rendered more perplexing by their claim never to have had one. Beware the historian who claims to have no theory, for there walks confusion. To elicit confusion from what an author deemed utterly transparent and obvious, however, frequently strains the text, and a patient evocation of snippets across many authors is likely to work better than a remorseless beating into submission of a recalcitrant empiricist who is determined to say nothing beyond what 'the facts' support. For the most part we can follow our modernists in their sense of themselves as practical people doing a practical activity: this is the world that they inhabited and the nature of that world is what has to emerge. Occasionally we shall need to think about a difficulty that they rarely sensed, such as the difference between 'sources' and 'evidence' which, despite the best efforts of their own theorists, Michael Oakeshott and R. G. Collingwood, they consistently blurred.[7] Two distinctions cannot wait, however, for they affect everything that will follow in these pages and considering them at the outset is perhaps especially necessary in a British context, as opposed to a European or American one, because a reluctance to draw them runs deep in British intellectual culture.

---

[7] This issue comes into play in chapter 8, pp. 207–11.

The first concerns 'historiography' as an idea and its difference from 'bibliography'. Thanks to modernist success in stamping its imprint on British education, this difficulty still baffles many working historians who live their lives convinced that to present the historiography of some theme or problem means to write down in chronological order what has been written about it. So they speak about 'the historiography' as synonymous with 'the literature' and regard the search for historiography as a passive act of description. This view of the situation is radically unhelpful. It would turn this book, for example, into a chronological list of books and articles with a little commentary on them indicating what they contained. Indeed, those readers doomed to disappointment by the present account will often base their disappointment on this flawed assumption, that the purpose of an historiographical study is to provide a description of what historians said about the past in order to contrast it, usually, with what we now 'know' and thus 'correct' the misinterpretations of Tout or Neale or Namier, of Helen Cam, or Eileen Power or Joan Thirsk. Beta-minus: must try harder. The starting-point here could hardly be more different. I take historiography to be a creative act of evocation intended to suggest why historical writing turned out the way that it did at the time and in the culture that it did. This book will not trundle its way through a list of authors, therefore, so much as consider some of the themes and generalizations to which their composite writing gives rise. It will supply not one narrative but a series of them seen from the perspective of those themes or generalizations. And it emphatically will not be a neutral or passive description but one person's engaged 'reading' of a historical genre and and a view of what makes it more than a random collection of texts.

A second distinction relates to 'facts' and their difference from 'events'. Modernists wasted little time on such matters and, at their hands, they came to mean almost the same thing. This fascinating confusion comments not only on an important disposition among these historians but, as Barbara Shapiro has brilliantly demonstrated,[8] on a deep structure in English analytical thought that had its origin three hundred years earlier. It began not in speculative reasoning or in the origins of scientific procedure but in *law*. The language of 'fact' as synonymous with the event under consideration by a court became pervasive in the wider culture, and in modern law lives on in a phrase such as 'accessory after the fact', indicating complicity after the crime in question. The assumption that facts live in the past along with the events

---

[8] Barbara Shapiro, *A Culture of Fact: England 1550–1750* (Ithaca, NY, 2000).

that they convey is a cardinal modernist assumption and difficulty. Why does it matter? It opens the possibility of thinking that grasping 'the facts' of a situation is to grasp the situation itself – to put one's hands on the past, as it were, and report how it was. The historian leaves the present and becomes immersed in past time where the events, and therefore the facts, are waiting to be discovered. So factuality becomes preferenced: it never changes, any more than the past does, and it legislates for all forms of 'interpretation'. What is odd about all this is that the generations of Carlyle and Macaulay had written superb essays showing that narratives, and the particular facts that one chose to sustain them, inhabited the historian's present. The past had to be *imagined*, not revisited. The whigs had understood this and given their public pictures and patterns. Modernism reverted to a sense of the past as an object of inspection, as we shall see in thinking about their method, and in doing so lost a critical distinction in historical thought that blurred lines between present and past and turned the historian into a time-traveller with an observer's confidence in what research had uncovered. To suggest to an Albert Pollard or Ernest Neale or Geoffrey Elton that they had mistaken the nature of the sixteenth century became a comment on their eyesight. They had been there and seen it. It was in the Public Record Office.

Once the historians had been removed from the picture, except as accurate observers and recorders of facts, the point of historiography disappeared except as a form of bibliographical exercise. It was a present-centred thing and did not penetrate to the 'real' history which was in the past; and, since the point of that history lay in getting the story straight by riffling though the past on one's desk, one could have little interest in people who got it wrong. Why read Macaulay on the late seventeenth century when he had been shown to have been mistaken about it? Why continue to venerate Stubbs when he had made a mess of the early medieval period? For these generations a sharp divide between history and historiography underpinned certainties about an emerging historical truth which, once demonstrated, no rational person could gainsay. Together, these related attitudes to the reality of the past and the dispensability of historiography confirmed the importance of the work undertaken and gave it a sense of breaking new ground. Often it did so. The disclosures and arguments of modernist historians achieved a degree of excitement and apparent irreversibility that lent their books weight and took the English historical profession to a peak of disciplinary success, whether in the vast series of volumes that they edited or in the periodicals to which they brought intellectual distinction or in the individual achievements – always impressive and sometimes quite as remarkable as any in the nineteenth century – that are still an object of envy among the working professionals of a different age. Only a fool, and a malevolent fool, would brush those achievements away. Yet all these people carried on their work (like the rest of us) under glass ceilings that it is the point of a critical historiography to bring to the attention of a later generation. If we miss them, then we miss what was unique in their world and fail to help the subject in its development for a new generation that is making its history under quite different conditions.

What seemed uncontentious to modernists lent their histories a distinctive form and register. If one looks at their work comparatively then its uniqueness shows through still more clearly. Precisely at the moment when English modernism went along the road of hardening present-centred facts into the past itself, some American historians went in the opposite direction, sensing the ambiguities of 'factual' knowledge and asking embarrassing questions about its provenance and reliability. Charles Beard's famous description of what, in effect, modernists wanted to believe as 'that noble dream' would have done nothing to raise their spirits had they acknowledged it.[9] Similarly in France, the movement towards a radical social history championed at Strasbourg by Marc Bloch and Lucien Febvre rejected from the beginning the formal method practised in the Sorbonne and Collège de France and always identified the task of the historian as an attempt to construct – not reconstruct, as the modernists wanted to say – a version of the past. If any European model of scholarship informed modernism, then it had to be that recommended by Leopold von Ranke with its mistranslated and misunderstood message to revive the past *wie es eigentlich gewesen*.[10] In the hands of Bishop Stubbs and then Lord Acton, this recommendation helped to dig a trench for twentieth-century English history. But there is a still more powerful comparison that one might make – not across space but across time. For, odd as it seems, the despised whigs again had a *better* grasp of these issues than did the modernists who succeeded them.

---

[9] Charles Beard, 'That Noble Dream', *AHR*, 41 (1935), 74–87. For the context see Peter Novick's account in *That Noble Dream: the 'Objectivity Question' and the American Historical Profession* (Cambridge, 1988), 258–78.

[10] These four words from the preface of Ranke's *History of the Latin and Teutonic Peoples* (Berlin, 1825) have done more inadvertent damage to historical studies than many volumes of theoretical writing. Ranke did *not* mean that the past could be brought back 'as it really was', and the word 'eigentlich' might better be represented, in its early nineteenth-century connotation, as 'essentially', or better still, 'in its essence'. But later generations mangled his meaning and treated his injunction as a guide to method. The story is explained in G. G. Iggers, 'The Image of Ranke in American and German Historical Thought', *H&T*, 2 (1962), 17–40.

Carlyle and Macaulay understood that narratives happened on one's desk and not in some metaphysical journey to the past as a foreign country available for tourism. Stubbs, for all his debt to Ranke, spread his 'sources' around him on his desk and wrote in the present tense, often, about what they had to say, leaving his own view as an informed but imaginative projection. Modernists came to believe that imagination weakened history by permitting speculation. They wanted their arguments to compel acceptance through their sheer force of evidence and depth of footnotes, as though a modernized history had no need for rhetoric.[11] They insisted that the new century wanted a history that was true, or as true as it could be made. Artistry could wait.

The empire shaken in 1902, the lives lost after 1914, the transformed culture after 1918, the sheer acceleration of ideas of time and space,[12] the leap forward in technology: none of these things needed a Lytton Strachey in order to depict how changed they were since the days of tired Victorians. Like Millie herself, the new historians adopted a self-image that was thoroughly modern and jettisoned a sentimental and sloppy reading of England's past. This made modernism not merely a persuasion but one with a mission: it had a *project* in a way that other forms of positivism did not. Many other walks of life had their brush with *Modernisierung* during the inter-war years and undoubtedly they had an important relationship with social change, economic transformations, the collapse of structures of authority and their replacement with newer and more ominous variants. But for the historical modernists their first obligation was to the reclamation of time and memory, their special media, with an imperative to 'move on' by rejecting the writing of previous generations and finding a way of modernizing it to meet a new culture. In doing so they made the past a different place, drained of its colour and picturesqueness, possibly, but charged with a new sense of reality and legitimated by procedures quite as rigorous as those found at the Cavendish Laboratory. By 1960 none of the topics precious to the whigs of the nineteenth century had any life left in the professionalized university, apart from a diluted sense of imperial history in the era of decolonization and a revived notion of military history. Yet neither the topics themselves nor the approaches to historical study on which they rested had been modernized in a single sweep. Modernizing England's past took years to accomplish and the process, for that is what it was,

---

[11] For a scintillating demonstration of how misguided they were, see Nancy Partner, 'The New Cornificius: Medieval History and Artifice', in Ernst Breisach (ed.), *Classical Rhetoric and Medieval Historiography* (Kalamazoo, MI, 1985), 5–59.
[12] See Stephen Kern's remarkable study *The Culture of Time and Space 1880–1918* (1983).

moved quickly in some areas and periods and slowly in others. Even when it did happen, its practitioners continued a dialogue of the deaf with writers who could not accept the new stringencies and who saw more point in making the past compelling than in making it definitive.

All of this implies that a book hoping to give an account of the process of modernization in English historiography will do well to avoid simple narrative and recognize that several narratives will arise depending on which part of the whig legacy one wishes to examine. Three intertwined themes played a critical role in what the whigs had said – constitution, religion and empire – and the first three chapters of this study are devoted to wondering what happened to them, posing questions in each case about the onset of modernization, its incidence and significance. Each section roots itself in the thought-world of the 1870s and tries to evoke events and moments over the next century that may have proved seismic. A fourth chapter then departs from historical thematization and enters a foggier world of memory and anticipation, if only to recall the human dimension of these extraordinary times. In turning more frontally to the modernists themselves, in the second half of the book, we discover the ability, range and novelty of these modernist historians and evaluate their achievement and context. This involves placing them in a social and economic environment about which they often wrote and within an ideological one that they constantly sought to combat. The tasks of explanation cannot avoid the whig issues of parliament and constitution, moreover, even in times that no longer deemed them urgent. Method, a subject that preoccupies the final substantive chapter, shows how central the ideas of historical procedure became in determining the subjects discussed by modernists and the accounts they gave of them. Finally, the scene changes to the historical climate in England after 1970 in order to suggest what it was that modernism could no longer modernize and propose how it was that a persuasion that had been designed to be endless found its end, not through demolition of the kind it had brought on the whigs, but in a curious infolding, as with a bloom at the end of its season.

Part I

The whig legacy

1 Constitution and nation

Any reader of history born after about 1955 is likely to have comparatively little knowledge of the constitutional history of England. Members of that generation who have grown up in the United Kingdom (outside Northern Ireland) or the United States will not normally have come across it in school, at least not as an insistent theme; they will not have taken courses in it if they have proceeded into higher education; they will certainly have been able to avoid, if ever they became threatened with, Magna Carta, the Glorious Revolution, the supposed tyrannies of Bad King John, Henry VIII and George III. Not so those previous generations who bore bravely or grudgingly their compulsory encounters with Stubbs's *Select Charters*, and with the constitutional histories and studies written by Bishop Stubbs himself, by Edward Freeman, Albert Venn Dicey, Sir William Anson, Sir David Keir, S. B. Chrimes, J. E. A. Joliffe, H. G. Richardson and G. O. Sayles, together with collections of constipating constitutional documents with the names of Tanner, Costin and Watson merely among the memorable.[1] For entire cohorts of schoolchildren in the century after 1850, by contrast, England's constitutional history functioned not as the accompaniment but as the explanation of her glory, while the crucial personalities in moulding that history – King Alfred, Simon de Montfort, Sir John Eliot, John Locke and a long list of modern embodiments of the will towards liberty – became the icons of textbooks and role models for their collective heirs, the British public. If any form of history might be described as *defining* the whig legacy, then constitutional history must surely take pride of place. Whigs believed in a continuity of institutions and practices since Anglo-Saxon times that lent to English history a special pedigree, one that instilled a distinctive temper in the English nation (as whigs liked to call it) and an approach

[1] J. R. Tanner, *Constitutional Documents of the Reign of James I* (Cambridge, 1930); *English Constitutional Conflicts of the Seventeenth Century* (Cambridge, 1928); *Tudor Constitutional Documents* (Cambridge, 1930). W. C. Costin and J. S. Watson, *The Law and Working of the Constitution: Documents 1660–1914* (2 vols., 1952).

to the world. Sometimes, as in the case of Edward Augustus Freeman,[2] this certainty brought a racial element, a sense of the superiority of English stock and blood. It always brought pride, patriotism, communion with forebears; it pricked the eye with sheer gratitude for a blessed heritage.[3] It issued in law and lent legal precedent a role in preserving or extending the freedoms of Englishmen. The whig story set out, in an unspoken but quite fundamental sense, not only what the history of England was about but what it *meant* as an account of an evolving national disposition. An educated person might feel ignorant of much in the English past but constitutional history supplied an irreducible minimum of what should be known: it excused ignorance by defining true knowledge and tested its acquisition in a hundred tests and examinations, a thousand lessons learned by rote.[4]

Where did it go, this devotion to constitutional history? And when did it depart? Dom David Knowles, Benedictine monk, Fellow of Peterhouse, Herbert Butterfield's college, and Regius Professor of Modern History at Cambridge from 1954 to 1963, thought the turn came after the Second World War. Looking back on medieval studies over the previous hundred years he chose a period between 1890 and 1950:

Until *circa* 1950 the studies and curricula of the Historical Schools in all British universities continued the rhythm set up at Oxford, and later at Cambridge, between 1890 and 1900 . . . English constitutional history still held pride of place. It provided a backbone of development with a considerable intellectual content, and it had its sacred books in Stubbs's *History* and *Charters*. It held sway at Cambridge between the wars with Gaillard Lapsley[5] and

---

[2] Edward Augustus Freeman (1823–92). Oxford but then private scholar for much of his life. *Saturday Review* 1860–9; Regius Professor of Modern History at Oxford in succession to Stubbs, 1884–92. *History of the Norman Conquest* (6 vols., 1867–79); *The Reign of William Rufus* (1882); *History of Sicily* (3 vols., 1891–2). Excoriated by the formidable John Horace Round: cf. Round, *Feudal England: Historical Studies in the Eleventh and Twelfth Centuries* (1895).

[3] I like John Burrow's acute remark that Freeman looked on the actors of the past as might a proud or anxious relative: J. W. Burrow, *A Liberal Descent: Victorian Historians and the English Past* (Cambridge, 1981; paperback edn, 1983), 199.

[4] For examples and development of this point, see Michael Bentley, 'The Organization and Dissemination of Historical Knowledge', in Martin Daunton (ed.), *The Organization of Victorian Knowledge* (Oxford, 2005), 173–97.

[5] Gaillard Lapsley (1871–1949). Born New York; graduated from Harvard, 1893, with Charles Gross his 'master'. Lived in England 1904–39. Tutor at Trinity College, Cambridge; Lecturer, then Reader in Constitutional History at Cambridge. No book; papers collected in Lapsley, *Crown, Community and Parliament in the Later Middle Ages*, edited by H. M. Cam and Geoffrey Barraclough (Oxford, 1951).

Helen Cam[6], and Sir Goronwy Edwards[7] was a pillar of the establishment at Oxford.[8]

In fact the syndrome of constitutional history lasted into the 1960s in most universities – including Knowles's Cambridge – though the extent to which it remained compulsory certainly varied and tended progressively to diminish. It is not hard to see why a study concentrating on law, precedent and ordered liberty might feel less than relevant to a world dominated by images of Auschwitz, the cynicism of the Cold War, the duplicities celebrated in the Suez crisis of 1956 or the ranting impatience of the student movement. One of Knowles's medieval historians, Maurice Powicke,[9] gave thanks towards the end of his life that the mould had broken, and wrote in a revealing private letter to Helen Cam that it had happened none too soon. 'Thank heaven,' he wrote in 1951, 'our rather narrow constitutional outlook *is* gradually affected by the wider medieval learning, just as it has become in the history of Law and thought . . . Lapsley seems to me to be the last & one of the best of the older constitutionalists unless we add Bertie Wilkinson and J. G. Edwards – who find anything called "Constitutional history" sufficient in itself; but they also look through the windows.'[10] Learning had become 'wider', partly through developments inside the discipline but also in reaction to what was going on outside the study in a world characterized by catastrophe and grief – one in which the gentle

---

[6] Helen Cam (1885–1968). Royal Holloway College, London. Bryn Mawr for a year; back to London to begin postgraduate work. Taught Cheltenham Ladies' College, 1909–12. Appointed to Royal Holloway 1912–21; Girton College, Cambridge, 1921–48. First Zemurray Radcliffe Professor, Harvard, 1948–54. Writings mostly on medieval England. Papers collected in *Liberties and Communities in Medieval England* (Cambridge, 1944) and *Law-Finders and Law-Makers in Medieval England: Collected Studies in Legal and Constitutional History* (1962).

[7] Sir (John) Goronwy Edwards (1891–1976). Son of a railway signalman in Salford. Moved to Flintshire, 1893, and Welsh his native language. Jesus College, Oxford, then Tout's Manchester, 1913–15. Fellow of Jesus College, 1919–48. Director of the Institute of Historical Research from 1948. Ford Lectures on *The Second Century of the English Parliament* (1960–1) published in 1979.

[8] M. D. Knowles, 'Some Trends in Scholarship, 1868–1968, in the Field of Medieval History', *TRHS*, 5th series, 19 (1969), 139–57 at 147.

[9] Frederick Maurice Powicke (1879–1963). Born Alnwick; father a Congregationalist minister. Named after the Christian Socialist F. D. Maurice. Manchester University and Balliol College, Oxford. Professor of Modern History, Queen's University, Belfast 1909–19; Professor of Medieval History, Manchester, 1919–28; Regius Professor of Modern History at Oxford, 1928–47. Daughter Janet married Richard Pares. Ford Lectures on Stephen Langton in 1926–7, but major work after the war in *King Henry III and the Lord Edward* (1947) and his volume on the thirteenth century for the *Oxford History of England* (1953).

[10] Powicke to Cam, 15 July 1951, Cam MSS 2/2/4.

increments of freedom discussed by Stubbs and Freeman fell upon an audience sadder and wiser than the readers of the 1880s and 1890s.

Impatience thus began long before 1950 and Knowles's treatment of the period smoothes out a rumpled sheet. The greatest constitutional crises facing Britain in the twentieth century took place, after all, in 1911 and 1936, and it would be surprising to find the constitutional history of the House of Lords or the monarchy unaffected by the Parliament Act or Edward VIII's abdication of the throne. One serious and knowledgeable historian of the constitution, who had written a much-admired treatise on Magna Carta, looked at the events of 1911 and saw in them a new constitution, one 'moulded by recent events', in which 'the undivided supreme power always lies with one or other of the parties that divide the State . . . [T]he same knot of politicians who control the Commons, likewise control the Cabinet . . . Sovereignty is no longer divided between King, Lords and Commons, but is concentrated in the leaders of the party in power.'[11] No one would find doctrine of this sort in Stubbs. For a Tory commentator like J. A. R. Marriott, on the other hand, the same events might be made to look like 'another stage in the long process by which power has been transferred from the Crown to a parliamentary Cabinet'.[12] Here is the Janus-face of constitutional history after the whigs: on the one side, a sense of departed certainties and new perspectives; on the other, a continuing tradition of argument reinforced in school and university curricula. It is part of the tension felt acutely by the generation of Butterfield and Namier and played its own role in the fuzziness which much of their history was intended in different ways to resolve. For the later Namier school, constitutionalism spelled innocence: a failure to see that real politics did not work like that. For Butterfield and those who thought like him, the ideals of continuity and finding a place for the nation in political argument remained values to cherish. Either way, the constitutional history of the whigs legislated to a remarkable degree for the generations that followed by imposing a shape on the history of England that almost everybody learned and ingested. To see the consequences of that, and the criticisms that post-whig historians brought to this mode of thinking, we have to do what the whigs themselves did by beginning at the beginning of their English story, but from an historiographical point of view; and in so many ways that means beginning with Stubbs.

[11] W. S. McKechnie, *The New Democracy and the Constitution* (1912), 25–6.
[12] J. A. R. Marriott, *The Constitution in Transition 1910–1924* (Oxford, 1924), 8.

The Stubbsian imprint

William Stubbs occupies a unique and central position in the constitutional historiography of England.[13] That he did not die until Queen Victoria did reminds us that he comes nearer the end of the whig persuasion in historical writing than its onset in Henry Hallam and Thomas Babington Macaulay between the second and fourth decades of the nineteenth century.[14] Indeed Stubbs and those who shared his generation – Edward Freeman, S. R. Gardiner,[15] James Anthony Froude,[16] J. R. Seeley[17] – saw themselves as critics rather than disciples of romantic whiggery in their superior scholarship drawn more from Germany than from their own country. Stubbs himself emphasized that aspect in having the works of Leopold von Ranke translated into English; the ideals of the founding father of German historical scholarship constantly emerge from Stubbs's texts in their searching for some inner essence in an historical period and a mastery of its surviving sources. In the *Constitutional History of England* (3 vols., 1873–8) and in his *Select*

---

[13] William Stubbs (1825–1901). Son of a Knaresborough solicitor and heir to a long line of Yorkshire yeomen. Ripon Grammar School and Christ Church, Oxford as servitor. High Churchman influenced by Pusey. Ordained 1850; vicar of Navestock, Essex: much writing and editing. Regius Chair of Modern History, Oxford, 1866. Bishop of Chester, 1884, and of Oxford, 1888. *Select Charters and Other Illustrations of English Constitutional History from the Earliest Times to the Reign of Edward I* (1870); *The Constitutional History of England in its Origin and Development* (3 vols., 1873–8).

[14] Henry Hallam (1777–1859). Father a prominent churchman, mother related to Provost of Eton. Eton and Christ Church, Oxford. Barrister and then Stamp Office in a sinecure. *The Constitutional History of England from the Accession of Henry VII to the Death of George II* (2 vols., 1827). Thomas Babington Macaulay (1800–59). Son of Governor of Sierra Leone, Zachary Macaulay, and Selina Mills, assistant to Hannah More, the evangelical writer. Trinity College, Cambridge, then reviewing, law and politics. MP from 1830, sporadic ministerial career. *History of England* (5 vols., 1849–61).

[15] Samuel Rawson Gardiner (1829–1902). Member of Catholic Apostolic Church; married Edward Irving's youngest daughter. Anglican in later life. Enormous narrative of foundational importance on seventeenth-century constitutional history, produced in spurts with different titles and covering the period from 1603 to 1656. Continued to 1658 by C. H. Firth in *The Last Years of the Protectorate* (2 vols., 1909).

[16] James Anthony Froude (1818–94). Brother of the Tractarian Hurrell Froude (1803–36). Oriel College, Oxford. Fellow of Exeter College; resigned over reception of *Nemesis of Faith* (1849). Married Charles Kingsley's sister; became professional author and travel-writer. Biographer of Carlyle. Regius Professor of Modern History at Oxford in 1892 at the age of 74. *History of England from the Fall of Wolsey to the Death of Elizabeth* (10 vols., 1856–70).

[17] John Robert Seeley (1834–95). Evangelical background in London. City of London School and Christ's College, Cambridge. Professor of Latin, University College, London, from 1863. Succeeded Kingsley in Regius Chair in Cambridge 1869 and held it until 1895. Some notoriety in mid-career from anonymous *Ecce Homo* (1865). Main historical works *The Life and Times of Stein* (1878), *The Expansion of England* (1883) and *The Growth of British Policy* (2 vols., 1895).

Charters and Other Illustrations of English Constitutional History from the Earliest Times to the Reign of Edward I (1870), both of these dimensions of Stubbs's approach found expression in works that would be consulted by and imposed on serious students of history for almost a century: they became his legacy – a whig legacy that critics of that style would need ultimately to confront and subdue. It does not matter to this argument that Stubbs was a Tory in politics. We are discussing not Whiggery as a political position but whiggery as an historical frame of mind. Not only did Stubbs perfectly represent many facets of that mentality, he did so with an intellectual luminosity and literary grace that made his work compelling in the way that a powerful recording of a familiar symphony becomes compelling: once heard, it cannot be unheard and other performances become tested against it. Stubbs imprinted on at least two generations of readers his own reading of English history between the Anglo-Saxon period and the Tudors. Partly this was achieved through the orientation of school and university curricula. Partly it happened vicariously because Stubbs conditioned the writing of other influential authors.[18] But the achievement also rested on the character of his own creation. He constructed a highly rhetorical text with its own inner and subliminal music that defied oblivion.[19] But far more compelling was his success in achieving two things: a way of thinking about the direction of English history and the moulding of a firm outline of the historical experience of the English nation. If we are to make sense of what modernists thought in the post-whig age, we must first understand the nature and persistence of this cumulative imprint.

At the heart of Stubbs's understanding of the English past lay the affirmation with which he closed the first volume of his *Constitutional History*, that 'the continuity of life, and the continuity of national purpose, never fails'.[20] Continuity, nation, purpose: three elements constantly combined. Institutions, law and custom – three other constants – best suggest the continuous experience that he finds fundamental in English history. Origin and development – the subtitle of the

---

[18] It is noticeable, for example, that one of the most widely consulted volumes on constitutional law in the early twentieth century took its 'historical outline' from Stubbs: Sir William Anson, *The Law and Custom of the Constitution* (2 vols., 1886–92), vol. I, 12–18; vol. II, 20–2.

[19] See Robert Brentano's remarks on 'The Sound of Stubbs', *JBS*, 6 (1967), 1–14.

[20] *The Constitutional History of England in its Origin and Development* (3 vols., Oxford, 1873–8), ch. XIII, §167, vol. I, 682. Editions abound of what will hereafter be referred to simply as the *Constitutional History*. I have used the following editions: vol. I, 6th edn (1897); vol. II, 4th edn (1896); vol. III, 5th edn (1896). In each reference I have supplied chapter and section numbers for readers who may have other editions available to them.

Constitutional History – indicate a conception of purpose that owes more to Darwin than Hegel, 'a process of natural selection . . . in constant working . . . exemplified in the gradual formation of the seven [Anglo-Saxon] kingdoms and in their final union under Wessex'.[21] The nation is more elusive – sometimes a mere category of persuasion to which Stubbs turns whenever, as Helen Cam noticed many years ago, he has a crisis to explain;[22] but often a real presence with the power of transfiguration. The emerging English lurk below the future's horizon: always there as a national spirit embodied in great personalities and institutions or besmirched by bad ones, but forever winning through in the end, as much because of adversity as despite it. Constitutional history is nothing if it does not tell this story in its own language, and it does so, as the first two sentences of the *History* tell us, by depicting the emergence of the constitution as 'the resultant of three forces, whose reciprocal influences are constant, subtle, and intricate. These are the national character, the external history, and the institutions of a people.'[23] Nation and people introduce themselves through notions of character and a capacity to construct their own arrangements; challenge comes from without, whether or not it is the French, as it usually is, or from unhealthy growths within the society such as royal tyranny, peasant revolt or misguided religion. The story, moreover, has a plot and inner logic that push the past towards the present and show how the English people came to be where they are and what they can learn from their journey. 'It presents, in every branch, a regularly developed series of causes and consequences, and abounds in examples of that continuity of life, the realisation of which is necessary to give the reader a personal hold on the past and a right judgment of the present.'[24] And in giving his reader a personal hold on the past, Stubbs gave himself a personal hold on the reader.

What the reader was meant to hold was a period, roughly between Henry II and Edward I, as a crucial moment in the development of the constitution; and a continuous tension in this period and elsewhere between 'substructure' (various elements of a national community and its modes of representation) and 'superstructure', basically the monarchy and the ecclesiastical-cum-baronial elite on which its immediate existence depended.[25] Before this hinge-period, the English people

---

[21] *Constitutional History*, ch. VII, §70, vol. I, 188–9.
[22] Helen Cam, 'Stubbs', *Cambridge Historical Journal*, 9 (1948), 129–47 at 134.
[23] Ibid., ch. I, §1, vol. I, 1.
[24] Ibid., preface to the three volumes, dated Christmas Day 1873, vol. I, iii.
[25] For this analysis see J. G. Edwards, *William Stubbs* (Historical Association pamphlet, General 22, 1952), 8ff. Edwards, however, sees the burden of Stubbs's text falling on the

struggled to manufacture coherence from a Germanic past. After it, an attempt at constitutional advance *before its time* led to disaster in the failure of the 'Lancastrian experiment' and its inevitable come-uppance in a 'Tudor despotism'. Only with the eradication of that back-sliding in a final confrontation with the king in the seventeenth century, a civil war, the king's execution and the eventual rescue of the country from foppery and Catholicism by William of Orange in 1689 could modern England emerge in the mature form already celebrated by Macaulay. Fleshing out these bones with some detail is necessary because those who came after Stubbs spent important years adjusting the smaller claims of volumes II and III even after they had reluctantly abandoned the assertions of volume I. Abandoned or not, this skeleton was the one in everyone's constitutional cupboard after 1914; and long after the flesh of detail had fallen away this configuration endured.

Volume I did not endure for long because it addressed a problem mostly mysterious in Stubbs's day: what was the original character of the English and where did they come from? By page two the reader has learned that they had enjoyed a prehistory in the German lands:

> They are a people of German descent in the main constituents of blood, charac-
> ter, and language, but most especially . . . in the possession of the elements of
> primitive German civilization and the commons germs of German institutions
> . . . In England the common germs were developed and ripened with the smallest
> intermixture of foreign elements . . . If its history is not the perfectly pure
> development of German principles it is the nearest existing approach to such a
> development . . . the purest product of their primitive instinct.[26]

These 'germs' were part of Stubbs's undoing in this part of his account in implying a commitment to what became called the 'germ theory' of constitutional development from a German parent and resting on the writings of respected German authors such as Gneist[27] that commanded widespread credence in the closing years of the nineteenth century. Many wanted to go further than this in drawing lines between Germany and England and Stubbs is often blamed for accepting a cluster of claims that he expressly rejected, the so-called theory of the Mark.

The idea of the Mark System, as it is called, according to which the body of kindred freemen, scattered over a considerable area and cultivating their lands in common, use a domestic constitution based entirely primarily on the community

---

period 1066–1215 whereas I take the late thirteenth century to mark the critical moment
in Stubbs's account for our present purposes.

[26] *Constitutional History*, ch. I, §§1, 5, 9, vol. I, 1, 6, 11.

[27] H. R. von Gneist, *Das englische parlament in tausendjährigen Wandelungen vom 9. bis zum Ende des 19. Jahrhunderts* (Berlin, 1886); *Englische Verfassungsgeschichte* (Berlin, 1882).

of tenure and cultivation, is an especially inviting one, and furnishes a basis on which a large proportion of the institutions of later constitutional life may theoretically be imposed.[28]

But it is important to keep reading. Although Stubbs thought that this system might have some application at the level of land use and the development of what Seebohm called the 'village community',[29] he pointed out that the idea had been announced, 'with his usual tendency to exaggeration', by Kemble in 1849 and then later enhanced by Sir Henry Maine and Seebohm himself.[30] Stubbs insisted that he rejected the *constitutional* implications of the Mark system in so far as it might be thought to explain English developments.[31] As so often with Stubbs, however, his right hand had already forgotten what his left hand had written fifty pages earlier where he had allowed that England did have 'germs and traces' of the Mark which, if they did not initiate the English constitution, may, with a tweak or two, have produced England's special form of feudalism which one day would 'rise into a great homogeneous people, symmetrically organised and united, progressive and thoroughly patriotic'.[32] The harm was done.

Alongside the rise of this great and homogeneous people, Stubbs presents the rise of a great constitution. His narrative implies, rather than asserts, important facets of this process: the reader is taken on one side much later in the story and told confidentially, as it were, what the story so far really means. Perhaps it will help a reader unfamiliar with Stubbs's text to undermine this rhetorical reserve and announce on the author's behalf two very important elements in the entire approach, one from the end of volume I, the other deep in volume III. First, we should note the place of representative institutions in the account as a whole:

The great characteristic of the English constitutional system, in that view of it which is offered in these pages . . . is the continuous development of representative institutions from the first elementary stage, in which they are employed for local purposes and in the simplest form, to that in which the national parliament appears as the concentration of all local and provincial machinery, the depository of the collective powers of the three estates of the realm.[33]

---

[28] Ibid, ch. II, §19, vol. I, 35.

[29] For Frederick Seebohm see his *The English Village Community* (1883).

[30] J. M. Kemble (1807–57) was best known for *The Saxons in England* (1849), the jurist Sir Henry Maine (1822–88) for his *Ancient Law* (1861) and his polemical essays on *Popular Government* (1885).

[31] See the long and very important footnote at ch. V, §39, vol. I, 89n. He associated himself with Gneist who was 'undoubtedly right in refusing to recognize the Mark as the basis of our polity'.

[32] Ibid., ch. II, §19, vol. I, 37, 39.

[33] Ibid., ch. XIII, §156, vol. I, 584.

Committing this passage to memory would remove much friction in the reader's mind in following the advances and regressions implied in the narrative. The second passage concerns the place of the constitution in the fabric of national life and its relationship with those who operate it.

> The great ship of state has its centre of gravity as well as its apparatus for steering and sailing, its machinery of defence, and its lading. And it is upon the working of these factors that any great crisis of national life must ultimately turn. Great men may forestall or delay such initial changes . . . But they do not create the conjunctures [that bring them about]: and the history which searches no deeper is manifestly incomplete. In the reading of constitutional history there is a primary condition: we have to deal with principles and institutions first, and with men, great or small, mainly as working the institutions and exemplifying the development of the principles.[34]

Nowhere in Stubbs's text is this vision of individuals absorbing and re-radiating the principles of nation and constitution not apparent when one knows to look for it. We find it in all the key moments of Stubbs's story: the development of Saxon kingship, the importance of the Conquest, the march of the barons towards their destiny at Runnymede, the admirable but premature struggle of the Lancastrian kings to make a constitutional polity.

Part of the Saxon difficulty lay in keeping Kemble at arm's length while having little else on which to rest the account apart from his correspondence with Freeman, whose mission it was to make the Anglo-Saxons racially English and the Normans honorary Englishmen. Freeman, rather than Stubbs, rhapsodized about the Witanagemot which he thought turned into the House of Lords – 'I can see no break between the two' – but which, despite its 'aristocratic' flavour he deemed 'democratic in ancient theory' and liable to become so again at moments of national excitement.[35] Stubbs went along with him far enough to see in the Witan a crucial part of the governing process, but stopped long before it came to resemble one of Gladstone's cabinets: it had a role in the issuing of laws, he thought (following Kemble), but he saw the council as, increasingly, a royal instrument.[36] It is the king who 'crowns the fabric of the state' as the social fabric changes through a process in which '[t]he Angel-cynn of Alfred becomes the Englo-lande of Canute',[37] and this intertwined strength of political and social

---

[34] Ibid., ch. XXI, §454, vol. III, 519.

[35] E. A. Freeman, *The Growth of the English Constitution* (1872), 59–60.

[36] *Constitutional History*, ch. VI, §56, vol. I, 148; §58, 157. He has the Witanagemot 'verging towards a condition in which it would become simply the council of the king, instead of the council of the nation' (157).

[37] Ibid., ch. VI, §59, vol. I, 158; ch. VII, §69, 184.

consolidation on which the Conqueror had to make his mark. He did so. There is none of that pretence, so strong in Freeman, that the Conquest never touched the heart of what it was to be English and merely became an incident in national development.[38] Stubbs speaks of a 'tremendous temporary sacrifice' similar to that imposed by the Viking invasions, out of which some good emerged through the drawing together of the nation.[39] But the crux of the story is already in place and the Anglo-Norman state acts as a partial regression in the rhythm of history rather than as a reversal of it. Unknown to the participants, a deep dialectic is already unfolding between baronial confidence and royal dependence. It is quickened during the reign of Henry II, falters during the absences of Richard I and plunges into dislocation when faced with the evil of John. It is a critical scene in the entire drama and Stubbs's paragraph on John, delivered as usual *after* he has narrated the events surrounding Magna Carta, shows how little 'the very worst of all our kings' had absorbed of the nascent constitution, as well as showing the depth of the bishop's emotion about his derelictions.[40] What John had most pointedly failed to absorb was what Magna Carta *meant*: it was not a buying-off of the barons, for Stubbs, so much as a compact between monarch and nation: 'It is the collective people who really form the other high contracting party in the great capitulation . . .'[41] And, once there, the collective people could never be erased.

Parliament marks their presence and the evolution of parliament their rise. When the justiciar and archbishop summoned representatives to

---

[38] He announces the thought on his very first page. 'The Norman Conquest brought with it a most extensive foreign infusion, which affected our blood, our language, our laws, our arts; still it was only an infusion; the older and stronger elements still survived, and in the long run they again made good their supremacy. So far from being the beginning of our national history, the Norman Conquest was the temporary overthrow of our national being.' Freeman, *History of the Norman Conquest of England, its Causes and Results* (6 vols., Oxford, 1867–79), vol. I, 1–2.

[39] *Constitutional History*, ch. VII, §77, vol. I, 222.

[40] Ibid., ch. XIV, §169, vol. II, 17. It is one of the great statements of Victorian historiography with a Carlylean love for the lethal: 'We need not ask whether poison, excess, or vexation hastened his death. He was the very worst of all our kings: a man whom no oaths could bind, no pressure of conscience, no consideration of policy, restrain from evil; a faithless son, a treacherous brother, an ungrateful master; to his people a hated tyrant. Polluted with every crime that could disgrace a man, false to every obligation that should bind a king, he had lost half his inheritance by sloth, and ruined and desolated the rest. Not devoid of natural ability, craft or energy . . . he yet failed in every design he undertook, and had to bear humiliations which, although not without parallel, never fell on one who deserved them more thoroughly or received less sympathy under them. In the whole view there is no redeeming trait: John seems as incapable of receiving a good impression as of carrying into effect a wise resolution.'

[41] Ibid., ch. XII, §§154–5, vol. I, 569–70.

their council at St Albans in 1213 they began, for Stubbs, the beginning of a career that the *Parliamentum Runimedae* continued and confirmed two years later.[42] Thereafter we call in at every 'parliament' as though in the hands of an over-zealous courier: 1244, 1248, 1249, 1253, 1254, 1255, 1257, and the two of 1258. The second one in Oxford gave rise to the famous Provisions with their stipulation that there should be three parliaments per year and precipitated tensions that erupted in the baronial wars against the king that were to last until 1265 – a signal moment for Stubbs in the new constitution following the battle of Lewes in 1264 and the calling of Simon de Montfort's historic parliament at Westminister in 1265, seven months before his death at the battle of Evesham. Stubbs contained himself in the face of all this destiny in a way that Freeman simply could not; the latter's love for Simon ran too deep:

The tyranny of our Angevin masters woke up English freedom from its momentary grave. Had Richard [I] and John and Henry [III] been Kings like Aelfred and Saint Lewis, the crosier of Stephen Langton, the sword of Robert Fitzwalter, would never have flashed at the head of the Barons and people of England; the heights of Lewes would never have seen the mightiest triumph of her freedom; the pavement of Evesham would never have closed over the mangled relics of her noblest champion.[43]

Stubbs's story had less colour but more subtlety. He believed that the thirteenth century lacked the 'constitutional programme' that the fourteenth would possess, albeit ineffectually, and for him the 'eighty years struggle' after 1215 marked a swinging of fortune back and forth between the forces, not so much of good and evil as of past and future.[44] Because he believed that the constitutional future lay with the knights of the shire, moreover, he pressed the critical moment of development forward into the reign of Edward I (1272–1307), partly out of a sense that then 'the nation rises to its full growth, in accord, for the most part, with the genius of its ruler', but still more because the voice of the nation is heard for the first time in the parliament of 1295 through its distinctive summoning of the knights, the Model Parliament, 'one of the landmarks in the history of representation' and 'the last formal step which established the representation of the commons'.[45] That is the moment when

---

[42] Ibid., ch. XII, §154, vol. I, 565–6; ch. XIII, §159, vol. I, 611.

[43] Freeman, *Growth of the Constitution*, 68.

[44] *Constitutional History*, ch. XIV, §168, vol. II, 1–2.

[45] Ibid., ch. XIV, §168, vol. II, 4–5; §179, vol. II, 114; §180, vol. II, 133. Cf. ch. XVII, §272, vol. II, 540: 'Both historical evidence and the nature of the case lead to the conviction that the victory of the constitution was won by the knights of the shires.' His footnote, however, points rather lamely to an opinion of Kemble's.

the English constitution as modernity would know it becomes firmly founded.

Progress is always a wave, however, and the wave now recedes, leaving behind the constitutional quietude – there was certainly no other kind – of Stubbs's fourteenth century. Kingship had to undulate through the trough of Edward II and the ascent of Edward III's domination as warlord. Nation, too, ran its curve through the terror of the Black Death at mid-century and into moments of false exultation in the revolt of 1381 and the errors of Lollardy. One of Stubbs's three determining elements of history – the force of the external in English affairs – came to its head in the Hundred Years War from the 1330s, with its pressure on finance and therefore on parliaments. But only in the reign of Richard II did all these lines and curves converge constitutionally in the reassertion of an authoritarian project, one which, granted the foundation of a parliamentary state, could only end in disruption and failure. The deposition of Richard in 1399 and the coming of the three Lancastrian kings (Henry IV, Henry V, Henry VI) might, on one anticipation, have heralded another great wave of constitutional advance. Never were the Commons so strong, we are told, as under Henry IV. No king so successfully became emblem of the nation as Henry V. And as for Henry VI, he was 'the last medieval king who attempted to rule England as a constitutional kingdom or commonwealth'.[46] Yet constitutional success and expanded liberty did not come about and could not have happened because their proponents acted, again, before their time. 'The failure of the house of Lancaster, the tyranny of the House of York, the statecraft of Henry VII, the apparent extinction of the constitution under Henry VIII, the political resurrection under Elizabeth, were all needed to prepare and equip England to cope successfully with the principles of Richard II, masked under legal, religious, philosophical embellishments in the theory of the Stewarts.'[47] Once again, too, the dialectical nature of progress announced itself in the relationship between Lancaster and York, both of them disastrous, both essential: 'the rule of the house of Lancaster proved that the nation was not ready for the efficient use of the liberties it had won, and that of the house of York proved that the nation was too full grown to be fettered again with the bonds from which it had escaped'.[48] So the civil war, as Stubbs understood it, of white rose and red and the rise of the over-mighty subject found their origins in an imbalance which nature would always reassert. She did so after 1485, via

[46] Ibid., ch. XVIII, §320, vol. III, 73; §363, 244; §341, 135.
[47] Ibid., ch. XVII, §297, vol. II, 653.
[48] Ibid., ch. XVIII, §363, vol. III, 240–1.

the Tudors, who stamped down Lancastrian pieties and created a monarchy that only 1689 (which Stubbs can now see in his mind's eye and from which he is reading backwards) could put in its proper frame. As he draws at last to the end of his great project, the sight of what is to come brings light to the dark days of the Tudors and subsumes the Stuarts in a compelling logic of his own.

> If the absolutism of the Tudors must in a measure answer for the sins of the Stewarts, and the sins of the Stewarts for the miseries of the Rebellion [of 1649–60], the republican government must in like measure be held responsible for the excesses of the Restoration . . . But . . . out of the weakness and foulness and darkness of the time, the nation, church, peers and people, emerge with a strong hold on better things; prepared to set out again on a career which has never, since the Revolution of 1688, been materially impeded.[49]

He thus hands the torch to Macaulay's ghost, his task complete.

Subverting Stubbs's 'system'

For all the veneration in which historians rightly continued to hold Stubbs, the internal logic and rhythm of his vision of English history came quickly under suspicion. The Germanism of the pre-Conquest material and its seeming dependence on fanciful theories of national origins supplied one thrust against him. A more immediate one came from those interested in the history of the medieval parliament and who saw it from two directions: one dominated by ideas of constitutional law, which was now finding itself treated historically by Maitland and Holdsworth,[50] the other, slightly later, from historians of land and society, who brought Stubbs's picture of 'the Lancastrian experiment' under critical review. Together these made the model appear fragile and by 1936 one constitutional historian could report the end of the road. 'Stubbs' great book is still the point of departure for all constitutional history after 1066', he wrote,' and those who neglect it do so at their peril. Yet it is true that Stubbs' "system" has been completely rejected.'[51] We shall see that the judgement was premature. It shows none the less the degree to which a professionalizing community of historians believed that they had dispatched Stubbs and his ideas by building a school of

---

[49] Ibid., ch. XXI, §455, vol. III, 524.
[50] Sir William Holdsworth (1871–1944). Reader in English Law, Oxford, 1910–22; Vinerian Professor thereafter. *History of English Law*, continued by A. L. Goodhart and H. G. Hanbury (17 vols., 1903–72).
[51] Gaillard Lapsley, 'Some Recent Advance in English Constitional History (before 1485)', in Lapsley, *Crown, Community and Parliament*, 1–33 at 1.

scientific research into constitutional history that owed much of its origin and all of its inspiration to Frederic William Maitland.[52]

Maitland's premature death in 1906 undoubtedly retarded the development of a powerful school of historical criticism in the constitutional historiography of England. What he accomplished, always against the grain of a frail physique and frequently collapsing health, seems so astonishing that one can only wonder how English history would have looked by 1918 had he been given the years necessary for its transformation. To all systems of thought he brought a cool scepticism and a forensic legal intelligence that could only corrode structures that did not meet his standards of verification or styles of documentation that looked uncertain in the light of his unrivalled knowledge of the contents of the Public Record Office. He had, needless to say, his own 'system' in his famous procedure of working from what was 'certain' to what remained 'uncertain': a rhetorical position of great authority until someone proves capable of showing that his certainty was not so certain after all if the matter were put in a different way. All the same, Maitland's grip on the particular undid pronouncements about the Roman villa system and its supposed relationship to feudal developments, and it arrested Stubbs in his striding towards a complete system of representative parliamentary institutions by 1295. It did not seem to do so at first because the trip-wire appeared in a technical publication far from the sight of the historical public. The Rolls Series – an expanding collection of primary historical material published by the government under the imprimatur of the Master of the Rolls – proposed to include among its volumes an edition of the *Memoranda de Parliamento* that gave an account of the 'parliament' of 1305. Asked to write an introduction to this publication in 1893, Maitland began a close scrutiny of its text and saw immediately that Stubbs's notion of parliamentary development after 1265 found little fit with what this so-called parliament seemed to be doing. It gave no hint of operating as a representative body but resembled instead a meeting of the King's Council, called to meet the king's purposes; it passed no 'legislation', but rather considered petitions or 'bills' as though acting as an ultimate court of justice. Not at all the forum of national public opinion and debate, it looked instead like a supreme tribunal with the king acting as supreme judge.[53] Maitland dealt with

---

[52] Frederic William Maitland (1850–1906). Eton and Trinity College, Cambridge: an Apostle. Bar and historical writing. Reader in Law, Cambridge, 1884; Downing Chair, Cambridge, 1888. *Domesday Book and Beyond: Three Essays in the Early History of England* (Cambridge, 1897); *Township and Borough* (Cambridge, 1898); *The Constitutional History of England* (Cambridge, 1908).

[53] Introduction to 'Records of a Parliament ...', (Rolls Series, 98, lxxxi–lxxxviii).

Stubbs gently, but if this analysis were correct then Stubbs's understanding of representative institutions would need to be recast. In a few lines
of an obscure publication, Maitland had brought about what Frank
Stenton later called '[t]he turning-point in the modern approach to
parliamentary history'.[54] Historians were not slow to see that significance. They saw it fastest in Cambridge, perhaps, but not in Cambridge,
England.

What Americans have done to English historiography over the past
century is an unexplored and important subject. By the turn of the
twentieth century, they had begun their own turn towards considering
the history of England as a way of enhancing their understanding of the
foundations of their country and its process of government.[55] Constitutional history played for them a critical role in that process and the
importance of their written constitution, plus the special place that it had
and has in the hearts of Americans, guaranteed that the history of constitutional matters would retain a fascination and significance for historians
in the United States even when it fell on hard times within British
culture. America, moreover, like France, embodied a distinctiveness
crucial to the consideration of how the constitution operated: it separated the function of the legislature, represented by Congress, from that
of the judicature, ultimately the Supreme Court, just as France had
suffered a less happy history in a society where the Estates supposedly
supplied representation and the *parlements* a judicial function. The thrust
of Maitland's analysis was that the medieval English parliament combined these two functions, and the implications of that observation
caught the eye at once of American historians, nowhere more so than
in Cambridge, Massachusetts, where a particular Harvard professor
became the focus for such study and trained others who would make a
major contribution to English constitutional history over the next
few decades. Remembered now mainly for his compilation of a major
bibliography of medieval studies or for his early work on medieval
merchant gilds, the name of Charles Gross deserves longer recollection
for its association with English history between 1910 and 1940.[56] This

---

[54] Frank Stenton, 'The History of Parliament', *TLS*, 6 January 1956, 2810.
[55] On the American background, see John Higham, Leonard Krieger and Felix Gilbert,
History: the Development of Historical Studies in the United States (Englewood Cliffs, NJ,
1965), and for the profession's sine-curve of 'objectivism', Peter Novick, *That Noble
Dream: the 'Objectivity Question' and the American Historical Profession* (Cambridge, 1988).
[56] Charles Gross (1857–1909). Jewish background. Williams College and Göttingen.
Thesis translated as *The Gild Merchant* (2 vols., 1890). Harvard from 1888. Wrote
mostly on municipal and legal history. First Gurney Professor of History and Political
Science at Harvard University. See Gross, *A Classified List of Books relating to British
Municipal History* (Cambridge, MA, 1891).

powerful and scrupulous teacher imposed his personality and interests on three men who would later record their debt to him when making their own statements about English constitutional history. They were James F. Baldwin,[57] Charles H. McIlwain[58] and – particularly important in England where he lived and worked for much of his life – Gaillard T. Lapsley.

McIlwain expressly drew attention in 1910 to the situation in the United States where the 'legislative' power of the Supreme Court had become 'a fact that is rightly attracting real attention at the present time' and argued that it must have some historical basis in a medieval English parliament that combined these roles. 'It both "legislated" and "adjudicated", but until modern times no clear distinction was perceived between those two kinds of activity.'[59] This meant that the term 'constitutional' demanded close scrutiny in its medieval context and a recognition that

the content of law, of which Magna Carta is the best example, was not entirely nor mainly 'constitutional'. 'Rigid' constitutions are a development of modern times. To us it seems natural to place the framework of government in a class by itself. We think of it alone as the fundamental law. We go as far as to make 'fundamental' and 'constitutional' practically equivalent terms. This was not done in medieval England.[60]

Not until the seventeenth century did he see, like his American colleague Wallace Notestein, a moment when 'modern times' encroached as parliament gained supremacy within the wider agencies of sovereignty in the English state; and that lent the trajectory of parliament a very different outline from the one supplied by Stubbs. His book and Baldwin's study of the King's Council then proved of material help to the English historian Albert Pollard,[61] who had been elected to a Fellowship at All

---

[57] James F. Baldwin, Professor of History at Vassar College. *The Scutage and Knight Service in England* (Chicago, 1897); *The King's Council in England during the Middle Ages* (Oxford, 1913).

[58] C. H. McIlwain, *The High Court of Parliament and its Supremacy* (New Haven, 1910); *The Growth of Political Thought in the West* (New York, 1932); *Constitutionalism, Ancient and Modern* (Ithaca, 1940). His collected papers were published by Cambridge University Press in 1939.

[59] McIlwain, *The High Court of Parliament*, viii–ix.

[60] McIlwain, 'Magna Carta and Common Law' in *Constitutionalism and the Changing World* (Cambridge, 1939), 127–77 at 177. Written in 1917, this essay drew attention to recent constitutional controversy over the Parliament Act of 1911 and argued that this recognition had never been more important to clarity of thought. See also H. L. Gray, *The Influence of the House of Commons on Early Legislation* (Cambridge, MA, 1932) and A. B. White, *Self-Government at the King's Command* (Minneapolis, 1933).

[61] A. F. Pollard (1869–1948). Methodist and Liberal background. Felsted and Jesus College, Oxford. Worked on *Dictionary of National Biography* for a decade after 1893.

Souls, Oxford, in 1908 specifically in order to conduct an extensive enquiry into the status of parliament under the Tudors.[62] Pollard continued the American theme, not only by attending to these authors but also in visiting Cornell in the spring of 1914 to deliver the fifteen lectures on his subject that he eventually expanded into one of his best-known books, *The Evolution of Parliament*, which he completed in 1915 though it was not published until after the war.[63]

It was left to Geoffrey Elton, many years later, to complain about parliamentary histories which took their direction from words such as 'growth' and 'evolution' because he disliked the linear and teleological accounts that they encouraged.[64] Pollard claimed that his account of the entire history of the representative institution began with Maitland's insight into the medieval parliament, 'a starting–point for us all'.[65] But in fact it began in the middle of his chronology with his deep knowledge of the status of parliament under Henry VIII and Elizabeth I. From there his mind worked back and forth from the Saxons to the present with the curve fixed by the Tudor co-ordinates that he had pre-set. This procedure gave him a result that was both revisionist *and* whig: he could declaim startling criticisms of Stubbs while confirming swathes of liberal sentiment about the later history of parliament from Macaulay, Gardiner and Firth. The former obligation was the more conscious, especially when the author declared it

the purport of these pages to show cause for thinking that parliaments in their infancy were much that parliament to-day is not, and little that it is; that legislation was not the original purpose of their being; that they existed before

Chair of Constitutional History, London, 1903–31. Founded Institute of Historical Research, 1921. *Henry VIII* (1902); *Factors in Modern History* (1907); *The History of England from the Death of Edward VI to the Death of Elizabeth (1547–1603)* (1910); *The Evolution of Parliament* (1920); *Wolsey* (1929).

[62] W. R. Anson to Pollard, 15 and 18 Mar. 1908, Pollard MSS 860 box 47. The offer originally envisaged Pollard's undertaking 'constitutional history of the whole or some part of the Tudor period'. Pollard asked for the topic to be limited to 'Parliament under the Tudors'.

[63] A. F. Pollard, *The Evolution of Parliament* (1920). His debt to McIlwain and Baldwin is recorded in the preface to the first edition. In introducing the second edition Pollard acknowledged missing an important article from the *Historische Zeitschrift*, which rather confirms the insulation of English scholarship from the greatest historical journal in Europe.

[64] G. R. Elton, 'Studying the History of Parliament', *British Studies Monitor*, 2 (1971/2), 4–14 at 8. He referred specifically to Pollard's volume. It should be noted that Kenneth Pickthorn had made the same point at the time of Pollard's second edition: 'The metaphors of *evolution* and *growth* are particularly dangerous because in practice . . . they tend towards fatalism . . .' (emphasis in original). Pickthorn, *Some Historical Principles of the Constitution* (1925), 9.

[65] Pollard, *The Evolution of Parliament*, v.

they contained any representative elements; . . . that parliament was at first a single chamber; that there was no 'house' of lords until after the close of the middle ages; that the 'house' of commons was not an original part of parliaments but yet is older than the 'house' of lords; and that the notion of three estates – so far from being the fundamental principle upon which parliaments were built – was borrowed from abroad and hesitatingly applied in the third century of English parliamentary history [i.e. under the Tudors] to an institution to which it was foreign in spirit and in practice.[66]

Dashing away with his smoothing-iron, Pollard levelled the contours of Stubbsian England and began a fashion for denying significance to medieval gatherings. The 'Model Parliament' of 1295 was no model; the 'Good Parliament' of 1376 was not much good.[67] Where we should place the correct emphasis instead does not need any guesswork, once Pollard's mission has become clear. 'The sixteenth century is indeed the great period of the consolidation of the house of commons, and without that consolidation the house would have been incapable of the work it achieved in the seventeenth. Under the Tudors it becomes a compact and corporate unit, and acquires a weight which makes it the centre of parliamentary gravity.'[68] His message was picked up by another of the Americans who contributed to this theme and a more celebrated one than the others – Wallace Notestein, who, in possibly the most famous British Academy Raleigh Lecture of the twentieth century, conceded the seed-bed of the Tudors, but located in the initiative of the House of Commons in framing legislation from the 1620s 'one of the essential changes in the growth of the English constitution'.[69]

---

[66] Ibid., 20. The 'third century' is made intelligible by Pollard's allegation that the Commons was not created by Simon de Montfort or Edward I but 'grew up during the fourteenth century' (113).

[67] Ibid., 55, for the model parliament that 'was not "model"'; cf. McIlwain's clearer perspective from 1936: 'If one thing in [Edward I's] reign more than another might serve to illustrate our changing historical views, it is what I would now probably speak of without risk as "the Myth of the Model Parliament".' 'The Historian's Part in a Changing World', in McIlwain, *Constitutionalism and the Changing World*. Even Stubbs, it is true, had soft–peddled on the Good Parliament which reached *sforzando* only in the 1920s with the (re)discovery of a new source: see below, pp. 41–2.

[68] Pollard, *The Evolution of Parliament*, 160.

[69] Wallace Notestein, 'The Winning of the Initiative by the House of Commons', *PBA*, 11 (1924), 125–75 at 126. Cf. Tanner's assertion at around the same time that 'the road which for the first Tudor had been only an ill-marked track had become to the feet of the first Stuart the beaten way of the Constitution'. Tanner, *Constitutional Conflicts*, 6. Of course, the momentous never seems so at the time. Twelve years after Notestein's lecture, one external examiner criticized the candidates from his host institution for their 'hav[ing] not fully grasped the significance of the work done on the English House of Commons by Notestein and his pupils'. George Potter to Theodore Moody (copy), 3 June 1936, Potter MSS box 22.

The early 1920s showed a confused mood in which the stamp of a new outlook and the Stubbsian constitutional imprint existed simultaneously. Eleanor Lodge, sister of Richard,[70] became principal of Westfield College, London, in 1921 and discovered that by no means all students there encountered constitutional history as a matter of course; even among those who did, she said, 'only a few take kindly . . . to Stubbs's Charters'.[71] The new administrative history pioneered by Tout at Manchester had more impact on *his* many pupils than memories of Stubbs. On the other hand, a young medievalist taught in Cambridge rather than Manchester not only enjoyed Tanner's lectures on constitutional history but found her notes very helpful when teaching at Newcastle before moving to Manchester itself.[72] Tanner must have felt the ambivalence of the current mood in trying to put together, with Charles Previté Orton, the revived volumes of the *Cambridge Medieval History* which had largely been commissioned before the war and run into the sands since then. None sounded so imprinted with the late nineteenth century as Doris Stenton whose covering letter enclosing her contribution on Henry I now reads for later generations as though she wanted to raise a laugh:

I have divided the chapter into two parts (i) the political aspects of the reign & (ii) an account of the administration . . . I have not found it possible to give any account of the social or economic conditions of the time. Neither have I said anything of the religious movements.[73]

But then compare the balance of Professor Caroline Skeel from London University, commissioned on the Stubbsian territory of the Lancastrian period. 'Constitutional development & social conditions must of course – after the narrative – be the main things,' she wrote. And she did not conceal her opinion that the fuss about the history of parliament had been overdone.[74] It was a moment of patchwork in which differing

---

[70] Sir Richard Lodge (1855–1936), son of Oliver Lodge, the physicist. Christ's Hospital and Balliol College, Oxford. Fellow of Brasenose College, Oxford, 1878–94; Professor of Modern History, Glasgow, 1894–99, and at Edinburgh, succeeding Prothero, 1899–1925. *The Close of the Middle Ages* (1901); *English Political History 1660–1702* (1909); *Great Britain and Prussia in the Eighteenth Century* (1923).

[71] Eleanor Lodge, *Terms and Vacations* (Oxford, 1938), 205.

[72] Margaret Deanesly to J. R. Tanner, 1 Nov. 1922, Tanner MSS CMH box 1.

[73] Doris Stenton to Tanner, 18 Sep. 1924, Tanner MSS CMH box 2.

[74] Caroline Skeel to Tanner, 13 July 1922, Tanner MSS CMH box 2. In the event she never wrote it. Peter Linehan wondered about 'a grievance against the editors' over the narrative issue ('The Making of the *Cambridge Medieval History*', *Spec.*, 57 (1982), 463–94 at 484 n.109 and 488 n.130), but equally plausible as an explanation is the depression that drove her out of academic life – see chapter 5 below, p. 121.

tendencies asserted themselves, just as they did in the political developments of the decade during which these opinions evolved.

Through that famous lecture in 1924 Notestein asked his audience to
think not only about developments in the 1620s but of the streams of
tendency that had fed into them – a point he made with reference to the
politics of his own day. 'Is it an exaggeration', he asked, 'to say that in the
Commons of 1924 you are reaping at length from the sowing of 1832,
1867 and 1884?'[75] If by that he hoped to catch a democratizing *Zeitgeist*
then he certainly missed it. He was right to look outside his texts, all the
same, for the new reading of parliament in history and right to think
about the politics of the moment informing the ways in which historians
were likely to think; but in the days of Baldwinian calm he stretched
credibility in seeing a great House of Commons there. Indeed contemporary authors were pointing to constitutional gloom. The epochal
importance of the Parliament Act of 1911, the admission of paid
Members of Parliament and the corruption that many believed would
ensue, the First World War with its disruption of constitutional relationships from the monarchy to the premiership,[76] the Coupon Election
with its blanketing majority, the sale of honours by Lloyd George to
anyone with enough money to buy one: none of these things enhanced
the plausibility of the Stubbs vision. The General Strike of 1926 hardly
made a manifesto for the success of parliamentary government or the
power of the House of Commons. Nor did the onset of fascism in Italy or
political violence in Germany do much to reassure observers that parliamentarism was faring better in Europe. These were years in which the
historical parliament would find little boost from modern conditions;
rather the reverse. By 1932, when Pollard himself attempted a summation of the current mood with the National Government firmly in place,
he had come to see the main architecture of parliamentary history as a
nineteenth-century creation with the twentieth century abandoning the
aisle 'for side-chapels and particular shrines'.[77] If Lewis Namier wanted
to see his eighteenth-century House of Commons as a gentlemen's club
insulated from principle as much as polemic, as his *magnum opus* of 1929
suggested at first blush,[78] then little in the current climate would lead

---

Whatever the cause, this ill-wind blew her chapter into the more powerful hands of
Bruce McFarlane. See McFarlane, 'The Lancastrian Kings, 1399–1461', *Cambridge
Medieval History* (1911–36), vol. VIII, 363–417.

[75] Notestein, 'Winning of the Initiative', 170.

[76] See, for example, Sir John Marriott, *The Constitution in Transition, 1910–24* (Oxford,
1924), 9, 39.

[77] Pollard, 'Parliamentary History', *TLS*, 13 Oct. 1932, 717–18.

[78] Lewis Namier, *The Structure of Politics at the Accession of George III* (2 vols., 1929).

him to take a different view. Indeed, the denial of Stubbs's understanding of parliament persisted and strengthened over the next few decades, reaching its apogee in G. R. Elton's work following *The Tudor Revolution in Government* of 1953.[79] Even among more measured commentators such as Goronwy Edwards, rescue seemed possible for only part of the Stubbsian thesis by the early 1950s, recognizing the damage done not only by Tudor historians such as Pollard, Neale and Elton but by medievalists themselves, in particular H. G. Richardson and G. O. Sayles through a raft of publications[80] that dismissed the importance of the 'representative' assembly when they could find it at all, dwelled on the judicial function we have seen emerging, and recalled the centrality of the Lords when 'parliament' could be shown to have had any serious role. Edwards, writing in 1955, wanted at least to make medieval representation sound like the beginnings of the parliamentary sovereignty that he remembered from Dicey.[81] 'But', he had to agree none the less, 'during the last sixty or seventy years there has been an unmistakable and growing tendency among some scholars, if not to write the medieval representatives *off*, at any rate very definitely to write them *down*.'[82] As we shall see later in this book, the mood encountered its critics and reversals but there was no denying its pervasiveness among modernists.

But the modernists hardly had it all their own way. 'Evolution' embracing decisive shifts, purposive continuity with winners and losers: the very language warns against any easy conviction that a whig sensibility had died. No wonder one observer had sent Notestein off to Yale with the thought that in a few years he 'would produce another group of young Gardiners'.[83] Revision there had certainly been, but the underlying thought in the work of most parliamentary historians about what historical narratives were supposed to do had not altered. Over the next few decades what we see instead is a spectrum of views about the history

---

[79] G. R., later Sir Geoffrey, Elton (1921–94). Born in Tübingen, son of the classicist Victor Ehrenberg. England from 1939. External London degree. War service (with new name). Cambridge after 1949 where he supervised more than seventy doctoral theses. Professor of English Constitutional History, 1967; Regius Chair, 1983. *The Tudor Revolution in Government: Administrative Changes in the Reign of Henry VIII* (Cambridge, 1953); *The Tudor Constitution: Documents and Commentary* (Cambridge, 1960); *Policy and Police: the Enforcement of the Reformation in the Age of Thomas Cromwell* (Cambridge, 1972).

[80] J. G. Edwards, *William Stubbs* (Historical Association pamphlet, Gen. 22, 1952), 19, was reduced to saying that Stubbs's account of parliament made up only one fifth of the text, which hardly made a compelling defence. For Richardson and Sayles, see pp. 94, 114.

[81] J. G. Edwards, *Historians and the Medieval English Parliament* (Glasgow, 1960), 42.

[82] Ibid., 27.

[83] Godfrey Davies to Notestein, 5 Feb. 1928, Notestein MSS 544/1/3/, 206.

of English representative institutions that has at one end a concern to shift decisive moments forward into the Tudor and Stuart periods and a countervailing brake that acknowledged the difficulties in Stubbs's arguments but wanted none the less to reinsert some of his perspectives by giving the later medieval period a weight that had become unfashionable. Two documents helped in this braking project. At one end of the argument, a guide to how parliaments should be called and arranged, the *Modus tenendi parliamentum*, gave rise to great discussion among political historians; at the other, a chronicle of the so-called Good Parliament of 1376, which remained unremarked until V. H. Galbraith published an edition of it in 1927, advanced the cause of protecting Stubbs's notion of popular representation.

The *Modus* got in the way of a post-Stubbsian revision. The master had put great stress on it and given it a predominant place in his *Select Charters* because it seemed to suggest that parliaments evolved early, had a representative component and that a clear procedure existed for their calling and operation.[84] Those who wished to follow Maitland in his scepticism had three ways to go: to declare the *Modus* a forgery; to declare it authentic but misdated; or to declare it derivative from a non-English source. All roads were followed, not least by the chief Stubbs-baiters of the twentieth century, H. G. Richardson and G. O. Sayles, who, in a spate of publications from the late 1920s onwards, tried to elbow the *Modus* out of the way.[85] Time worked against them, however, as evidence mounted that its provenance was English and not, as they hoped, Irish, and that its date was earlier than felt comfortable, perhaps the early decades of the fourteenth century. The *Anonimalle Chronicle* helped sustain that instinct, meanwhile, by providing an eye-witness acccount of the Good Parliament of 1376 that at least

---

[84] The idea of *representation* as a clear function of the medieval parliament remained powerful through the 1930s in the works of historians such as May McKisack (*The Parliamentary Representation of the English Boroughs during the Middle Ages* (Oxford, 1932)) and Maud Clarke (*Medieval Representation and Consent: a Study of Early Parliaments in England and Ireland, with Special Reference to the 'Modus tenendi Parliamentum'* (1936)).

[85] H. G. Richardson and G. O. Sayles, 'The Irish Parliaments of Edward I', *Proceedings of the Royal Irish Academy*, 38 (1928–9), 128–47; Richardson, 'The Preston Exemplification of the *Modus Tenendi Parliamentum*', *Irish Historical Studies*, 3 (1942), 187–92; Sayles, *The Medieval Foundations of England* (1948); Richardson and Sayles, *Parliament in Medieval Ireland* (Dundalk, 1964); Sayles, '*Modus Tenendi Parliamentum*: Irish or English?' in J. F. Lydon (ed.), *England and Ireland in the Later Middle Ages: Essays in Honour of Jocelyn Otway-Ruthven* (Blackrock, 1981), 122–52. Cf. N. Pronay and J. Taylor, 'The Use of the *Modus Tenendi Parliamentum* in the Middle Ages', *BIHR*, 47 (1974), 11–23; W. C. Weber, 'The Purpose of the English *Modus Tenendi Parliamentum*', *Parliamentary History*, 17 (1998), 149–77.

superficially implied, in the assertion of an impeachment procedure, 'the assurance of their successors in the seventeenth century'.[86] Taken together with the Provisions of Oxford of 1258 with their requirement of three parliaments a year *pur ver le estat del reaume et pur treter les cummuns besoinges del reaume et del rei ensement*, the early school of analysts had enough straw for their bricks and made revisionists think harder about their propositions for the sixteenth and seventeeth centuries. Even granted the weakness of arguing from the Provisions of Oxford to a form of public pressure on the king, the new resources of social and economic history in the post-war world could come in with assistance to reinvigorate Stubbs. Yes, the baronial revolt had been about barons.

But social and economic facts drove both king and barons to consider the people who would have to supply military and fiscal resources in time of need – the knights of the shire and the burgesses of the towns. And so Maitland's high court of Parliament has to be reinforced by Stubbs' 'concentration of local communities' and 'assembly of estates' . . . [T]he involvement of the commons in the process of law-making is bound up with the original character of the parliaments.[87]

One historian who wanted to go in the opposite direction was J. E. (later Sir John) Neale, who would become very important in the history of Tudor institutions: indeed his infatuation with all things Tudor and with Elizabeth in particular became the butt of undergraduate jokes.[88] For all his insistence on the primacy of Tudor experience in the history of parliament and commitment to some whig characteristics, he inadvertently helped the other side through an interesting twist. When he learned that Galbraith had discovered the chronicle of the Good Parliament, he asked to borrow Galbraith's working transcription of the chronicle and wrote an essay with it in mind, on the Commons' privilege of free speech, for a volume of Tudor essays published in 1924.[89] The essay fell into the hands of a very young Bruce McFarlane who found himself moving towards his own revision of Stubbs as a result. To a degree the familiar critique rested on what followed the fifteenth century: the attempted constitutional experiment was supposed to go under the wheels of Tudor tyranny and the historical undoing of that tyranny, originally by Froude but more persistently by the Pollard school, had

---

[86] F. M. Stenton, 'The History of Parliament', *TLS*, 6 Jan. 1956, 2810.
[87] H. M. Cam, *Law-Finders and Law-Makers in Medieval England* (1962), 18.
[88] For Neale see chapter 4, p. 106, note 55.
[89] J. E. Neale, 'The Commons' Privilege of Free Speech in Parliament', in R. W. Seton-Watson (ed.), *Tudor Studies, Presented to A. F. Pollard* (1924), 257–86. He refers to Galbraith's transcriptions at 257.

made the Lancastrians look less distinctive. Now McFarlane, the formidable Tutorial Fellow in Medieval History at Magdalen College, Oxford, rested his rejection of the Lancastrian experiment on a denial that anything was new in the nature of kingship, governance and bureaucracy during the century in question. In so far as novelty obtained, it did so in social and legal developments relating to the landed aristocracy which made the political history of the period work differently. What drove his own judgement about the period, indeed, was a new understanding of what a real political history might look like – a subject to which we must return in thinking about social and economic history and its methods in the twentieth century.[90] It would definitely differ from what Stubbs regarded as constitutional history which bled out of the account much that affected events and carried within itself a whig prejudice that McFarlane was the first to see in the very important terms in which he expressed it. The usual complaint – that Stubbs saw 'an appearance of maturity and completeness which [was] in fact illusory'[91] – was well taken by most authors after the First World War. McFarlane saw deeper and discovered a critical asymmetry in how Stubbs thought about the 'constitution' as a developing form. He defined it least guardedly in a letter to Helen Cam in 1949:

The real trouble about Stubbs's Lancastrianism, it seems to me, arises from his vague & even ambiguous use of the word 'constitutional'. For him it means much more than 'according to the law and custom of the constitution'; it is usually made to include the yielding of the king to parliament and nation of a most uncustomary share in government. [He then quotes the *Constitutional History*, vol. III §§320 and 343.] . . . But for Stubbs concessions to parliament are always much more constitutional than the king's attempts to vindicate his rights. It doesn't seem to occur to him that concessions wrung from a reluctant Henry IV were strictly speaking as unconstitutional as the usurpation [of Richard II] itself. Yet a Tory ought to have been the first to realize that Stubbs the historian was indeed an arrant whig.[92]

---

[90] See below, chapter 5, pp. 120–42.

[91] Theodore F. T. Plucknett, 'The Lancastrian Constitution', in Seton-Watson, *Tudor Studies* (1924), 161–81 at 161. This volume was important in McFarlane's own vision of this period; he singled out Neale's contribution to it as the beginning of a revisionist approach. See McFarlane, 'Early Paper on Crown and Parliament', in K. B. McFarlane, *The Nobility of Later Medieval England: the Ford Lectures for 1953 and Related Studies*, edited by J. P. Cooper and J. Campbell (Oxford, 1973), 288–9. He rightly reasoned that Neale's purpose was to make the Tudors appear creative.

[92] McFarlane to Cam, 30 Mar. 1949, Cam MSS 2/2/12. Similar attacks on constitutional history itself occur throughout McFarlane's essays and papers, as in the last paragraph of his Ford Lectures on the English nobility: 'The root trouble about most late-medieval constitutional history is its assumption that the interests of king and nobility were opposed, that conflict could not be avoided.' McFarlane, *The Nobility of Later Medieval England*, 120.

McFarlane's suspicions about the nature of constitutional history itself may stand as warning that it will not do merely to consider ways in which its late Victorian variant had become superseded by 1950. Undoubtedly the forensic analysis of parliaments through their membership, their administrative procedures and the 'civil service' on which they depended continued to undermine the Stubbsian model, nowhere more so than in the massive work of Thomas Frederick Tout on administration and the yet more massive *History of Parliament* initiated by Josiah Wedgwood in an act of whig piety which was readily turned by a Namierite collection of enthusiasts into a monument to other gods who ground slow but exceeding small.[93] Yet these new elements have to be located in a wider view of political history that envisaged ways of approaching the past that made Victorian historiography sometimes seem less distant and foreign. Herbert Butterfield proved quite as interested in putting the constitution and nation back into modern history as Lewis Namier felt in removing them. Grinding out histories of the House of Commons struck Butterfield as less urgent than re-establishing links between Commons and constituency, principle and party, and relating their story in a narrative with direction and shape. It would be premature to dismiss that instinct, or to forget its relationship with a widening sense of nation, simply because its focus had widened into social and economic issues unfamiliar to Stubbs. It would be premature, equally, to write the constitution off or to write it down in the world-view of English historians, just as it would tempt Providence to declare their God dead.

---

[93] T. F. Tout, *Chapters in Administrative History* (4 vols., Manchester, 1920–33); Hon. Josiah Wedgwood (ed.), *History of Parliament* (1936–). Julia Namier recalled how her husband had rapidly revolted against Wedgwood's Stubbsian assumptions. 'Long talks with Wedgwood soon convinced Lewis that in the fifteeenth century the stream that fascinated them both had been so unlike the one he knew [in the eighteenth century] that, loosely speaking, it was a different stream.' *Lewis Namier: a Biography* (Oxford, 1971), 199–200.

2 Church and state

A Protestant state

If a particular view of the importance of the English constitution became a whig legacy, so did a series of contentions about the church and its place in the struggle for freedom. And if the one contention demands examination in the light of what was to follow, then so does the other, for it may be that a retreat from the ideals of a Protestant state impinged on the ability of whig historiography to reproduce itself. Stubbs had, after all, been a bishop and had seen no incongruity between wearing the episcopal mitre and an academical gown; Gardiner married a daughter of Edward Irving[1] and escaped the church no more willingly than Stubbs; James Anthony Froude's Protestantism lacked a certain humility, but it galvanized his sense of Henry VIII's reasonableness and interfered constantly with the rest of his political judgements. The issue goes further, for all that, than curiosity about the personal religion of a few historians in inviting any sensitive observer of late nineteenth-century historiography to think about the connexion between Protestantism and the English state as it had developed since the Reformation. It is clear enough that a simple model of secularization among European historians, familiar from Owen Chadwick's path-breaking work on the secularization of the European mind and more recently from ecclesiastical histories of Britain in the twentieth century by Adrian Hastings and Callum Brown among others, will not work for the English as compellingly as it does for the French and Germans.[2] It

---

[1] Edward Irving (1792–1834). Born in Annan, close to Carlyle's future birthplace and on the same day as Shelley. Taught (and remained in love with) Jane Welsh Carlyle. Moved to London in 1822. Removed from Regent Square chapel in 1832 following his tolerance of 'speaking in tongues' and founded the Catholic Apostolic Church with his own church in Gordon Square.

[2] Owen Chadwick, *The Secularization of the European Mind in the Nineteenth Century* (Cambridge, 1975); cf. Michael Bentley, 'Victorian Historians and the Larger Hope', in Bentley (ed.), *Public and Private Doctrine: Essays Presented to Maurice Cowling* (Cambridge, 1993), 127–48. It should be noted that Chadwick gives religion a longer

will not do to assume, as Vivian Green did in his book about religion in Oxford and Cambridge many years ago, a process of 'steady attenuation' through the twentieth century.[3] Not only a persistent concern with religion among professional historians, one as familiar in the generations of Patrick Collinson[4] and Eamon Duffy[5] as among Victorians, but a tradition of identifying religion as a key determinant of how that English state turned out in its mature form guaranteed that the subject retained a certain vitality through the century after 1870. But it did not retain it in the same way or to the same degree or with the same consequences that it infected Stubbs's world; it became the subject of a divided polity in the wake of Catholic reaction and Dissenting protest; it had to learn to cope with lapsed faith and frank atheism from various parts of the historical community; and it had to find links and connexions that connected present and past more subtly than the Victorian historians had felt any need to emulate. Whether that story is pregnant for the understanding of whig history can be left for later judgement. What is blatant from the beginning is that the story cannot be cast as a linear trajectory of decline and attenuation.

Stubbs himself, whom one historian saw as a new Mabillon who captured 'the single-minded, wonderful Benedictine scholarship of a former age',[6] became the point of departure for so much in this story and lends depth to the contention of continuing religion by reflecting always two levels of description in his histories. The first and normally more prominent perspective was the light in which the church saved the nascent state of medieval England. His narrative revealed fragmentation in the state in the years after the Conquest, but the church carried continuity forward. 'The unity of the church', he insists, 'was in the early period the only working unity; and its liberty . . . the only form in

---

life in England in the essays collected as *Spirit of the Oxford Movement: Tractarian Essays* (Cambridge, 1990). Cf. Adrian Hastings, *A History of English Christianity 1920–1985* (1986) and, more contentiously, Callum Brown, *The Death of Christianity in Britain: Understanding Secularization 1800–2000* (2001).

[3] V. H. H. Green, *Religion at Oxford and Cambridge* (1964), 341.

[4] Patrick Collinson, CBE, FBA (1929–). King's School, Ely; Pembroke College, Cambridge; London PhD (1957). Lecturing posts in Khartoum, 1956–61, King's College, London, 1961–9, Chairs in History at Sydney, 1969–75, Kent 1976–84, Sheffield 1984–8; Regius Professor of Modern History, Cambridge, 1988–96. *The Elizabethan Puritan Movement* (1967); Ford Lectures: *The Religion of Protestants* (Oxford, 1982); *Godly People: Essays on Elizabethan Protestantism and Puritanism* (1983).

[5] Eamon Duffy, Professor of Church History and President of Magdalene College, Cambridge. See in particular *The Stripping of the Altars: Traditional Religion in England c.1400–c.1580* (New Haven, 1992) and *The Voices of Morebath: Reformation and Rebellion in an English Village* (New Haven, 2001).

[6] Charles Bémont, 'Bishop Stubbs', *Quarterly Review*, 202 (1905), 1–34 at 18.

which the traditions of the ancient freedom lingered. It was . . . to unite Norman and Englishmen in the resistance to tyrants, and educated the growing nation for its distant destiny as the teacher and herald of the world.'[7] Distant destiny strikes the most obtuse historian as a significant narrative ingredient; but note, too, its vehicle as it trundles back and forth through the three volumes of the *Constitutional History*. Judging the years of Henry II's reign, his mind goes most readily to Langton and Beckett and the balm they had brought to a bleeding polity. 'They had bound up the wounds of the perishing State,' in Stubbs's words. 'No doubt there were evils in the secular employments of these great prelates; but if for a time the spiritual work of the Church was neglected, and unspiritual aims fostered within her pale, the State gained immensely by being administered by statesmen whose first ideas of order were based on conscience and law rather than on brute force.'[8] Nothing in the next three hundred years of his account dissuades him from the conclusion that church and state must be read as an historic and moral fusion that does not merely accompany the story as a decorative motif but explains much of its optimism:

Second, but only second, to the influence of the crown was the influence of the Church . . . In more ways than one the ecclesiastical power in England was a conserving and uniting element . . . To those who knew anything of the political history of the past, the Church had great historical claims to honour; her champions had withstood the strongest and most politic kings and her holiest prelates had stood side by side with the defenders of national liberty . . . Rich, wide-spread, accumulating for centuries a right to the national gratitude working in every class of society, the clergy were strong in corporate feeling and in the possession of complete machinery for public action . . . If we may judge of the class by the character and conduct of the foremost men, they ought to have the full benefit of the admission which their bitterest critics cannot withhold. They worked hard for the good of the nation; they did not forget the good of the Church; but they rarely if ever sacrificed the one to the other.[9]

Thus the great bishop about other great bishops. The second level of penetration in his religion ought not to be obscured, all the same, by shadows thrown by the church as an institution. The narrative is crafted precisely to reveal 'higher laws, more general purposes, the guidance of a Higher Hand'.[10] At every turn it is coloured by Christian values and

---

[7] William Stubbs, *The Constitutional History of England in its Origin and Development* (3 vols., 1873–8), §90, vol. I, 268.

[8] Ibid., ch. XVIII, §166, vol. I, 676–7.

[9] Ibid., ch. XXI, §464, vol. III, 539–41. His huge chapter on 'The Clergy, the King and the People' fills almost a hundred pages of volume III (294–387, §§374–405).

[10] Ibid., ch. XVII, §298, vol. II, 654.

teaching whether or not Stubbs is discussing the church. It may not have been necessary to give Henry VI twelve adjectives – 'pious, pure, generous, patient, simple, true and just, humble, merciful, fastidiously conscientious, modest and temperate';[11] he undoubtedly thought it natural to make nine of them carry a Christian weight. But in any case – and the point for our purpose – history had to be written as theology-teaching by example. '[T]he study of Modern History', he said in his later Oxford lectures,

is, next to Theology itself . . . the most thoroughly religious training that the mind can receive. It is no paradox to say that Modern History, including Medieval History in the term, is co-extensive in its field of view, in its habits of criticism, in the persons of its most famous students, with Ecclesiastical History. We may call them sister studies, but, if they are not really one and the same, they are twin sisters, so much alike that there is no distinguishing between them . . . It is Christianity that gives to the modern world its living unity and at the same time cuts it off from the death of the past.[12]

Smoothing discontinuity and keeping the past alive were and remained whig-historical aspirations and it would be a rash commentator who ignored their formative role in thinking about English history during Stubbs's lifetime.

One of Mandell Creighton's successors in the Dixie Chair of Ecclesiastical History in Cambridge, J. P. Whitney,[13] developed in 1893 Stubbs's fanciful thoughts about the German germs of the constitution and turned them into the German germs of the church:

the task of the middle ages was the training of the northern nations by the Latin church. The Teutons were wild and lawless, but their very vices were the vices of strength rather than of weakness. They were better stuff to work on than the effete old heathen society. They could at least welcome with enthusiasm the love of Christ which had sought them out in their northern forests; and a strong man's enthusiasm has always been both power and weakness to the English and the German.[14]

---

[11] Ibid., ch. XVIII, §341, vol. III, 134.

[12] William Stubbs, *Seventeen Lectures on the Study of Medieval and Modern History and Kindred Subjects delivered at Oxford* (Oxford, 1886), 13, 15–16.

[13] James Pounder Whitney (1857–1939). Owens' College, Manchester and King's College, Cambridge. Priested 1885. Rector of Milton, Cambridge, 1885–1900. Chair of Ecclesiastical History, King's College, London, 1908–18. Dixie Chair, Cambridge, 1919–39.

[14] Whitney, *The Gospel and Society: Three Lectures* (Cambridge, 1893), 18. Whitney also commented on the constitutional importance of the church in insisting on episcopal government that avoided 'alike a Papal tyranny or individual anarchy'. See his *The Episcopate and the Reformation* (1917), 166–7, 172.

This partnership between race and nation, church and destiny held out the promise of a delicate balance between church and state of the kind Stubbs wanted – 'the identity between the good man and the good citizen'[15] – but even by his day the balance had come under threat from the events of his own century. In his tedious constitutional history of the Church of England, published in German in 1894, a Berlin lawyer called Makower stressed the degree to which the relationship had entered a period of flux once civil rights had been given to Catholics and Dissenters.[16] The revival of a powerful Catholic historiography we shall examine shortly. But it would be a mistake to lose sight of Nonconformity as an energy-centre of thought about Church and state from an aggressive, often whig stance. Dissent had benefited, after all, from Whig politics after 1689 and the celebration of rights wrung from a disapproving state had an historical form in the work of English historians wishing to distance themselves from the state. Herbert Butterfield's *Christianity and History* (1949) does not scream Methodism; but a slim and spare Methodist heritage played its part in generating the message of indifference to all things except cleaving to Christ: its famous last sentence. No less important were those Dissenting historians who carried the lamp of entire communities to illuminate their own, partial past. Churchmanship underpinned versions of whig language in the historical writings of Gordon Rupp[17] or Bernard Lord Manning[18] and any view of whig sustainability would be weakened without their inclusion in the reckoning.

Among Anglicans, on the other hand, Richard Hooker's ideal of an ecclesiastical polity, one reinvigorated by Coleridge and then Gladstone in the 1830s,[19] had begun by the 1870s to tip over into something resembling a political ecclesia: an Erastian reworking of the Reformation in which the state rightly played a predominant role that ought to be

---

[15] Stubbs, *Constitutional History*, §374, vol. III, 296.

[16] Felix Makower, *The Constitutional History and Constitution of the Church of England* (New York, 1895): 'the exclusively protestant character of state constitution was gone' (98–9).

[17] Gordon Ernest Rupp (1910–86). Wesley House, Cambridge: First Class in Theology. Methodist ministry and then teaching at Richmond Methodist College, 1938–52. Cambridge 1952–6 and Professor of Ecclesiastical History, Manchester, 1956–67. Dixie Chair, Cambridge, from 1968 and Principal of Wesley House, 1967–74. *Studies in the Making of the English Protestant Tradition* (Cambridge, 1947); *The Righteousness of God; Luther Studies* (1953); *Patterns of Reformation* (1969), etc.

[18] Bernard Lord Manning (1892–1941). Father Congregationalist minister: remained convinced Congregationalist. Semi-invalid. Caistor Grammar School and Jesus College, Oxford; later Fellow and Senior Tutor. *The People's Faith in the Time of Wyclif* (1919); *The Making of Modern English Religion* (1929); *Essays in Orthodox Dissent* (1939).

[19] Samuel Taylor Coleridge, *On the Constitution of the Church and State, according to the idea of each* (1830); W. E. Gladstone, *The State in its Relation to the Church* (1838).

Chillingworth's celebrated remark that the Bible was the
Protestants underwent simultaneously a certain slippage in
:neutics of the German school of theology, in Strauss's
Leben Jesu (1835), translated no less notoriously by George
in the English *Ecce Homo*, projected a few years before
Stubbs's *History* in 1868, or vomited from the jaws of hell as Lord
Shaftesbury preferred to put it, by the anonymous John Robert Seeley.
The latter went on to the Regius Chair in Cambridge, wedged
chronologically between a cheerful Protestant in Charles Kingsley
and a progressive Roman Catholic in Lord Acton, embodying as
Seeley did 'the "natural religion" of the average educated middle-aged
Englishman',[20] continuing his evacuation of the Protestant state into
little more than a state that happened to contain Protestants and
developing an insight redolent of Durkheim that religions should be seen
as 'nationalities in an idealized form'.[21]

Early modern historians – they would not have recognized the
appellation – punched home the message of state encroachment in the
last twenty years of the century, though with varying levels of approval.
The period from the Reformation to the Civil War became a platform for
views about the power of religion to dislocate as well as inspire and the
rightful needs of a developing state to regain control of it. Creighton,
recovering from his *History of the Papacy*,[22] discovered tolerance within
the umbrella of a civilized state – the one implied by T. H. Green and the
Oxford Idealists more than anything the sixteenth century could offer. 'A
State need not necessarily maintain a lower standard of moral rectitude
than the Church,' he told his Cambridge audience in the Hulsean
Lectures of 1893–4. 'The Church welcomes the gradual transference
to the State of many departments of social activity which have been
quietly organised by her offices . . . Ecclesiastical power will never
be revived; but any lingering desire after it prevents the growth of
ecclesiastical influence.'[23] For James Anthony Froude, similarly,

---

[20] George Unwin, 'The God of History', in Unwin, *Studies in Economic History* (1927),
407–28 at 407.

[21] J. R. Seeley, *Natural Religion* (1882), quoted in Deborah Wormell, *Sir John Seeley and the
Uses of History* (Cambridge, 1980), 37.

[22] Mandell Creighton, *A History of the Papacy during the Years of the Reformation* (5 vols.,
1882–94); *A History of the Papacy from the Great Schism to the Sack of
Rome* (6 vols., 1897).

[23] Mandell Creighton, *Persecution and Tolerance: Being the Hulsean Lectures Preached before
the University of Cambridge in 1893–4* (1895), 129–30, 138. Looking back on these
lectures six decades later, Norman Sykes saw in them a last moment 'when the Liberal
State was still enjoying the Indian summer of its prosperity.' *Man as Churchman*
(Cambridge, 1960), 166.

recovering from the twelve volumes of his *History of England from the Fall of Wolsey to the Death of Elizabeth,* and speaking in Oxford while Creighton spoke in Cambridge, the Puritan Revolution (as Gardiner had made everyone call it, with his view of the seventeeth century as a struggle for 'divine order' and Calvinism as its quickener[24]) and the Liberal party (both of them good things) sprang from the same root. 'To Macaulay and Buckle', he admitted, 'Cranmer is the basest of mankind.' But they had missed the point. ' [T]he Liberals . . . are the lineal successors of the Long Parliament. The Long Parliament came straight from Cranmer and his friends, the Marian martyrs. Their existence as a party grew out of the struggle between freedom of thought and ecclesiastical authority, and without the Marian martyrs they would perhaps never have been a party at all.'[25] Gratitude to Henry VIII was not universal, but Froude had made it at least respectable. A younger, better scholar of the period, and a future parliamentary Liberal candidate, was Albert Pollard. He found much to lament in the Tudor handling of religion but nothing to throw doubt on its momentous consequences for future relations between church and state. Writing towards the end of the Boer War, with the imperial glory of the Tudors looking now frailer than once it had, Pollard reverted to tyranny as his noun, the one that whigs had always used.

This was the real tyranny of Tudor times; men were dominated by the idea that the State was the be-all and end-all of human existence. In its early days the State is a child; it has no will and no ideas of its own, and its first utterances are merely imitation and repetition. But by Henry VIII's reign the State in England had grown to lusty manhood; it dismissed its governors, the Church, and laid claim to that omnipotence and absolute sovereignty which Hobbes regretfully expounded in the *Leviathan* . . . The service of the State tended, indeed, to encroach on the service of God, and to obliterate altogether respect for individual liberty.[26]

Good or bad, the whig historical temperament saw by turn of century a Protestant state very different from that confessional state intended by Gladstone or the enthusiasts of the Oxford Movement in the 1830s and

---

[24] S. R. Gardiner, *History of England* (10 vols., 1883–4), vol. x, 78–9; Gardiner, *The First Two Stuarts* (1876), 63. The phrase, 'the Puritan Revolution', persisted throughout the first half of the century: the lecture notes of A. S. Turberville at Leeds University mention it three times in three paragraphs in his lecture on Charles II (Turberville MSS 149/15). J. P. Kenyon memorably described it as Gardiner's greatest disservice to historical studies in the first sentence of *The Stuart Constitution 1603–1688: Documents and Commentary* (Cambridge, 1966).

[25] J. A. Froude, *Lectures on the Council of Trent* (1896), 4. Cf. his *History of England from the Fall of Wolsey to the Death of Elizabeth* (12 vols., 1856–70).

[26] Albert Pollard, *Henry VIII* (1902), 433.

1840s, who had recently been celebrated by Dean Church despite
Froude's dismissal of it as 'the grimacing of a dead superstition . . .
struggling out of its grave'.[27] Changing contexts had already
problematized the task of discovering historically the rise of individual
liberty within Protestantism as the cornerstone of English progress.

Challenges

That these trajectories could be made to coincide – religion, state,
liberty – reflected an intellectual optimism that now seems virtually
beyond recapture. The muscular Christianity of frank and manly public
schoolboys somehow coalesced with a view of the state as the representation of man's better self and produced a special freedom dependent on
responsibility and – the catchword of the period – decency. If the present
required constant division of one's contemporaries into sound men and
cads, so did the past, which readily yielded to a search for them. Has
there ever been a more plangent celebration of sound men than a
publisher's series entitled 'English Worthies' or 'Heroes of the Nation'?
There has certainly never been a more formidable cad-hunter than Lord
Acton inflicting, with total confidence, punishment on past wrong. One
may wonder what happened to these entwined confidences. An easy
answer, and a mistaken one, lies ready to hand in the First World War.
It feels plausible enough that the worst cataclysm known to man, fought
in circumstances not only of human degradation but also with a sense of
apparent pointlessness, would generate all the secular attitudes familiar
ninety years later and produce histories and historians dominated by
cynicism and without trajectory, a sort of retrospectively conceived waste
land in which all Aprils had proved cruel, each promise empty. The war
did indeed produce some of that aggression, as we shall see, and, when it
did not, the experience of it among young people finding their way, such
as the schoolboy Herbert Butterfield at Keighley during those years,
remained indelible. But it produced also the opposite: an intellectual
society in which religion recharged *because* of what it had been made to
endure, and to a manifest degree that ought to curb the determination of
later generations wanting to show that English historiography became

[27] For the concept of a confessional state, see Perry Butler, *Gladstone: Church, State and Tractarianism; a Study of Gladstone's Religious Ideas and Attitudes* (Oxford, 1982), 77–123. R. W. Church, *The Oxford Movement: Twelve Years, 1833–1845* (1891). For the quotation from Froude, see his 'Times of Erasmus and Luther' in Froude, *Short Studies on Great Subjects* (4 vols., 1867–83), vol. I, 39–153 at 153. Cf. Froude, 'Condition and Prospects of Protestantism', in ibid., vol. II, 146–79 and 'Revival of Romanism', in ibid., vol. III, 130–206.

secular from 1918. There are other problems, too. If whig optimism about the Protestant state came under overt challenge after 1914, it had felt some of that undermining long before the war started. These earlier initiatives strike us far more strongly than they impinged on contemporaries. In the longer view, never the less, they merit remark if the twentieth century is to be seen as a whole. Two strands help a sense of perspective: the appearance of a style of social Christianity whose state would be Protestant but not Liberal; and the beginning of an important dialogue between Protestants and a Catholic version of the past that the whig establishment had largely concealed. Both began before the First World War and both straddled it.

A style of Christian belief that oriented English history differently from the vision of Stubbs or Froude began not so much with the 'Christian Socialism' of Maurice and Ludlow in the 1840s, which lacked a coherent historical dimension, but rather with the economic critiques of writers influenced by the German school of economic history – especially the elder Arnold Toynbee with his pioneering account of the industrial revolution and William Cunningham's evocation of modern society.[28] These portraits, from two committed Anglicans, went far beyond dispassionate descriptions; they revealed moral issues about inequality and deprivation to be dealt with on a sub-theological level. Concerns of this kind did not have to lead in the direction of a Christian critique: they could inform secular and liberal accounts of industrialization and urbanization in the way that J. L. and Barbara Hammond wrote about the agricultural and industrial labourer.[29] But in one pair of hands in particular they became clay thrown on a quite different wheel. For R. H. Tawney the problems of the modern age could only be investigated historically and in a spirit of Christian sympathy for the oppressed classes which issued in a hard-edged doctrine about state and church. Like Froude, he thought that the partnership could not be equal, but for reasons that Froude would not have recognized. 'There must be a Church as well as a State,' he wrote in his

[28] Arnold Toynbee (1852–83). Born Savile Row, son of a surgeon. Pass degree from Balliol College, Oxford. Disciple of Ruskin and Green. Always infirm; died of meningitis at the age of thirty-one. See his *Lectures on the Industrial Revolution in England* (1884). For William Cunningham (1849–1919), see Audrey Cunningham, *William Cunningham: Teacher and Priest* (1950). His *magnum opus* was *An Essay on Western Civilization in its Economic Aspects* (2 vols., Cambridge, 1898), but see also *Christianity and Social Questions* (1910); *Christianity and Economic Science* (1914); *Christianity and Politics* (1916).

[29] J. L. and Barbara Hammond, *The Village Labourer* (1911); *The Town Labourer* (1917); *The Age of the Chartists* (1930). He was the son of a rector in Yorkshire, she the daughter of a vicar and probably the stronger historical mind of the two. Journalism and writing occupied their life together.

commonplace book in 1913. 'But the church must not be above the state, not because it is too bad but because it is too good . . . It must be free to be a servant . . . The ancient question [of church and state] finds its solution in a free church refusing the temporalities for the sake of the spiritualities.'[30] Temporalities meant money; and for the rest his life Tawney obsessed about money, interest, acquisitiveness and the various evils that flowed from them. He began with God and that meant he began with equality because '[i]n order to believe in human equality it is necessary to believe in God . . . What is wrong with the modern world is that, having ceased to believe in the greatness of God, and therefore the infinite smallness (or greatness – the same thing!) of *man*, it has to invent or emphasize distinctions between *men*.'[31] In order to re-establish a true moral order, such as that of the middle ages, in which, he thought, one might be poor but one's conscience was not every day revolted by the unfairness of society,[32] another revolution was necessary – one that may turn out as messy as the seventeenth century's attempt but whose eventual benefits he deemed assured:

when we cut off the heads of our industrial Lauds and Straffords, we shall probably for a century or so have to put up with political jobbery and ineptitude which at present is limited by the fact that large spheres of national life lie outside politics altogether. But if one is asked 'Was the Great Rebellion worth while?', there are few decent Englishmen would not say 'Yes'.[33]

These private thoughts, written in a notebook and not for publication, suggest how far removed Tawney's historical state might be from those of the blander whigs. He wanted a state based on moral foundations, certainly, but those of equality and fairness secured under law: not a liberal vision but a socialist one.

Tawney then had his war; and the private became public in a volume that captivated a generation of historians for whom religion had become a dubious asset. *Religion and the Rise of Capitalism*, delivered as the first [Henry Scott] Holland Memorial Lecture in 1922, appeared in 1926 with a foreword by Charles Gore, baptizing social Christianity in the way that his episcopal predecessors had tried to baptize Darwinism. The famous thesis linking the development of Protestantism with the value-structure of nascent capitalism reiterated in historical form the

---

[30] Commonplace book, 1 Dec. 1913, in J. M. Winter and D. M. Joslin (eds.), *R. H. Tawney's Commonplace Book*, *Economic History Review*, Supplement 5 (Cambridge, 1972), 71.

[31] Ibid., 6 Mar. 1913, 54.

[32] Ibid., 10 June 1912, 19.

[33] Ibid., 3 June 1912, 11.

insights of Weber's 'celebrated essay' on the Protestant ethic.[34] Along the way, however, Tawney supplied a sort of whiggery-in-negative with a continuity of process driving the argument forward but towards a dark conclusion – usury and exploitation – which his pre-war work had anticipated and which his style of Anglicanism endorsed. The medieval church had suffered from corruption and a narrow spirit, it was true, but at least it had reined in Tawney's true devil, commerce. 'A man must be sure', in this teaching, 'that he carries it on for the public benefit, and that the profits which he takes are no more than the wages of his labour.'[35] This view has the extra virtue of making Aquinas responsible for the labour theory of value and thus rendering Karl Marx 'the last of the Schoolmen'.[36] But then Puritanism took religion into new and dangerous waters, losing sight of 'the insistence of medieval thinkers that society is a spiritual organism, not an economic machine, and that economic activity . . . requires to be controlled and repressed by reference to the moral ends for which it supplies the material means'.[37] One can almost hear his loathing for modern man in his depiction of the driven Puritan:

Called by God to labour in his vineyard, he has within himself a principle at once of energy and order, which makes him irresistible both in war and in the struggles of commerce. Convinced that character is all and circumstances nothing, he sees in the poverty of those who fall by the way . . . a moral failing to be condemned, and in riches . . . the blessing which rewards the triumph of energy and will.[38]

Worse still, Anglicanism has 'surrendered' to these forces and degenerated into 'a kind of pious antiquarianism'.[39]

True Christianity, this polemic implied, would not associate itself with the story of moral abdication but rather announce its lack of complicity; and that was now the trouble with whigs like Gardiner or Froude or Trevelyan: they connived with the darkness at the heart of the plot. This kind of message had considerable power in the twentieth century and must be borne in mind when considering whig vulnerabilities. It has a presence – more subtle and understated but present all the same – in Helen Cam's earlier years when her Christian socialism left part of her mind examining medieval society for its proto-trade unions and another part impelling her to send what little money she had to the Viennese hungry. It presumably inhabited the moments when Beatrice Webb was on her knees in that '"habit of prayer" she

---

[34] R. H. Tawney, *Religion and the Rise of Capitalism* (1926), xi.
[35] Ibid., 32.   [36] Ibid., 36.   [37] Ibid., 61.
[38] Ibid., 230–1.   [39] Ibid., 135.

speaks of'.[40] It can weigh too much on one's mind, of course, if we forget the sublime English principles of apathy and ignorance. A decade or so after the publication of Tawney's book, the good news had not quite reached the lodge of New College, Oxford, whose warden, H. A. L. Fisher, betrays a certain vagueness about it all. 'It is certainly a matter of importance,' he wrote to a correspondent. 'R. H. Tawney has dealt with it at length in one of his excellent books, the title of which for the moment I cannot recall. I am afraid I do not know Max Weber's essay but I shall certainly read it . . .'[41]

But then Fisher impresses his biographer as a rationalist of the 'high and dry kind' who had written a slashing attack on Christian Science, 'an extraordinary farrago of nonsense',[42] and who resisted manfully the countless attempts of his editor, Douglas Jerrold, to make his *History of Europe* better reading for Catholics. Jerrold[43] and his contemporary Christopher Dawson[44] stood heirs to a tradition of Roman Catholic historiography which provided a second challenge to the more comfortable assumptions of whigs about the Protestant state. Persecution, recusancy and secrecy do much to explain the lack of such a tradition before the remarkable John Lingard, whose *History of England* inaugurated a significant strand of writing that showed Lingard to be an author of discrimination and intelligence, if never quite the 'English Ranke' claimed by his biographer.[45] He was little regarded by his contemporaries, despite the re-establishment of the Catholic

---

[40] F. M. Unwin to R. H. Tawney, 2 Apr. 1945, Tawney MSS 24/2.

[41] Fisher to Henry M. Andrews (copy), 29 May 1935, Fisher MSS 71 f.15. Herbert Albert Laurens Fisher (1865–1940). Born into the intellectual aristocracy: father private-secretary to the Prince of Wales, mother a Pattle, Maitland his brother-in-law, Virginia Woolf a cousin, Julia Cameron an aunt. Edward Grey's fag at Winchester. Gilbert Murray his closest friend. Warden of New College, Oxford, from 1924 after brief ministerial career in Lloyd George's governments.

[42] Fisher to A. J. Balfour (copy), Fisher MSS 66 f.157. Cf. his entry by Alan Ryan in the *Oxford Dictionary of National Biography* (*ODNB*), vol. XIX, 677–83, at 681.

[43] Douglas Jerrold was director and later chairman of Eyre and Spottiswoode. He wanted Fisher to increase in particular the coverage of Gregory the Great and Aquinas who, he thought, ought to have at least twice as many pages as Wycliffe. Jerrold to Fisher, 28 Apr. 1932, Fisher MSS 69 ff.93–4.

[44] Henry Christopher Dawson (1889–1970). Son of a Yorkshire landowner and an archdeacon's daughter. Winchester and Trinity College, Oxford. Conversion to Roman Catholicism after Oxford. Prolific author; admiration for Cardinal Hinsley and Bishop Bell. Professor of Roman Catholic Studies, Harvard, 1958–62. *The Making of Europe* (1932); *Medieval Religion* (1934); *Religion and the Rise of Western Culture* (1950).

[45] Lingard's *History of England from the First Invasion by the Romans* (8 vols., 1819–30) found a sympathetic continuator in Hilaire Belloc who extended the narrative to 1910. Cf. Donald F. Shea, *The English Ranke: John Lingard* (New York, 1969).

episcopal hierarchy in 1850 and the public stature of Newman and Manning, though he attracted some attention among inter-war Catholics;[46] and Lord Acton, who *was* so regarded, struck English observers none the less as a European aristocrat with an unattractive message of retrospective retribution. Only after Acton's death in 1902 did the culture begin to absorb a Catholic presence, mostly through the popular literary figures cut by Hilaire Belloc and G. K. Chesterton. From the historians' point of view Downside Abbey played an important role through two of its spiritual leaders, Dom Aidan, Cardinal Gasquet[47] who made an important mess of editing Acton, and the house's later abbot, Cuthbert Butler, whose treatise on the Benedictine monastic life, published in 1919,[48] remained significant as a background and target for the Downside renegade, the Benedictine monk Dom David Knowles. Indeed the inter-war years suggested a Catholic confidence among the clerisy of England, and not only in the confined circles of an Evelyn Waugh or Graham Greene or among the Anglo-Catholic mysteries of T. S. Eliot. Few attained the assertiveness of Romney Sedgwick, collaborator with Lewis Namier in editing eighteenth-century primary sources, who, despite direct descent from Adam Sedgwick of geology fame, was 'not only a Roman Catholic . . . but a colonel in the Swiss Guard at the Vatican'.[49] Less spectacular were quiet advances institutionally, perhaps especially in Oxford with the establishment of Campion Hall in 1918

---

[46] An example was Edmund Bishop who 'told me he found old Lingard the best historian of the Early Church, because, being a Roman Catholic, he thoroughly understood the practices and point of view of the Church he was dealing with . . .' Kenneth Sisam to F. M. Stenton, 13 June 1935, Stenton MSS 8/18/1/. Bishop (1846–1917) was a Catholic convert and formerly Carlyle's amanuensis. Collaborator of Gasquet (see below). Papers published posthumously with Sisam's help as *Liturgica historica* (1918).

[47] Francis Neil [Aidan] Gasquet (1846–1929). Vast output, mostly of edited primary materials, but see also *The Eve of the Reformation* (1900); *English Monastic Life* (1904); *Henry III and the Church* (1905); *Parish Life in Medieval England* (1906); *England under the Old Religion and Other Essays* (1912). On Acton see Gasquet's *Lord Acton and his Circle* (1906).

[48] Rt Revd Cuthbert Butler, *Benedictine Monachism: Studies in Benedictine Life and Rule* (1919). Butler was willing to see historical work as satisfying the Rule's requirement that the monk should labour. But of course '[t]his means laborious study and comparison of original sources, the Fathers, the early authorities for history; it means working among archives and records, transcribing documents, collating manuscripts – all of it painful, exacting, unexciting work' (377–8).

[49] Denys Winstanley to J. R. M. Butler, 10 Feb. 1940. 'When the Prime minister and Lord Halifax visited the Pope,' Winstanley went on to recall, 'he acted as their interpreter . . . He dined with me one evening and was quite pleasant, though very ultramontane.' Butler MSS A1/147.

(and the presence there from 1927 of Martin D'Arcy SJ, who converted Waugh) and of Greyfriars in 1921.

These currents washed over into higher reaches of Anglicanism. So unmysterious (and unhistorical) an archbishop as Cosmo Gordon Lang saw that the Prayer Book of 1549 and 1662, reduced to ashes by the revision of 1928, must remain an important document in Anglican sensibility.[50] A lesser light shining from the Society for the Promotion of Christian Knowledge, and himself the son of a bishop, caught a powerful mood on New Year's Day, 1922, ruminating to a future Professor of St Andrews about the possibility of union between the Churches of England and Scotland. Note the weight in his remarks not so much of doctrine as of *history*:

> We want, above all things, to be Catholic. We look upon the Reformation as a temporary break in Church tradition, but we are not very much interested in it. The teeming life of the medieval towns before the advent of Tudor centralization seems to us more full of lessons for the 20th century than are the 17th and 18th centuries. Similarly in church matters, St Augustine, St Thomas Aquinas, St Anselm & St Francis mean more to us than Cranmer and Laud . . . It is the Church Catholic, which is common to the Church of all ages, & especially to the undivided Church, which attracts us . . . As to episcopacy, we cannot budge. Prelacy most of us dislike as much as the Scotch but primitive episcopacy, never questioned till the 16th century, we dare not touch.[51]

This fertile soil readily accepted David Knowles's portrait of the religious orders of England (and especially the black monks) acting as 'the very heart and soul of the rebirth of the country' in the time of Edgar and Dunstan, and remaining until the Reformation 'an element of great importance to the religious, social and economic life of the nation'.[52] It also has a presence, on the Protestant side, in the very early work of Geoffrey Dickens in his studies of continuing Romanism in post-Reform Yorkshire that he hid away in the *Yorkshire Archaeological Journal* between 1938 and 1941.[53] None of

---

[50] Lang to Claude Jenkins, 17 Oct. 1923: it was 'a genuine bit of Church history'. Jenkins MSS 1634 f.163.

[51] W. Lowther Clarke to J. B. Baxter, 1 Jan. 1922, Baxter MSS 36940/282a-b. Lowther Clarke was Canon of All Saints', West Dulwich, and editorial secretary of the Society for the Promotion of Christian Knowledge from 1915.

[52] M. D. Knowles, *The Monastic Order in England: a History of its Development from the Times of St Dunstan to the Fourth Lateran Council 943–1216* (Cambridge, 1940, 1949), 680.

[53] A. G. Dickens, 'Royal Pardons for the Pilgrimage of Grace', *YAJ*, 33 (1938), 397–417; 'Some Popular Reactions to the Edwardian Reformation in Yorkshire', *YAJ*, 34 (1939), 151–69; 'The First Stages of Romanist Recusancy in Yorkshire, 1560–1590', *YAJ*, 35 (1941), 157–82. These studies culminated in *The Marian Reaction in the Diocese of York*

these contentions helped perpetuate the myth of the Protestant state. By the time Knowles moved towards rescuing Gasquet's tattered reputation as an historian in 1956, an important slice of argument had moved away from Victorian susceptibilities.[54]

The person from whom Gasquet needed by then to be rescued had himself been called into being as an historian by Roman Catholic currencies, or as he himself would have put it, by papist lies and deceit. If ever an historic thesis generated its antithesis, then the Catholic historiography of the 1920s provoked into existence the terrible George Gordon Coulton. All Coulton's obsessions led to discomfort: his attempts to make the British government raise an army on the Swiss model; his passion for eating over-ripe pears out of their skins with a spoon; his invention of a strange kind of cocoa; his commitment to slaying Roman Catholics whenever they mentioned the past without wearing sackcloth. Just for a moment – say the decade after 1923 when his multi-volume diatribe called *Five Centuries of Religion* began to appear[55] – the Protestant state found a twentieth-century defender in the mould of James Anthony Froude. The Reformation he thought an inevitable product of Catholic failure. Before he had even moved beyond the preface to volume I, Coulton had told the reader his straight and unvarnished truth. 'In Chaucer's day', he said, 'the people themselves had plainly begun to find the monk less necessary; God was more evidently deserting the cloister. Little more than a century later, in [Thomas] More's day, the conjuncture only awaited some prince strong enough in his own self-will and the general obedience of his people . . . If anything can be called inevitable in history, this is that inevitable thing.'[56] But Catholics, for reasons he could not begin to understand, would not accept a truth he found palpable; and by volume II their attitude had become an affront not only to common

---

(2 vols., 1957). But Christopher Haigh saw whiggery in his later work in reaction against the 'anti-Froudian, neo-Tractarian reaction which swept across English Reformation Studies between 1890 and 1940'. ('A. G. Dickens and the English Reformation', *Historical Research* [special issue on Dickens], 77 (2004), 24–38 at 32.)

[54] M. D. Knowles, *Cardinal Gasquet as Historian* (1957), 22–3.

[55] G. G. Coulton, *Five Centuries of Religion* (4 vols., Cambridge, 1923–50). The first volume comprised lectures delivered as early as 1910 (xxxiii). Coulton (1858–1947) seems to have picked up a form of school Protestantism at Felsted, or at least 'the spirit of devotion' ('My changes of belief', holograph sheet dated 25 Feb. 1886, Coulton MSS, box 3). Ordained deacon 1883 but never priested. Curacies and then schoolteaching. Married an Ilbert, like H. A. L. Fisher. Cambridge career came very late: Faculty of English and Fellow of St Johns from 1919. Spiritual position in later years 'somewhere between Deism and Christian agnosticism'. *ODNB*, vol. XIII, 654–6 at 655.

[56] Coulton, *Five Centuries*, vol. I, xxxv.

sense but to faith itself: 'by whatever other name we may call it, whatever excuse or palliation we may seek for it, the avoidance of unpleasant facts is unfaith; and, still worse, the denial or distortion of unpleasant facts'.[57] When he went to Liverpool, of all places, to lecture on 'The Defence of the Reformation' in 1930, he chose attack, as usual, as the best means of defence and proved so successful in upsetting half the city that the Catholic bishop felt it necessary to organize a series of 'reply lectures'. Coulton replied to the reply, as usual, with a book stuffed with appendices drawing on primary documentation that he deemed unanswerable.[58] That was the method and he berated all his critics with it. There is a Yorkshire saying that a kind of personality exists who would rather have a fight than a breakfast. Coulton seems regularly to have missed breakfast. And the point of all this lay not only in the demolition of opponents but in seeing in the Reformation narrative the dawn of a freedom that Catholic culture had stifled. He seems genuinely to have considered that before the Reformation English society contained Anglicans, Presbyterians, Baptists, Congregationalists, Methodists and Quakers *in utero*, waiting for their moment to come into the world.[59] Of course he did not represent anything so timid as Anglicanism. But as one leafs through (say) Norman Sykes's lecture notes on the Reformation composed in the late 1930s or at the beginning of the Second World War, the sense of Protestant message has a Coultonian flavour. '*Morality*; world had overcome ch[urch]; Renaissance popes scandalous whether explained with white gloves by Creighton or denounced by Acton . . .'; 'PAPACY: . . . omnipresent influence in Eng[lan]d, and not for good.'[60]

From an Anglican point of view Coulton and his sympathizers at least thought that Protestantism mattered and that it had some potential for theological integrity. But of course the twentieth century threw up active and influential historians who had neither time for nor truck with any view of the past resting on Christian assumptions about grace and providence, Protestant or Catholic. Macaulay himself had said much about the church that could be read as Enlightenment contempt for religion and his redactor Charles Harding Firth remained a materialist to the end. Maitland left in the mind of an intimate friend the sense that he was 'a very Protestant agnostic' and he seems to have settled for

---

[57] Ibid., vol. II, 423.

[58] G. G. Coulton, *In Defence of the Reformation* (1931). The appendices cover almost a hundred pages and are longer than the lectures themselves.

[59] Coulton, *Five Centuries*, vol. III, xl.

[60] Lecture notes on 'The Continental Reformation' and 'Religion in England 1485–1588', Sykes MSS.

that.[61] In the twentieth century, whether or not God had deserted the medieval cloister, he had unquestionably washed his hands of Edwardian Bloomsbury and those evenings in Gordon Square that had become a seminary for secularism, never more so than in he who would later make Victorian notables look as flawed as they were eminent. Lytton Strachey's langorous eyes looked on religion as a form of cholera which modern sanitation would surely eradicate. He hated Christians of all kinds, which gives his social thought a pleasing symmetry, but reserved the lowest shelf of his hell for those whom he called 'wobblers': intellectuals who knew that they ought to know better but continued believing out of fraud, fabrication or fear. A. L. Rowse once pointed out that Strachey did not merely dislike religion but had no idea of what it might be like to have a religious experience.[62] One may be moved to add that it takes one to know one, though Rowse himself occasionally found religious sites personally moving before snapping out of his reverie with a dismissive sneer.[63] It is important, however, to avoid the periphery of professional history, exemplified by men such as Strachey[64] and Rowse,[65] and think rather of those closer to the centre of the historical world who embodied the distinctive methods and approaches of modernism in a distinctively secular way. Rowse's Oxford offers three such names at once in his All Souls enemy E. L. Woodward, his Magdalen friend Bruce McFarlane and his friend-cum-enemy at Oriel, Hugh

---

[61] Quoted in Helen Cam's introduction to Maitland, *Historical Essays* (1957), xx. She sees in J. H. Round 'a Protestant of a very different kidney' (xxi). R. L. Poole, in a similar generation, is harder to place, but it is easily forgotten that he wrote a *History of the Huguenots* (1880).

[62] A literary commentator, Rupert Hart-Davis's friend George Lyttelton, came to exactly the same conclusion. 'The real flaw in S. is not that he had no religion, but he had no understanding at all of anyone who had; he didn't know what it, or they, *meant*' (emphasis in original). Lyttelton to Hart-Davis, 21 May 1958, in Roger Hudson (ed.), *The Lyttelton–Hart-Davis Letters 1955–62: a Selection* (2001), 137.

[63] 'I lingered in the chancel [of the University Church, St Mary's, in Oxford] before the spot where Newman's mother is buried. It makes a curious impression on one's mind to linger in a place where the life of centuries has flowed through, but now is left high and dry; it is so obviously forgotten by our generation and counts for nothing much.' Rowse's diary, n.d. [?March/April 1926], in Richard Ollard (ed.), *The Diaries of A. L. Rowse* (2003), 15–16.

[64] Lytton Strachey (1880–1932). Member of considerable Strachey network among the intellectual aristocracy and central member of the Bloomsbury Group formed out of contacts at Trinity College, Cambridge. *Eminent Victorians* (1918) made him financially secure for life. *Queen Victoria* (1920); *Elizabeth and Essex* (1928).

[65] A. L. Rowse (1903–1997). Son of china clay worker and shopkeeper in Cornwall. Christ Church, Oxford, and All Souls until 1974 after which he spent most of his time in America. Vast number of publications on the Tudor period – most of them dismissed by academia – and on Cornish culture.

Trevor-Roper. Each in his own way subverted the Protestant state by subverting the spiritual claims on which any Protestant past rested.

Woodward[66] worked on the official histories of the Second World War, but made his name with a volume of the *Oxford History of England* that ran from 1815 to 1870 and ought to have conducted the reader through the most intense spiritual crisis of modern times. He did his best but the private man comes through.[67] Once a believer, Woodward had felt his faith silently withdraw before the First World War rather like, as he deftly put it, a retreating tide might leave one stranded on a sand-spit.[68] The private man wrote a stream-of-consciousness reflection in his curious volume *The Twelve-Winded Sky* (1930), in which he recounts his mood on returning from Oxford to his house on the south coast and revisiting the familiar parish church:

The church is the last sign visible here of medieval England. For many centuries a priest at the high altar under this window, or at the side altars in the transepts, used every day the words of imperial Latin in re-enaction of the sacrifice of the Cross. The miracle of the Mass was accepted, for fear or hope, for quiet or trouble of mind. Then came an age when this whole order of sacrifice and incarnation, oblation and forgiveness was overthrown.

And then comes this remarkable outburst:

Is there no end to the procession of medicine men, witch doctors, weavers of spells, masters of rain, prophets and prophetesses of runes and oracles, augurs of good and evil fortune?[69]

No such outbursts from McFarlane. His antipathy to God, like his attraction to his own sex, remained constricted and suppressed. But he told his pupil Gerald Harriss that he was 'that rare thing, the unbelieving son of an unbeliever'; while his pupil and close friend, John Cooper, insisted after McFarlane's death that 'he did not weaken in rejecting the consolations of religion'.[70] Only once did he unbutton before the

---

[66] E. L., later Sir Llewellyn Woodward (1890–1971). Merchant Taylor's School and Corpus Christi College, Oxford. Fought in First World War. All Souls College, Oxford, 1919–44. Professor of International Relations, Oxford, 1944, and of Modern History, 1947. Princeton 1951–61. *The Age of Reform, 1815–1870* (1938); co-edited *Documents on British Foreign Policy, 1919–39* (1946–); *British Foreign Policy in the Second World War* (1970–6); of which he saw only the first volume in print through delays in clearance at the Foreign Office.

[67] See his jaundiced and often unevidenced remarks in his chapter on 'Religion and the Churches' in *The Age of Reform 1815–70* (Oxford, 1938), 483–509. He had been an Anglo-Catholic for a time in earlier years, oddly, and lived for a while in Pusey House.

[68] E. L. Woodward, *Short Journey* (1942), 217.

[69] E. L. Woodward, *The Twelve-Winded Sky* (1930), 127–8.

[70] Bruce McFarlane to Gerald Harriss, 2 Dec. 1954, in K. B. McFarlane, *Letters to Friends 1940–1966*, ed. Gerald Harriss (Oxford, 1997), 118; cf. John Cooper's introduction at xxxii.

historical public when in his first book on *Cardinal Pole* (most of the copies of which he later bought up to prevent their circulation) he saw in Reformation England 'that spirit of liberty characteristic of a new humanism and of the reform movement'.[71] It was not much but already too much in going beyond what he could *prove* – the abiding passion, recommendation and limitation of McFarlane's historical vision.

Trevor-Roper,[72] unlike Woodward or McFarlane, wobbled – at least for a while in the 1930s when he fell, like so many Oxford gents, under the spell of Anglo-Catholicism and Campion Hall. Or at least that is probably what lies behind the first book, another embarrassment, on Archibishop Laud, which appeared in the dark days of 1940. By the time he came to write it, whatever had stimulated the subject in the first place had failed to produce any sympathy with the object and the biography had turned into a Gibbonian rant[73] against not merely Arminians but against all religion. Page six celebrates 'that secular spirit from which alone an impartial view can come'. Page fourteen has the monasteries cumbering the ground just as Coulton had advised: 'the scraps which should have gone to the poor were frequently kept to feed the monastic pack of hounds'. Laud himself dies by a thousand cuts and proceeds to his withering judgement only at the end. 'Thus Laud has had his defenders against the charges of Macaulay and Hallam: but these defenders have been clergymen, who have confined their interest in their hero to those aspects of his career which they can understand . . .'[74] This is where Trevor-Roper remained, encased in a string of funny, lacerating remarks against Catholics (especially Jesuits and converts) and adopting a mock form of Protestantism with a mock form of biblical scholarship. 'Look after yourself', he wrote typically to Jack Plumb in 1981, 'remembering (for I am sure that you are, like myself, punctilious in the reading of Scripture and hearing of sermons) I Timothy v.23.'[75] He dismissed a modern liberal churchman such as George Kitson Clark as

---

[71] K. B. McFarlane, *Cardinal Pole: the Stanhope Prize Essay, 1924* (Oxford 1924), 18.
[72] Hugh Trevor-Roper, later Lord Dacre of Glanton. Born 1914. Charterhouse; Christ Church, Oxford (Student 1946–57). Regius Professor of Modern History, Oxford, 1957–80. Master of Peterhouse 1980–7. Married General Haig's daughter, Alexandra. *Archbishop Laud 1573–1645* (1940); *The European Witch-Craze of the Sixteenth and Seventeenth Centuries* (Harmondsworth, 1978); *Catholics, Anglicans and Puritans* (1987); *History and Imagination* (Oxford, 1980). Many essays and editions of great authors. Superb essayist.
[73] Trevor-Roper maintained a deep veneration for Gibbon and, if anything, an even stronger one for Giannone. Many passages in *Laud* have the ring of Gibbon's prose.
[74] H. R. Trevor-Roper, *Archbishop Laud* (1940), 6, 14, 433.
[75] Trevor-Roper to J. H. Plumb, 27 Dec. 1981, Plumb MSS. 'No longer drink only water, but take a little wine for the sake of your stomach and your frequent ailments.'

an 'ass' and felt most comfortable in a secular society among people of his own class and taste. But it produced problems for him, too. A set of televised lectures in the 1960s had alienated the audience, according to Munia Postan, through 'his gratuitous and offensive references to religion'.[76] His commitment to a secularized form of modernist scholarship guaranteed, as if by come-uppance, that his lapse over the Hitler diaries would seem beyond absolution, just as his acceptance of the Mastership of Peterhouse – the College of Cosin and Perne as well as of Edward Norman[77] and Maurice Cowling[78] – showed more bravado than sense.

Revival and attenuation

Even these few examples will question the vitality of any argument that claims a simple persistence of a middle-of-the-road Protestantism of the kind that Stubbs or Froude or Creighton had taken themselves to be addressing. When the successor volume to Woodward's in the Oxford History of England came out in 1936, one churchman wrote to its author, Robert Ensor, to express strong agreement with the curve of religious decline that the Fabian socialist Ensor had provided, 'a watershed at 1870 evangelical all the way up to that date, and more and more nothingarian all the way down the other side'.[79] But we have seen that that simplicity does not work, either, when one comes to examine the historians and their understanding of a Protestant past. At just the time that our cleric was endorsing Ensor's pattern of rise and fall, Maurice Powicke must have been preparing his beautiful reflections on *History, Freedom and Religion* that he delivered in Durham in 1938. The free-born Englishman comes out of those addresses predictably well

---

[76] Herbert Butterfield's journal, 4 Dec. 1963.
[77] E. R. Norman (1938–2005). Selwyn College, Cambridge; Fellow, 1962–4, and Jesus College, 1964–71. Ordination and Dean of Peterhouse, Cambridge, 1971–88. Dean of Chapel, Christ Church College, Canterbury, 1988–95. Canon Residentiary, York Minster, 1995–2003. *Anti-Catholicism in Victorian England* (1968); *Church and Society in Modern England* (1976); *The English Catholic Church in the Nineteenth Century* (1983); *Roman Catholicism in England* (1985), etc.
[78] Maurice Cowling (1926–2005). Battersea Grammar School and Jesus College, Cambridge. Fellow of Peterhouse, 1963–93. Reader in History, University of Cambridge. Best known for two trilogies: *1867: Disraeli, Gladstone and Revolution* (Cambridge, 1967), *The Impact of Labour 1920–1924* (Cambridge, 1971), and *The Impact of Hitler 1933–1940* (Cambridge, 1975); and *Religion and Public Doctrine in Modern England* (3 vols., 1980–2001).
[79] Revd J. C. Pringle (Charity Organization Society) to Ensor, 9 Feb. 1937, Ensor MSS box 4.

and manifested what Helen Cam called the 'fourth-dimensional quality'[80] that Powicke's concern with religious ideas brought to his history. 'The presence of God is more satisfying to him than the unknown outcome of an illogical historical process,' Powicke reminded his audience. 'He sees that law and order are not impositions upon him but the expression of his desire to live and let live . . . the lasting conditions of the good life.'[81] For Powicke, and later Richard Southern,[82] the world of medieval Catholic culture formed the basis of their spiritual judgements, but these, too, could help the Reformation's status in modern society if one were to argue that Luther and Calvin rescued that culture from itself and represented its more authentic continuator. Several historians took up that role both before and after the Second World War. Norman Sykes, again in 1938, argued that the apostolic character of the reformed religion revealed itself in a paucity of Catholic martyrs. After acknowledging Fisher and More and a number of other 'illustrious exceptions', he dwelt on their exceptionalism and announced breezily that 'the vast majority of clergy, secular and regular, not only accepted the changes but retained office throughout the even greater changes to come in the next reign'.[83] Similar continuities in the national past were urged by the Liberal-Tory Anglican Kitson Clark in his account of *The English Inheritance* (1950) which placed the Protestant churches – Dissenting as much as Established – at the centre of English national life and swam against the tide of secular assumption contaminating the national heritage. 'This cuts us off from our past,' he said, echoing Stubbs's phrase. 'It cuts us off as a nation from many of the moral assumptions on which our institutions are based.'[84] He dedicated his book to a Cambridge friend, the Anglo-Catholic priest Charles Smyth who, among other services to the nation, taught the young Maurice Cowling.[85] And when Smyth himself came to draft a narrative

---

[80] Helen Cam, 'The Study of English Medieval History Today', in Cam, *Law-Finders and Law-Makers* (1962), 176–87 at 181.

[81] F. M. Powicke, *History, Freedom and Religion* (Durham, 1938), 34.

[82] The celebrators in his *Festschrift* dwelt in their dedication on the love of God, 'of a mind at rest thinking of home in a strange land, the pieties which kept life sweet . . .': a beautiful passage which sounds like Southern: R. W. Hunt, W. A. Pantin and R. W. Southern (eds.), *Studies in Medieval History presented to Frederick Maurice Powicke* (Oxford, 1948), dedication.

[83] Norman Sykes, *The Crisis of the Reformation* (1938), 114. It should be said that Sykes also, however, discerned 'the failure of the Tudor ideal of a national church coterminous with the civil kingdom . . .' (133).

[84] G. Kitson Clark, *The English Inheritance: an Historical Essay* (1950), 171.

[85] For Smyth and Cowling see the latter's *Religion and Public Doctrine in Modern England* (3 vols., 1980–2000), vol. I, xi–xxiv.

about church and nation in 1962, he drove his continuities back through
the Reformation and through the middle ages into Anglo-Saxon
England, drawing out a whig story of which Stubbs would have been
proud, one in which Henry VIII, by creating suffragan bishoprics out of
his booty in 1534, resumed the work of Willibrord and Boniface and
linked arms with those Victorian suffragans who made the story complete in a land whose every village has a church that goes back a
thousand years.[86]

One might have thought that a major *dis*continuity in the experience of
all these people – the Second World War with its assertion of the state at
a level of totalitarianism that Hitler would have envied and with the
impetus towards a leftward politics of assimilation within it – would have
destroyed any conception of a Protestant state with a normative history.
Yet the ambivalence that characterizes the century of historical thought
about religion in England after 1870 comes through here, too. Few
shared Martin Wight's depiction of the conflict as 'a divine judgment
on European civilization for corporate sin'.[87] On the contrary many felt
the undertow of spiritual intensity at a moment of distinctive British
destiny, one that brought the Englishman and his history together, as
Herbert Butterfield implied in his book of that title in 1944. War experience among thinking historians turned on reasserted identity discovered in a junction of people and state in moral endeavour. It sent
the European historian A. J. Grant to ruminate in his diary about Jerome
and Augustine and 'a world in which religion was the chief interest'.[88] It
played a major role in establishing the mature patterns of thought found
in Butterfield and Arnold Toynbee. And probably – the contention runs
beyond evidence – it increased rather than diminished the unremarked
faith of men like the medievalist Charles Previté-Orton – 'a churchman',
G. N. Clark later commented, 'satisfied with the central Anglican
tradition, and displeased with extremism of any kind'.[89] Butterfield's
election to the Chair of Modern History in Cambridge in 1944 carried
some of this mood with it. Post-Beveridge Britain manifested a variety of
ethical forms of which traditional religious observance was only one and
perhaps not the most influential. But there is nothing to suggest that the
war heralded the end of a Christian historical perspective about the

---

[86] Charles Smyth, *The Church and the Nation* (1962), 29, 35.
[87] Quoted in Ian Hall, 'Sir Herbert Butterfield, Arnold J. Toynbee and Martin Wight and
the Crisis of International Politics: a Study in International Thought', unpublished
doctoral thesis, University of St Andrews (2003), 30.
[88] Grant's diary, 10 Jan. 1940, Grant MSS.
[89] G. N. Clark, 'Charles William Previté-Orton', *EHR*, 62 (1947), 433–7 at 437.

British past and we have considerable evidence that implies survival and even rebirth in the 1950s. Take one arresting thought about the post-war world and one of the commanding heights of academic history, the Regius Chair of Modern History in Cambridge. G. N. Clark's appointment to it after the war brought to Cambridge a sensible and calm Anglican convert from Methodism and the editor of the Oxford History of England.[90] His successors though the 1950s, '60s and '70s were, in chronological order, a Benedictine monk, a former Methodist with College Anglican tendencies and an Anglican priest.[91] Not until the appointment of G. R. Elton in 1983 did the church lose its hold and even that fall was reversed when he was succeeded by the godly Patrick Collinson.

Of course these people spoke to a changing audience and led a profession markedly different from the pre-war model in its structures. A. H. Halsey showed some years ago how the grip of Oxbridge on the English university system weakened strikingly, at least in its proportionate weight in teachers and students, in the decade before 1950;[92] and the 1960s were to see an explosion of higher education in which voices from a college system with its chaplains, deans and chapels had little say. Sixties' Marxism and the student movement made the state look more like a capitalist oppressor than a Protestant inspiration and turned its history into a sociological, even anthropological enquiry. Where Christian history remained pervasive was in departments of medieval history which always attract those with pre-Reformation sympathies; and perhaps among the decaffeinated pages of the new *Journal of Ecclesiastical History*, founded noticeably and significantly late in 1952, the same year as the not-at-all Protestant *Past and Present*. Time was, of course, that ecclesiastical history and the history of state and society had been taken to be inseparably intertwined: the history of the church for someone like Gwatkin at the beginning of the century had represented 'simply the spiritual side of universal history'.[93] Instead, dismissive reductionism characterized much of the

---

[90] Clark himself, however, saw no connexion between his religion and his history which cannot provide, he said, 'a philosophy, or a religion, or a substitute for religion, or even an adequate excuse for doing without a religion'. G. N. Clark, *Historical Scholarship and Historical Thought* (Cambridge, 1944), 11. There seems no reason to follow him in this judgement, *a fortiori* when retrospecting his own work.

[91] Dom David Knowles, Sir Herbert Butterfield, Owen Chadwick.

[92] A. H. Halsey, *The Decline of Donnish Dominion: the British Academic Professions in the Twentieth Century* (Oxford, 1992), 58–88 and especially the graphs at 62 and 64.

[93] Norman Sykes, *Man as Churchman* (1960), 6. H. M. Gwatkin (1844–1916). Shrewsbury and St John's College, Cambridge. Three First Class degrees in the same

public discourse about religion in these years, and in the wake of John Robinson's *Honest to God* in 1963 the church itself seemed to have landed on rollers. Vatican Two, sitting through precisely the same period, even tried to fit the Catholic hierarchy with rollers and provoked deep introspection. 'What bores these papists are!' Trevor-Roper had exploded a few years earlier,[94] and his lack of understanding as much as sympathy stamps the epoch. When Geoffrey Elton, of all people, sent a manuscript to *Past and Present* in 1961 alleging that religion had become 'a dirty word in these pages', the editor told him to delete the phrase;[95] but in the same year in which those pages contained Keith Thomas's famous article on 'History and Anthropology',[96] perhaps Elton had not been far off the mark. Ten years later, Thomas's *Religion and the Decline of Magic*[97] became a cultic statement of modernist secularism, albeit one better concealed than Trevor-Roper had bothered to affect in his attack on Laud.

Those secular certainties did not endure, however, and neither did the modernist historical method on which they sometimes rested. As late-modernity slid unknowingly towards post-modernity, different suscepti-bilities appeared in historical writing about identity, culture and history, and not all of it was as innovative as its practitioners believed. The point about their forebears that has been made here lies in the suggestion, first, that the historical world against which Herbert Butterfield reacted so effectively in *The Whig Interpretation of History* in 1931 and which he sought to correct in *Christianity and History* in 1948 had its own history and rhythms that repay attention. It argues, second, that the historical milieu familiar to us in *The Stripping of the Altars* by *Godly People*[98] did not take its shape from a vacuum but had its origins in a style of historiography that runs back into late Victorian Britain. The story implies, finally, that an important whig legacy in the conjuring of an idealized, indeed mythological Protestant state did not go under the

---

year; his fourth – theology – in the following one. Fellow of St John's. Lecturer in theology and history, Cambridge 1874–91. Succeeded Creighton in Dixie Chair. International reputation for knowledge of the radulae of snails. Deaf, increasingly blind, conversationally challenged, but a major scholar.

[94] Trevor-Roper to Plumb, 8 Sep. 1956, Plumb MSS.

[95] Trevor Aston to G. R. Elton, 27 Apr. 1961, Elton MSS.

[96] Keith Thomas, 'History and Anthropology', *Past and Present*, 24 (1963), 3–24.

[97] Keith Thomas, *Religion and the Decline of Magic* (1971).

[98] Eamon Duffy, *The Stripping of the Altars: Traditional Religion in England, c.1400–c.1580* (New Haven, 1992); Patrick Collinson, *Godly People: Essays on English Protestantism and Puritanism* (1983).

wheels of secularization significantly before 1960 and that it supplies, from the standpoint of the historical intelligentsia, some reinforcement for Callum Brown's chronology of sudden decline from that moment. Rather than offer an image of prolonged burial for Christian historiography, the narrative helps assert a persistent canon that helps explain – partially but crucially – how a whig understanding of the past endured in an historical community that supposedly had lost God.

3   Empire and war

Constitutionalism and churchmanship never faltered in exerting their special pressure on history in twentieth-century England: always under challenge but always there. Painting in the context of historians after the whigs requires other shapes apart from these, of course, though many of them must remain beyond the borders of the present small canvas that allows only a silhouette. The legacies of the whigs should detain us, all the same, until two further elements enter the picture because they dominated the mind and practice of the late nineteenth century and were to play roles of the utmost significance in the twentieth – one of them as a supposed attenuation, like religion, the other as a spreading stain in the consciousness of every man and woman. Whigs were born to empire. Modernists were prone to war. Between them, these evolving conditions comprised a critical conditioning for a specific present within which an English past acquired form. They did not stand outside the developments we have been examining. Rather, they merged with and reflected them in important ways. If they do not occupy the centre of the composition, they permeate all of it through their changing light and shade.

Empire

In the generation of John Robert Seeley and James Anthony Froude the reality of empire was a constitutional fact as much as a category of aspiration and the history of it took some of its colour from the procedures of constitutional historians. When as late as 1953 a respected imperial historian could described the foundation document of the second British empire – the Durham Report of 1839 – as 'the Magna Carta of colonial self-government',[1] he acknowledged a tradition of thought among historians of empire that would endure for two generations after the last great names of whig history. Amid grandiose

[1] Eric Walker, *The Second British Empire* (1953), 56.

plans for drawing colonial possessions into the ambit of British parliamentarism and the rhetorical exercises of Joseph Chamberlain insisting that it would make practical politics to do so, constitutionalists felt that their account of British representative institutions would be incomplete without an imperial perspective, against the coming day – Britain's imperial day was still coming –when MPs from Australia and Canada would join dark-skinned representatives from India and Africa in an expanded Westminster parliament, *pater familias* to most of the civilized world. One future parliamentary candidate, the constitutional historian Albert Pollard, avoided the more mystical attractions of empire in his chapter on 'The British Realms in Parliament'; but perhaps there is greater significance in his feeling it necessary to include one at all in what was meant to be a constitutional history of Britain.[2] With the whig subject came a whig method, as the most famous pair of modernist critics would later allege, one that ensured that its Victorian creators 'regarded the empire of kinship and constitutional dependence as an organism with its own laws of growth',[3] just as they saw the history of Kings, Lords and Commons as a story of linear evolution driven by the call of freedom and responsibility. That sentiment did not die in the First World War. Distinguished constitutional historians and theorists such as Sir Arthur Berriedale Keith[4] and Sir Kenneth Wheare[5] kept the Stubbsian flag flying over imperial studies between the wars. Even thereafter, with India gone and nationalist movements elsewhere destabilizing a patrician approach to the imperial past, it is possible to find whig certainties and models in the historical literature. 'A typical colony', Frederick Madden announced in an opaque moment in 1970, 'moves from a period of absolute royal, "crown colony" government to representative, to responsible government and on to dominion status.'[6]

---

[2] A. F. Pollard, *The Evolution of Parliament* (1920), 359–79.

[3] R. Robinson and J. Gallagher, 'The Imperialism of Free Trade', *Economic History Review*, 2nd series, 6 (1953), 1–15 at 1.

[4] A. B. Keith (1879–1944). Royal High School, Edinburgh and Edinburgh University. Classics and Sanskrit at Balliol College, Oxford. Bar 1904. Colonial Office, 1901–14, then Regius Professor of Sanskrit at Edinburgh for the rest of his life. Wrote more than fifty books. See in particular his *Constitutional History of the First British Empire* (1930) and R. F. Shinn and R. A. Cosgrove (eds.), *Constitutional Reflections: the Correspondence of Albert Venn Dicey and Arthur Berriedale Keith* (1996).

[5] K. C. W. Wheare (1907–79). Born Victoria, Australia. University of Melbourne. Rhodes scholar: Oriel College, Oxford. Beit Lecturer, 1935–44. Fellow and Tutor at University College, 1939–44. Gladstone Chair of Government and Public Administration from 1944. Anglican. See *The Constitutional Structure of the Commonwealth* (1960).

[6] A. F. C. Madden, '1066, 1776 & All That: the Relevance of English Medieval Experience of "Empire" to Later Constitutional Issues', in John E. Flint and Glyndwr Williams (eds.), *Perspectives of Empire: Essays Presented to Gerald S. Graham* (1973), 9–26 at 24.

Seeley could not have detected the 'drift' of British history more emphatically in his studies of the growth of British policy almost a century before.

But the British empire struck Victorian historians as more than a constitutional structure. It radiated mission; it embraced a destiny. The mission and destiny might imply a form of racial superiority. They might assert a Darwinian inevitability. They asserted no less often, however (and to a degree rarely observed through the lenses of a later age), a view of Christian involvement in the world. The author of *The Expansion of England* and *The Growth of British Policy* was also the author of *Ecce Homo* and owed his Regius Chair to his Christianity more than to his imperialism. One might declare Seeley *sui generis* were it not for Froude, who might have had his *Nemesis of Faith* burned in the streets of Oxford many years before but whose patriotism never lost its Protestant urgency. His imperial tour of the 1880s – the one that gave rise to his elegiac *Oceana* in 1886 – could have left him with the impression that the empire amounted to constitutional nuts and bolts in faraway places, or scattered pockets of kith and kin. 'But', ran his reply, 'in theological language, it is the saving of our national soul, it is the saving of the souls of millions of Englishmen hereafter to be born that is really at stake; and once more the old choice is again before us, whether we prefer immediate money advantage . . . by letting the empire slide away, or else our spiritual salvation.'[7] The white man's burden transcended the taking of responsibility and insisted on the importance of witness with its symbols and sacraments. Reflecting on the coupling of empire and church in English experience from the side of ecclesiastical history, J. P. Whitney looked forward to a better future for both in an emotional meditation during the First World War by looking back at what the history of the early church seemed to teach:

we must expect the common life of the Church to impress itself with growing power upon our Empire. It is astonishing, for instance, to see how strong, even in the more distant branches of the Church, is the love (respect is too weak a term), for the Mother see of Canterbury. It is a sentiment of extraordinary power, and may yet do for our Empire what the see of Augustine did in the olden days for our own island.[8]

Just how mistaken it is to terminate such Christian confidence in the twentieth century we have already seen. It is no less mistaken to abort imperial historiography in the age of modernism by turning it into a

[7] J. A. Froude, *Oceana: or England and her Colonies* (1886), 388.
[8] J. P. Whitney, *The Episcopate and the Reformation* (1917), 167.

wasteland of monopoly capitalism, survival of the fittest and desiccated diplomatic calculation.

The Victorians were different for all that and different in four ways. First, their historians wrote from *within* the idea of the British Empire (always with capital letters) as a remarkable and sometimes almost metaphysical presence – one which they could all recognize and none quite explain. Their seminal texts from the 1880s – Seeley's *Expansion of England* and Froude's *Oceana* – testified to British inadvertence, the famous 'fit of absence of mind', during which the empire, according to Seeley, had been acquired. Some may have preferred Mary Kingsley's diagnosis ('a coma accompanied by fits'[9]), but it came to the same thing: the reverse of an argument from design. Duty, character, responsibility, leadership, liberation – these are the nouns that Seeley and Froude, plus a range of fiction from Rider Haggard to Kipling, Henty and the young John Buchan, thrust forward in their understanding of Britain's imperial power. They extended the scope of the imperial past beyond the embarrassments of the eighteenth century, with its loss of America, in order to recapture the mood of Tudor maritime greatness associated with Ralegh and Drake.[10] And the suffusive character of their message in the last twenty years of the century brooks no denial. Joseph Chamberlain always said that the *Expansion* was what turned him into an imperialist and the effect of this environment on a brilliant young scholar like Alfred Milner is familiar to all students of the period.[11] But it reached lesser lights, especially in Oxford, which was to retain its sympathy with the continuities of empire over the next fifty years. The future economic historian George Unwin held no brief for imperialism, yet he looked back on his undergraduate days with a clear recollection of the mood. 'In the middle 'nineties', he reminisced, 'when I was an undergraduate at Oxford, Seeley's *Life of Stein* was recommended to me, along with the works of Captain Mahon, by earnest young neophytes of Liberal Imperialism, as containing the *arcana* of that doctrine of which the simpler elements were contained in *The Expansion of England*.'[12] There was no

[9] Quoted in A. P. Thornton, 'The Shaping of Imperial History', in R. W. Winks (ed.), *The Oxford History of the British Empire, vol. V: Historiography* (Oxford, 1998), 612–34 at 622.

[10] See John Burrow's demonstration of this late Victorian sea-change in his *A Liberal Descent* (Cambridge, 1981), esp. chapter 9, 231–50.

[11] For Chamberlain see Peter Marsh, *Joseph Chamberlain: Entrepreneur in Politics* (New Haven, 1994); Richard Jay, *Joseph Chamberlain: a Political Life* (Oxford, 1981).

[12] George Unwin, 'National Power and Prosperity', in Unwin, *Studies in Economic History*, edited by R. H. Tawney (1927), 336–44 at 342. For the deeper meanings of Seeley on Stein, see R. T. Shannon, 'John Robert Seeley and the Idea of a National Church', in R. Robson (ed.), *Ideas and Institutions of Victorian Britain: Essays in Honour of George Kitson Clark* (1967), 236–67.

getting away from it. Possibly Llewellyn Woodward missed the point when he complained half a century later about Seeley's failure to establish a school of imperial historians – he had been 'too didactic and too much a partisan'[13] – because the moment seized by Seeley was one demanding doctrine and commitment rather than the balanced prognoses favoured by a less charged age. And out of Seeley's commitments came a variety of enthusiasms that were to survive into that age and rebel against its caution.

Compared with Froude, he was in any case a model of sobriety. Turning to his own purposes Sir James Harrington's seventeenth-century description of England, Scotland and Ireland as 'oceana', Froude produced in 1886 a book that functioned partly as travelogue, partly as jeremiad, partly as imperial manifesto. He had all of Seeley's assumptions about progress and liberty; he had no doubt from the historical record that true Anglo-Saxons, 'wherever they went . . . would carry with them the genius of English freedom'.[14] They needed to go at once (never was it more urgent) with their hard-won privileges in their pockets to colonize other parts of the world beyond India and create a Greater Britain as Sir Charles Dilke had urged two decades before.[15] Australia had already shown what could be done in creating communities of expatriates who now seemed '*ipsis Anglicis Angliciores*'.[16] They would have their critics, of course, but Froude reassured colonizers about the validity of their purpose by imposing an odd form of class analysis on the argument. '[T]hose fortunate ones who could afford parks and deer forests and yachts in the Solent', they would always deny the force of the imperial argument because they already had the good things of life. But what about the poor in Britain's teeming cities, people who lacked access even to sun and fresh air? Where were they to go to improve the life chances of themselves and their children?[17] So imperialism became a sort of modern social theory at one remove, providing an outlet for urban energies currently blocked by processes of industrialization and urbanization. Exporting the British stock, however, would not be enough. One had to recognize the other side of the coin by acknowledging the rights of other colonists, none more so than those of the much-maligned Boers of South Africa, Froude thought. Even before 1880 the message of South Africa seemed plain to him, though he nursed few illusions about the

---

[13] E. L. Woodward, *British Historians* (1943), 45.
[14] Froude, *Oceana*, 2.
[15] Sir Charles Dilke, *Greater Britain* (2 vols., 1868).
[16] Froude, *Oceana*, 151.
[17] Ibid., 8–11.

likelihood of an intelligent response from the British government. The importance of the issue weighed in his mind not only because of its significance in itself, but because South Africa would become for him what India had already become for others – a crystal ball in which one could see the wavering outline of Ireland.

Since at least 1874 the appeal of a party committed to Home Rule in Ireland threatened to subvert this second major element in whig psychology. For Whigs with a capital 'W' the issue promised pain because that sector of Liberal politics owned so many acres in Ireland. For whig historians and liberal intellectuals without capital letters it commented on the imminent weakening of a great imperial idea. If Britain could not hold on to her closest colony, what price her retaining India and slices of Africa? The argument reached its crescendo, naturally, in 1885–6 when Gladstone sprang on his colleagues and the world the desirability of rescinding the Act of Union and granting Dublin its parliament. He lost the intelligentsia overnight, snuffing out all those lights that should have been liberal to the end, including Ireland's best-known historian, W. E. H. Lecky.[18] But Froude had seen it coming long before then and had heard in South Africa the distant echoes of Ireland's complaint.

We annexed Ireland; we sent colonists there to govern it; we gave the colonists a Parliament; we gave them the management of native affairs there. The result was a series of laws which we would not allow to be executed; we had the weakness of an oligarchical administration without its strength, wars, rebellions, confiscations, quarrels with the colonists, quarrels with the native race, misgovernment, poverty, misery; and finally the Ireland that we know, which is the disgrace of British administration. The state of Ireland is no extraordinary mystery. It is as much the product of causes clearly ascertainable as a famine or the cholera. And yet step by step we are treading on the old course, and are creating exactly and literally a second Ireland in South Africa.[19]

In his latter instance the empire had proved stiff-necked. In the former it would soon show its weakness, mixing imperialism with democracy in a hopeless stirring of oil and water. Lord Salisbury, no Whig, declared the Irish a western tribe of Hottentots whom the British should govern for their own protection, an unfair, offensive but clear-headed proposition. Whig historians knew that they had to say the reverse in order to placate their gods of liberty, responsibility and democracy, and found themselves incapable of clarity. They froze in face of a call they could not resist in order to achieve an object they could not countenance. Froude

---

[18] See Christopher Harvie, *The Lights of Liberalism: University Liberals and the Challenge of Democracy, 1860–1886* (1976).
[19] J. A. Froude, *Two Lectures on South Africa* (1880), 80.

did not freeze because he had the courage to separate empire from democracy and ultimately to resist an important element in whig historical thought. For him, by 1886, democracy had become the instigator of cultural decline rather than its treatment, a false flowering of sentiment that betokened a coming fall.

Hitherto this has been the history of every democratic experiment in the world. Democracies are the blossoming of the aloe, the sudden squandering of the vital force which has accumulated in the long years when it was contented to be healthy and did not aspire after a vain display. The aloe is glorious for a single season. It progresses as it never progressed before. It admires its own excellence, looks back with pity on its earlier and humbler condition, which it attributes only to the unjust restraints in which it was held. It conceives that it has discovered the true secret of being 'beautiful for ever', and in the midst of the discovery it dies.[20]

Hard reading for whigs, this. It is as though a treasured ideal of empire has run into another view of the English past which forces a choice between democracy and destiny. In choosing destiny, as most whig historians did, something was lost or confused in their message in a way that helps explain the discomforts of imperial historiography in a democratizing world.

Yet other aspects of the Victorians' situation helped promote that very style of historiography and to give it its particular flavour. One of them – the third in our account – concerns the historians themselves and their place in society. Long gone were the days of Gibbon and Macaulay when a man could be both a minister of the crown and a prolific historian virtually simultaneously, unless one counts G. M. Trevelyan's father, George Otto, who was Gladstone's Chief Secretary for Ireland. It remained possible to use family connexion and tradition to assist informal governing of the empire, while the bureaucracy needed to run an expanding government and empire after the 1860s not only remained but offered a major formal platform for historians to learn their trade from the inside. True, the eye falls first on a Seeley or a Froude who represents the Victorian model of part-gentleman-scholar, part Oxford or Cambridge don. But the next generation produced a different man who made his way through the higher imperial society or the higher civil service and who reflected on the history of empire in the light of that experience. Take the case of Sir Hugh Egerton (1855–1927). With a parliamentary father and an aristocratic mother, a mid-range public school (Rugby) and a mid-range Oxford College (Corpus Christi), Egerton proceeded to his First in Greats like so many of his ability and

---

[20] Froude, *Oceana*, 155.

social class and from there to the Bar. But Egerton was connected. He was the direct descendent of a Lord Chancellor (Ellesmere) and first cousin to a Stanhope; so when Edward Stanhope, son of the historian,[21] became Lord Salisbury's Secretary of State for the Colonies and needed a bright young man to act as his assistant private secretary, he knew at once where to turn. Add in *The Expansion of England*, by which the young Egerton declared himself affected, and a trajectory opened through a *Short History of British Colonial Policy* (1897) and a racy biography of Raffles (1897) to his election to the Beit Chair in Oxford (of which more later) in 1905 – its first holder. For the formal side of the argument one might look sideways to an almost precise contemporary, Sir Charles Lucas (1853–1931). He was more middle than upper class in his origins; his father was a doctor in Wales. Winchester and Jowett's Balliol knew how to pour young men into their own moulds, for all that. Lucas's First appeared in the same list as Egerton's in 1876. He did not reach the Colonial Office by connexion, however, but by examination: top of the list in 1877 and straight into the Office where he rose to assistant under-secretary twenty years later. He ran the Dominions Department from 1907, retired at fifty-eight and then edited and wrote a good deal of *The Empire at War*[22] during his retirement at All Souls.

New people, then; but their impact would have lessened had they not had access to new forms of support for the study of imperial history, a final and very important element in these years. Oxford was its major beneficiary. Perhaps the Queen and Disraeli's drift towards a more grandiose imperialism played its part in encouraging the foundation there of the first Readership in Indian History which was to be held by S. J. Owen for thirty-five years.[23] Another foundation a few years later would prove of more permanent significance. The Indian Institute, opened in Oxford in 1884, brought a major library within the grasp of scholars, complementing in some ways the Pitt-Rivers collection that the Ashmolean Museum had acquired the previous year.[24] Thereafter the accent swung away to the African continent, thanks to two bequests that

---

[21] Philip, 5th Earl Stanhope, *History of England from the Peace of Utrecht* (7 vols., 1830–54); *Life of the Rt. Hon. William Pitt* (4 vols., 1861).

[22] Sir Charles Prestwood Lucas, *The Empire at War* (5 vols., 1921–6).

[23] S. J. Owen (1827–1912). Repton and Worcester College, Oxford. Bar. Professor of History, Elphinstone College, Bombay, 1856–60. Reader in Indian History, Oxford, from 1872. *India on the Eve of the British Conquest* (1872); *The Fall of the Mogul Empire* (1912).

[24] For these developments see Frederick Madden, 'The Commonwealth, Commonwealth History and Oxford, 1905–1971', in Madden and D. K. Fieldhouse (eds.), *Oxford and the Idea of Commonwealth: Essays Presented to Sir Edgar Williams* (1982), 7–29.

demonstrated the power of money in changing the face of scholarship. The earlier is too famous to demand much stress. A century's experience of Rhodes scholars makes it obvious at once how impoverished would have been intellectual contact between the metropolitan power and the Empire had the last will and testament of Cecil Rhodes not contained its startling provisions. Fifty-seven students from beyond the United Kingdom to go to Oxford each year: twenty from the Empire, thirty-two from the United States and – still thinkable in 1902 – five from Germany.[25] Together with the building of Rhodes House after the war and the opening of its impressive library in 1929, this transfusion of imperial enthusiasm did much to keep the subject of colonial history prosperous. Less celebrated outside academia, but more significant still for the future of imperial historiography, a bequest from Alfred Beit, a German mining magnate who had made a fortune from Kimberley diamonds, enabled the establishment of two posts from 1905 – a new Chair in colonial history with Egerton as its first incumbent, and a lectureship which soon became a powerful entry position for young talent. All of this largesse may have had a consequence beyond grants and buildings. Oxford absorbed and then radiated imperial sympathies which helped produce a style of historiography that dwelt on continuities and emerging virtues that looked not unlike the whig verities that the twentieth century would come to bemoan. John Darwin may well be right to suggest that, in gaining so much from imperial contact, Oxford lost detachment of the sort found elsewhere in colonial studies between the wars.[26]

Elsewhere meant London, where both the London School of Economics (LSE) and the newly founded School of Oriental and African Studies (SOAS) (1916) developed a cutting edge; or perhaps Edinburgh where Arthur Keith held the Chair of Sanskrit and Comparative Philology. But Oxford's domination of the field continued until at least the departure of the Australian W. K. Hancock from All Souls to the Chair of History at Birmingham in 1934. The domination turned on a new kind of man whose emblem might be (Sir) Reginald Coupland, whose name is often associated with this period of imperial history, or a completely new kind of woman in the fearless and formidable (Dame) Marjory Perham. They produced, moreover, a new kind of book: closer

---

[25] The latter provision was abrogated in 1916. India was later brought within the scheme.
[26] I take this thought from John Darwin, 'A World University', in Brian Harrison (ed.), *History of the University of Oxford* (8 vols., 1984–94), vol. VIII, 607–36 at 620. 'This concept of continuity', Madden commented, 'became the peculiar stamp of imperial history at Oxford.' *Oxford and the Idea of Commonwealth*, 11.

to events on the ground in Africa than previous writers and written from an almost proconsular perspective. Doyen of the mood was a genuine proconsul in Sir Frederick Lugard, whose entanglement with both the East Africa Company and the Royal Niger Company lent particular authority to his *Dual Mandate in Tropical Africa* (1922), whose very title entered the language as a colonial mantra with its implication that the British object in Africa lay in protecting the 'natives' and developing the region economically through the wisdom of the district officer, hero of many an imperial romance, father of many imperial sympathizers in the next generation, and often (puzzlingly) Scottish. From this focus ultimately came 'area studies' in the 1930s which promised to say more about the essential history of the territories under review than the armchair word-spinning of those seeking British destiny in the previous generation. They did not abandon, however, the constitutional and Christian commitments of that generation; neither did they abandon a form of whig history. Indeed one could make a persuasive case that the last pocket of determined whig resistance to the inroads of modernism had dug itself deeper into imperial historiography than any other, with its headquarters in Oxford.

Politics had something to do with that. Milner's South Africa had provided sanctuary for imperially-minded intellectuals and publicists before the war, and the return of the famous *Kindergarten*[27] to Britain and their incorporation into Lloyd George's Garden Suburb – the collection of huts he had built in the garden of 10 Downing Street after he became prime minister in December 1916 – brought some of them to the core of government.[28] For the *Round Table*, a journal with a pressure group of distinguished imperialists and with Milner and Lionel Curtis as its driving force, these were years of opportunity.[29] In a sense this effervescence departed after the war not because its proponents had too little commitment but because they had too much. Curtis, in particular, offended sceptical and perhaps more balanced minds through his all-encompassing visions. The empire had become for him history's destination and consummation, a transfiguration of Christ's purposes. When *Civitas Dei* began to appear in 1934, the same year as Arnold Toynbee's first three volumes of *The Study of History*, it created discomfort more than admiration among historians of empire and the

---

[27] See Walter Nimmocks, *Milner's Young Men: the 'Kindergarten' in Edwardian Imperial Affairs* (1970).

[28] See John Turner, *Lloyd George's Secretariat* (Cambridge, 1980).

[29] Cf. Alexander May, 'The *Round Table* 1910–66', unpublished D.Phil. thesis, University of Oxford, 1995.

unintended successor-volumes did nothing to ease it.[30] The proposition that Jesus had a political programme that he could not explain to Galilean fishermen, a programme for a commonwealth whose recommendations were best represented by the modern British empire, seemed to discriminating readers not so much provocative as mad. Even if one could 'see in the light of history the kind of society which in the course of time slowly but surely increases the sense of duty in men to each other' – a large claim – it stretched most readings of scripture to make Jesus or Moses its prime mover.

> The Kingdom of Heaven, as Jesus conceived it, consisted of men serving God by serving each other, the desire to serve increasing by exercise, and depending for guidance on experience of facts interpreted by reason and conscience . . . We can see . . . that a community, a sufficient proportion of whose members had realized to a certain degree a capacity for putting the interest of others on a level with their own, could govern itself . . . Self-government is primarily a question of character, and the ultimate problem of politics is how to develop that character. A commonwealth is simply the sermon on the mount translated into political terms.[31]

The trouble was that Aramaic, Jesus's language, 'contained no word to convey that idea',[32] so the penetrating modern observer had to supply a vocabulary for divine intention. The British empire had already shown what could be done. Tomorrow, perhaps, the world would see the light, or it seemed likely by the end of volume III. 'If an international commonwealth built from countries within the British Empire came to include countries in Europe which had never been part of that Empire,' Curtis speculated, 'the most difficult stage in its growth to a world commonwealth . . . would have been crossed.'[33] No wonder sober imperialists had begun to cross the street.

Rarely has the *Cambridge Modern History* been accused of insobriety. It formed the model for a *Cambridge History of the British Empire*, which began to appear from 1929 under the editorship of two Cambridge dons, E. A. Benians and J. Holland Rose, and the Rhodes Professor of Imperial History in the University of London, A. P. Newton. The preface, signed by all three, put the roots of empire in water:

> Though the seed of England's later imperial power may be found in the unity, the law, the institutions, and the sea instinct, of which she became possessed in the Middle Ages, it was not until late in the fifteenth century that her oceanic expansion began. It is therefore with the Tudor period that the History

---

[30] Lionel Curtis, *Civitas Dei* (3 vols., 1934–7).
[31] Ibid., vol. I, 164, 285.
[32] Ibid., vol. II, 524.
[33] Ibid., vol. III, 111.

opens. Out of the ambitions of that adventurous age, when men dreamed great dreams for England and set out to realize them, grew the maritime State which . . . has developed in the twentieth century into the British Commonwealth of Nations.[34]

Familiar names brought *gravitas*: Sir Charles Lucas in the Introduction and Egerton in a concluding chapter, but there were also Charles M. Andrews of Yale, Lillian Penson of Birkbeck, W. F. Reddaway of King's College, London and Harold Temperley as member of the home team with a chapter on the Peace of Paris.

Oxford made its presence felt in two chapters from one of the formative influences on imperial history in the twentieth century, Vincent Harlow.[35] His later *magnum opus*, two volumes on *The Founding of the Second British Empire*, imposed a personal 'shape' on the history of colonial development from the eighteenth century and ran into criticism from modernist scholars for that reason. In the meantime his lectures in Oxford 'were infused with a staunchly Christian interpretation and a deep sense of legacy'; he upheld in the Beit Lectureship those values and approaches that he had gained from his teachers, C. H. Firth and Hugh Egerton, offering students the perspective of 'a pro-consul *manqué*'.[36] He has some claim to the title of last imperial whig, perhaps, but the inter-war years threw up several contestants. Reviewing those years half a century later, and after a lifetime's immersion in the sources, William Roger Louis found his mind reaching back to the whig paradigm as a model for the age. 'Like their Victorian predecessors', he writes, – 'above all, Stubbs and Maitland – historians such as Curtis, Coupland and Perham, along with Keith, continued to view imperial history from the perspective of British constitutions and administration. Historians of the inter-war years, with varying degrees of scepticism, continued to affirm the whig idea of progress.'[37] They took into the Second World War a collection of certainties about the reality of the imperial project that the war would undermine to a degree that the First World War had seemingly failed to achieve.

---

[34] *The Cambridge History of the British Empire* (8 vols., 1929–36), vol. 1, 5.
[35] Vincent Harlow (1898–1961). Durham School and Brasenose College, Oxford. Beit Lecturer, Oxford, 1930–5; Ministry of Information during war; Rhodes Professor of Imperial History, King's College, London, 1938–48. *The Founding of the Second British Empire, 1763–1793* (2 vols., 1952–64).
[36] Madden, 'The Commonwealth, Commonwealth History, and Oxford', 18–19.
[37] William Roger Louis, 'Introduction', in Robin W. Spinks (ed.), *The Oxford History of the British Empire* (5 vols., Oxford, 1998–2001), vol. v, 1–42 at 27.

War

Not that whigs necessarily believed war to be immoral or counterproductive. Their style of understanding embraced the possibility that a war might defend justice and express the national character in some elevating way; and the past that they celebrated had thrown up many wars that had contributed, in their eyes, to periods of English development towards becoming a nation – 'periods at which', according to Stubbs, 'the history of its wars is the true history of the people, for they are the discipline of the national experience'.[38] If the war against colonial America fitted this model badly, the resistance to Napoleon reinstated it. The Crimea entrenched lessons across English culture from Tennyson to Kinglake,[39] and these still had their power in 1914 despite the messiness of the Boer War. They ran far beyond the need for bravery. Valour there had to be, of course, but also decency, 'character' and a patriotism so lofty in spirit that death in its name became *dulce et decorum*. Everyone knows that the manner and conditions of the fighting made these ideas hard to realize in the trenches of Flanders. Brutality and cynicism, squalidness and despair: these products of that environment did nothing to sustain the values of liberal gentlemen; and they received such an amplification over the next two decades from those who wrote about the war that to claim a permanent element of cultural collapse in English values does not seem hyperbolic. On the other hand, that same collection of liberal opinions dovetailed into an ideology of collective security among dissident historians, as we shall see later,[40] and the contention misses important aspects of non-dissident opinion. It makes Lytton Strachey more important than he was and throws into shade the plodding work and pain of those – much the majority – who thought the war a disagreeable necessity that had to be seen through. It remained possible to imagine that the war did not touch the historians except in their personal sense of loss. Writing in the middle of the next war, Llewellyn Woodward thought that the special gifts of people like himself had been overlooked on both occasions.

It is a queer thing that, in the last war when we were young, we saw the ablest and best of our contemporaries killed as junior officers when they should have been singled out for high military responsibilities, and, in this war, when we have

---

[38] William Stubbs, *The Constitutional History of England in its Origin and Development* (3 vols., 1873–8), ch. 16, §257, vol. II, 392.

[39] Sir Alexander Kinglake, *The Invasion of the Crimea* (8 vols., Edinburgh and London, 1863–87).

[40] See chapter 7, pp. 169–93.

behind us years of experience, and of the exercise of judgment and authority, we cannot get into the key positions controlling policy and executive action within the sphere of our special competence.[41]

He was wrong, all the same.

Naturally, the historical profession did not find itself pulled bodily into positions of military responsibility between 1914 and 1918, any more than it ascended the summit of civil power after 1939. Luminous figures such as Lord Bryce[42] did find themselves called upon to contribute advice to government and to the incipient movement for a post-war League of Nations. Or one might wonder whether, in other circumstances, H. A. L. Fisher would have found the prime minister on the other end of the telephone at the end of 1916 asking him to become Minister of Education. More important than anecdotal evidence about individuals, however, is a deeper point about the historical community in general. England went into the First World War as a liberal state ostensibly defending Belgium against aggression and trusting the word of one representing a great Whig dynasty, Sir Edward Grey, that the decision to intervene rested on the most cherished traditions and values of free-born Englishmen. Historians followed where Grey led, unless committed to a different view of social democracy in the manner of H. N. Brailsford or the Hammonds, and brought with them an assumption that the history of the war's origins would show the justice of the British cause. When H. W. C. Davis examined the responsibility of German historians for the German mentality, in order to boost the war effort, he made his enquiry 'very limited in scope – no "deeper causes" of the war [were] investigated, unless German political theory [was] a deeper cause'.[43] This small beginning led to greater interventions. Come the end of the war, historians were called upon to enquire into the resemblances between the Congress of Vienna and the proceedings at Versailles. For some, it inaugurated an historical journey to a spiritual Geneva in which all history now became the story of advance towards the League of Nations

---

[41] E. L. Woodward to Charles Webster, 8 Aug. 1942, Webster MSS 1/23/1.

[42] James, Lord Bryce (1838–1922). Family Presbyterian Ulster Scots. Glasgow University and Trinity College, Oxford. Bar; Regius Professor of Civil Law, Oxford, 1870–93; parliament; eventually ambassador to Washington. *The Holy Roman Empire* (Oxford, 1864); *The American Commonwealth* (3 vols., 1888); *Modern Democracies* (2 vols., 1921). For a perspective on war and history see his first Raleigh Lecture, 'World History', *PBA*, 9 (1919–20), 187–211.

[43] H. W. C. Davis to T. F. Tout, 27 Sep. n.y. [?1915], Tout MSS 1/264/19. Davis's account appeared as *The Political Thought of Heinrich von Treitschke* in 1914. For Davis's imperial perspective see his Raleigh Lecture on 'The Great Game in Africa, 1800–1844', *PBA*, 12 (1926), 227–56.

with Canning its inspiration.[44] For a more cautious figure such as J. R. M. Butler, author just before the war of a study of the Great Reform Act, 1815 and 1919 bore no resemblance to one another because this time there was only one right answer, as his scribbled note insists: 'There was no picture [in 1919] of an innocent G[ermany] wh[ich] c[oul]d be held up, as t[he] traditional France c[oul]d be set up in 1815 ag[ain]st rev[olution]ary France. To t[he] Allies G[ermany] was always a *militaristic* power . . . Liberal Germany had always been laughed at.'[45]

Here was a strange form of oblivion. Liberal Germany had once been the very icon of excellence for the English intelligentsia who visited, studied and marvelled in the land of Goethe and Hegel. But Germany's war guilt had now become part of historical consciousness and England's historians found themselves in a closer relation to their own state than they may have deemed possible or desirable in 1914. The consummation of that relationship came in 1926 with the beginning of *British Documents on the Origins of the War*,[46] edited by a confirmed whig in G. P. Gooch and a modified one in Harold Temperley, a series intended to show the transparency of English intentions if not of policy. At the same time, the Royal Historical Society had embarked on its own Camden series on diplomatic history, whose demise brought joy to Rose Graham in 1933.[47]

Institutional development confirmed this pattern of drawing military historians towards the post-war state just as it had drawn the imperial. If SOAS dated from the central years of the war, so did the Imperial War Museum with its long reach of commemoration over the following generations. The Royal Institute of International Affairs at Chatham House also offered a new base for historical thinking in London, just as the establishment of the Chichele Chair of Military History at Oxford allowed the inventor of the tank to breach the defences of All Souls. Both institutions call distinguished names to mind. The Royal Institute of International Affairs owed something, not only to Arnold Toynbee, its director, but also to a young man with a background in the League of Nations Union who would take on the onerous edition of *Documents on*

---

[44] No one more so than Charles Webster. We return to the theme of internationalist liberalism in chapter 7.
[45] Note by J. R. M. Butler (1926), Butler MSS E1/6; I, p. 5.
[46] *British Documents on the Origins of the War, 1898–1914* (11 vols., 1926–34).
[47] Rose Graham to F. M. Stenton, 11 Mar. 1933, Stenton MSS 8/16/1. Rose Graham (1875–1963) was a medievalist close to Powicke, Knowles and E. F. Jacob. Lived in London most of her life – presumably a private income – and wrote on ecclesiastical history.

International Affairs for Chatham House between 1929 and 1936. But then John Wheeler-Bennett held the advantage of having missed Oxford because of illness and of therefore having been thrown into the company of General Sir Neill Malcolm, head of the British military mission in Berlin after the armistice, whom he served as a personal assistant. His visit to Germany again in 1929 brought him the acquaintance of Papen and some intimacy with Brüning. Efforts to help Germans afflicted by the new regime after 1933 cast him also into the company of Sir Robert Vansittart, permanent under-secretary at the Foreign Office until he was kicked upstairs at the beginning of 1938, and deepened his hostility to appeasement. So it became almost an inevitability that the Second World War would project him further into the state's orbit in the Political Warfare Mission and then the Political Intelligence Department. Although he had the outward appearance of a wealthy Oxford don after the war – teaching at New College and residing at Garsington Manor – the books that flowed from him (especially *The Nemesis of Power*[48]) brought together the virtues and vices of a participant and an insider. The new Chichele Chair, meanwhile, prompts the name of Norman Gibbs, deeply military in background and connexion, who held the chair from 1953 to 1977, and whose books about the Committee of Imperial Defence and the first volume of *Grand Strategy* in the official history of the war[49] testified to his experience in the historical section of the Cabinet Office after 1943. None of these initiatives had the historiographical significance of Michael Howard's Department of War Studies at King's College, London, founded in 1964, and it is well to remember W. K. Hancock's warning as late as 1960 that he still found, as he had in the 1930s, a reluctance in Britain to think about war as an historical problem.[50] But the point about convergence remains and, though it was not a style familiar to the whigs of Victorian England, it promised a certain approach and mood in defending the honour of the state in face of criticism.

Despite their own remarks distancing the historical profession from the state and from war, Llewellyn Woodward and Hancock ought

---

[48] Sir John Wheeler-Bennett, *Munich: Prologue to Tragedy* (1948) and *The Nemesis of Power: the German Army in Politics, 1918–45* (1953). In similar vein see R. W. Seton-Watson, *Europe in the Melting Pot* (1919); *Britain and the Dictators: a Survey of Post-War British Policy* (Cambridge, 1938); *Munich and the Dictators: a Sequel to 'Britain and the Dictators'* (1939).

[49] N. H. Gibbs, *The Origins of the Committee of Imperial Defence* (1955); *Grand Strategy: Rearmament Policy* (1976). For Gibbs see Michael Howard (ed.), *The Theory and Practice of War* (1965), 187–212, and Flint and Williams, *Perspectives of Empire*, 172–88.

[50] W. K. Hancock, *Four Studies of War and Peace in this Century* (Cambridge, 1961), 121.

peculiarly to have felt an undertow the other way since they both played an important part in the official history of the Second World War. Woodward wrote the five volumes of *British Foreign Policy in the Second World War* (1970–6), originally drafted for official use between 1942 and 1950, with a shorter version published in 1962. It proclaimed the importance of rejecting 'after-knowledge' so that the account could be viewed as a description of what was known at the time.[51] Hancock, meanwhile, edited the entire run of volumes on the non-military side of the conflict which covered all government departments except for the three service ministries and the Foreign Office. 'The historians began work in 1942', Hancock recalled, 'and for some years there were only ten of them . . . [W]hen the war ended, most of the historians returned to their universities. They have since then done part-time work on the official histories, particularly in their vacations, and with such limited research assitance as could be made available to them. It has been for all of them a formidable labour.'[52]

It was all something new in English historiography: a government-sponsored initiative helped, sometimes hindered, by a section of the Cabinet Office set up for the purpose, huge in scope and preoccupying some post-war historians for much of the rest of their working lives. *The Times* announced in November 1946 that J. R. M. Butler of Trinity College, Cambridge, would join W. K. Hancock in putting together the necessary teams – Butler undertook to supervise the strategic and military aspects of the war history – and work full-time on the project for a year.[53] And as the often-enormous volumes rolled from the press, a repository of correct thinking about the British war effort, encouraged but also to a degree controlled by the state, ought to have impinged on the consciousness of historians more generally; or so Woodward himself had hoped. By 1957 Woodward could not suppress 'a certain amount of surprise at the relative level of attention paid by our fellow academic historians to this kind of work which is not only important and authoritative in itself but is also of great technical interest in that it is a new development in historical writing'.[54] In fact, some of the volumes became notable publications in their own right and assumed importance outside the framework of the official history. Few people nowadays think

[51] E. L. Woodward, *British Foreign Policy in the Second World War* (5 vols., 1970–6), vol. I, vi.
[52] W. K. Hancock and Margaret Gowing, *British War Economy* (1949), x.
[53] *The Times*, 26 Nov. 1946. The Treasury had offered Butler a high salary (£2000), but he failed to negotiate the two years full-time that he was after. Edward Bridges to Butler, 8 Aug. 1946, Butler MSS E3/6/1.
[54] E. L. Woodward to Butler, 14 Sep. 1957, Butler MSS E3/6/2.

of Richard Titmuss's *Problems of Social Policy* (1950) as a contribution to the Civil Series or of Hancock and Gowing on the war economy (1949). Michael Howard's volume on *Grand Strategy* (1972) similarly took on a life of its own outside Butler's series, as did Stephen Roskill's four volumes on *The War at Sea* (1954–61).

Yet all these significant historians could miss, with Woodward, the extent to which this development struck some of his fellow historians as unfortunate in inviting the creation of a historiography in which difficulties might be ironed out by the need to please the government. Butterfield wrote one of his more violent papers against the whole idea and contended that 'official' history was an oxymoron.[55] Other criticisms, if less pointed, accumulated in the 1950s and 1960s as a generation of military and strategic historians wanted to see the Second World War in a different light and felt that the official volumes had been, well, muted. It was Michael Howard's word, precisely selected for its placidity but more than enough to draw fire from an irritated Noble Frankland.[56] Howard, who had to alter a couple of sentences because of Foreign Office scruples and who knew that pressure from the military and civil service had been brought to bear on Gibbs in his volume of *Grand Strategy*, justified himself to the editor of the official series in 1971:

Noble Frankland . . . took me to task over what I said about the Official Histories but I am afraid that I am unrepentant! The word which I used, 'muted', was very carefully chosen to express what does seem to me to be the result of the perfectly legitimate pressures brought to bear by official bodies on Official Histories . . . I certainly did not mean to imply that in any of the Official Histories, pressure from Service and Diplomatic quarters resulted in a distortion of the truth.[57]

Leaving aside the problematic of 'truth' and 'distortion', his remarks reflected a professional modernism that had moved on from some of the whiggish assumptions underpinning the Official Histories as a project for packaging the English past for a particular public under the scrutiny of the state.

---

[55] Herbert Butterfield, 'Official History', in *History and Human Relations* (1951), 101–30. It should be recalled that he particularly resented the time spent on the history of the mercantile marine by his close friend Betty Behrens: it occasioned one of their rows.
[56] Anthony Noble Frankland (1922–). Born Westmorland. Sedbergh and Trinity College, Oxford. RAF 1941–5. Air Historical Branch, Air Ministry, 1948–51; Cabinet Office, 1951–8. Director of Imperial War Museum, 1960–82. *The Strategic Air Offensive against Germany* (with Charles Webster, 4 vols., 1961); *The Politics and Strategy of the Second World War* (8 vols., 1971–4). Cf. Frankland, *History at War: the Campaigns of an Historian* (1998).
[57] Howard to Butler, 6 Oct. 1971, Butler MSS A1/207.

Yet (again), a whig presence made itself felt and not merely in the well-known wartime texts of Stenton and Butterfield. The private correspondence of historians enveloped in the crisis of existence after 1938 breathes pride in English values of the kind caught and poeticized in Arthur Bryant's *English Saga* (1940) and allows a depth of emotion unnatural in English gentlemen. Perhaps it breathed most vigorously when addressing the Land of the Free. Wallace Notestein's little book on *English Folk* (1938), much read during the war, brought an American freshness to the portrait of a nation at precisely the moment when colours seemed to have faded. And he did it in a *whig* way by reversing the chronology of his pen-portraits so that the reader encountered the story backwards from the nineteenth century to the sixteenth.

For the political historian it is best in following a closely-related series of events to move forward in order of time. Yet journalists and story-tellers are likely to begin at the conclusion or in the middle of a narrative and then go back to explain how matters came to the pass that they were in. It is even the technique of some of our modern novelists. It is an order in which the mind works, from what is to how it came to be. It is the order we use in setting forth a situation to a friend; we are concerned with a present and we proceed to give it a setting.[58]

He knew that war and empire had played a part in filtering the 'English character' whose depiction he saw as his purpose. He contended that his thirteen portraits suggested something trans-temporal about what it meant to be English and, as the war became the backdrop to his book, his contention seemed plausible to historians, even rather moving. With fighters filling the sky in the summer of 1940, Vivian Galbraith did homage to Notestein in this startling and emotional message.

For I did not need to read your English Folk . . . to know how you understand England. Indeed, Powicke apart, I don't remember anyone who taught me as much about the association of English country & English history as you have (which you'll admit is odd!) & your acquaintance with our Poetry is almost indecent in its depth & reaches to the heart of things. As a matter of fact I rather think the rock-bottom feeling with which we are meeting this tragedy is pretty much what you have set out in your 'English Folk'. Simple chaps do prize their old, ?unheeded way of life: and I think will fight like tigers to preserve it. All this is rather debauched & deflowered by the BBC with its old school tie broadcasts & quotations from Henry V – but most of us just turn off when we've heard of the daily 'bag' of Messerschmidts [*sic*] and Junkers & so on, & our 'Postscripts to the News', Pep Talks and Propaganda is [*sic*] mainly heard, I believe, by Haw Haw & the Neutrals.[59]

[58] Wallace Notestein, *English Folk* (1938), 15.
[59] Vivian Galbraith to Notestein, 21 July 1940, Notestein MSS 544/1/3/285.

Modernism this is not. Nor was the original intention to get Trevelyan to participate in the Official Histories.[60] A doctrine about a little island 'crammed with heroes' needed to be given historical form just as its great wartime leader, the last of the Tudors in the eyes of J. E. Neale, demanded commemoration in the anxious months of the Blitz and association with his only conceivable comparator.

How many of his sayings will be immortal! I think he has seized the drama & romance present in these sordid days & personifies the nation as no one since Q. Elizabeth has done. (By the way, have you ever thought of the Catholics in Elizabeth's day as the exact parallel of Hitler's Fifth Column to-day? I think those interpretations in my 'Queen Elizabeth' which looked like prejudice in me when I wrote the book carry conviction to-day. What do you think?)[61]

War could thus embody the whig historical message as much as compromise it.

By 1960 W. K. Hancock, war's editor and tribune, could look sideways from the podium on which he was declaiming the history of war in the twentieth century to notice how *passé* had become not only the empire but the commonwealth that had become its heir. In a world changing rapidly something sempiternal still hung around the commonwealth's sense of itself, something resembling 'Hooker's *Ecclesiastical Polity*, Halifax's *Character of a Trimmer* and much other writing of a distinct English flavour; we find it embodied in the legal and constitutional practice which still remains dominant . . . in the majority of Commonwealth countries'.[62] He was the same Hancock who had written a Penguin Special on the idea of empire in the middle of the war,[63] an idea long unworkable by 1960. For some imperial historians the writing remained unread on the wall out of a sense of the genuine loss that they thought the disappearance of the British empire would entail – not only in Curtis's overcharged sense of mission, but in the quiet notion that imperialism in its British form always took its tone from 'those moral considerations which, to the annoyance of rivals, have rarely been lacking when the British think aloud'.[64] Absence of mind or thinking aloud, it made little difference to the empire's integrity as an *idea*, for all the faults of execution, and even in these days following the 'Axis war'

---

[60] Charles Webster's diary, 29 Oct. 1943. The idea was to produce a one-volume version after the war that would reach a wider audience. Hancock and Webster 'agreed this would be a boon on the Ministry of Information level'. Webster MSS 29/10.
[61] J. E. Neale to Notestein, 8 Feb. 1941, Notestein MSS 544/1/6/536.
[62] Hancock, *Four Studies of War and Peace*, 112.
[63] W. K. Hancock, *Argument of Empire* (Harmondsworth, 1943).
[64] Walker, *The Second British Empire*, 80.

with its language of *Lebensraum*, Eric Walker saw freedom where critics saw tyranny, 'a spirit sprung from a love of personal freedom, a leaning towards tolerance that has been inculcated by the abiding necessity of coming to terms with one another in their own islands, a respect for tradition and prescriptive rights . . .'[65] Indigenous nationalist movements were to blow away sentiment as though it were candy-floss and the next quarter of a century would show the illusion of a moralized commonwealth united by a vision. But for a while it remained strong enough to make a continuing whig past available and usable until currents within the historical profession at home found themselves in league with critics overseas.

Perhaps Vincent Harlow found himself the last whig in those post-war years. His two volumes on *The Founding of the Second British Empire* had an inner drive of shape and purpose: the empire had moved away from dominion to trade and it had, in his echoing phrase, swung to the east in its focus.[66] His sources were public records like those used by any nineteenth-century whig; his rescuing of empire from disreputability followed their model. It formed an undeniable achievement, 'an almost monolithic rock of prescribed and undodgeable reading', as a later scholar put it. But between volumes I and II the entire conception ran into reefs within the imperial historical fraternity. Modernists who had had good wars – Richard Pares and Lucy Sutherland at the Board of Trade, Ronald Robinson and Jack Gallagher in the armed forces – brought a very different sensibility to the study of the empire. The first two supplied different arguments from Harlow's, especially Pares who knew about west as well as east. The second two did more damage by starting somewhere else. Their 'The Imperialism of Free Trade', when it appeared in 1953,[67] looked important and has been made seminal. This was silly on the authors' own assumptions. The fifteen pages were meant to supply an interesting case about continuity in imperial power across the division between protection and free trade within Victorian political economy. They were not supposed to be seminal because the sharp end of the argument was about dispensing with seminality and replacing it with cases resting on explicit assumptions. They wanted to make the history of the British empire a *conceptual* issue, the place at which Harlow and his forebears ran aground:

---

[65] Ibid., vii. For *Lebensraum*, see p. 49.
[66] Harlow, *The Founding of the Second British Empire*. The 'prevailing *drang nach osten* [*sic*]' occurs at p. 8 of vol. I and chapter 3 is called 'The Swing to the East': vol. I, 62–102.
[67] R. Robinson and J. Gallagher, 'The Imperialism of Free Trade', *EcHR*, 6 (1953), 1–15.

The imperial historian, in fact, is very much at the mercy of his own particular conception of empire. By that, he decides what facts are of 'imperial' significance; his data are limited in the same way as his concept, and his final interpretation itself depends largely upon the scope of his hypothesis.[68]

This is what sets fire to what had gone before. Their own conclusions were radical: by defining empire as a tissue of informal connexions and controls, imperial history found itself turned away from constitutionalism in a search for an *histoire totale* that could integrate formal and informal empire.[69] But what makes the conclusions possible is the set of governing assumptions within which the argument took form; and these not only avoided whig formulations but consciously contested them. It was not the end, of course. Robinson and Gallagher's major monograph on *Africa and the Victorians* did not reach book form until 1961 and another decade would be required to bring about transformation in imperial studies as much as in war studies. As in so many other areas of argument within English historiography, by 1970 the ghosts of Victorian England walked with less confidence than they had enjoyed in the years of their creation.

[68] Ibid., 1.   [69] Ibid., 6–7.

4   Ghosts and intimations

Legacies are a matter of memory. Intimations concern the future. Modernists had perpetual encounters with both dimensions and much would disappear from their world if their location became at the hands of posterity little more than a checklist of received attributes. In our own day the recommendations of Hans-Georg Gadamer and Reinhart Koselleck urge the importance of 'horizons of expectation' in history: the need to give participants the sense of future (and therefore of past) that we readily give to ourselves. The whig understanding of history in the twentieth century cannot itself be understood without this procedure because it took its nature from acts of recollection and imagined futurity among those trying to preserve or relinquish it. There is a subconsciousness that matters and which sensitive historians can occasionally depict. That is why we must pause before considering modernist historiography in its own terms for, in the light of a century's perspective, its own terms concealed illusions and repressions, not least over the continuities that it was the point of a whig outlook to foster. The coupled characteristics of a whig legacy that we have been reviewing – constitution and nation, church and state, empire and war – formed the stuff of recollection and intimation when twentieth-century observers spoke of the whigs. But stuff is not form and the raw material of memory and received wisdom had to await its sculptor. It was hard for contemporaries to see how, for example, when Herbert Butterfield so compellingly described the 'Whig interpretation of history' in 1931, he also in a very real sense created it.

Perhaps some of the earlier contributors to his asserted paradigm would have recognized themselves as whig historians – Henry Hallam, possibly, or Macaulay in his more self-aware moments. Most would not; and none would have seen himself as confined by a model nor his history cast in a mould. Those tendencies that Butterfield lamented – the triumphalism, the judgementalism, the presentism, the Protestantism, the persistent urge to 'abridge' narratives until they became compressed into rigid chipboard[1] – these were not characteristics that the nineteenth century accepted, at least not in the negative form that Butterfield lent them. Arraigned at some posthumous bar of historical judgement and faced with posterity's charges, the ghosts of Hallam and Macaulay and Kemble, Freeman and Green and Stubbs, Seeley and Gardiner and Firth, Froude and Creighton and Acton might reasonably have raised their palms and shrugged their shoulders. What *else* were they supposed to do? Nor should their apparitions be sentenced without a proper hearing. A particular weakness of Butterfield's paradigm, after all, is that it includes just about everybody, once we have left out Carlyle, who fits no one's model; and a description that describes everybody and everything becomes prone to what the philosophers call 'vacuous contrast'. In the *twentieth* century, on the other hand, Butterfield's message took on great point and turned into an important intimation that historical writing was undergoing an act of becoming. One of that century's most important historiographers, Brian Wormald, father of the medieval historian Patrick Wormald, still held, as a nonogenarian, that Butterfield's statement seventy years ago remained the most influential and important book he had encountered over a long life of historical reflection.[2] It spoke to its time and of its time, and said as much between its lines about its surrounding generations and their ambitions as it did about its more distant victims. How, the question arises, and when, and with what success, did historians transcend the world pilloried in the *Whig Interpretation* and convert its polemical force into the conventional wisdom of two generations of English scholars? And why did that wisdom in turn begin to look, as we have already seen at several points in this study, less than eternal by the 1960s, leaving behind a talented and significant cohort to suffer the ultimate disparagement of looking 'transitional' between one great age of communication with the public and another, more spectacular, one for which the immediacy of a Schama[3] or

---

[1] Herbert Butterfield, *The Whig Interpretation of History* (1931; Pelican edn, 1973), esp. ch. 2, 16–31.

[2] B. H. G. Wormald in conversation with the author. Wormald was arguably the first English historian to offer, from 1957, serious instruction in historiography within a university syllabus. See his acute study of *Clarendon* (Cambridge, 1951) and *Francis Bacon: History, Politics and Science, 1561–1626* (Cambridge, 1993). Patrick Wormald (1947–2004), formerly Student of Christ Church, Oxford, had embarked on a huge history of early English law: see *The Making of English Law: King Alfred to the Twelfth Century*, vol. I (Oxford, 2000), especially the first chapter, for a masterly survey of the historiography. He died prematurely – a disaster for historical scholarship – in September 2004, and his father followed in 2005.

[3] Simon Schama (1945–)is best known for his television series on the history of Britain but is also a prolific author: see in particular *The Embarrassment of Riches: an Interpretation of*

Starkey[4] or Ferguson[5] now throws into shadow texts formative of entire generations, such as *The Structure of Politics at the Accession of George III* or *King Henry the Third and the Lord Edward* or *Elizabeth I and her Parliaments?*[6]

Oddly enough, the discoverer of the whig interpretation contributes to the difficulty of these questions by his adoption of the very method of abridgement that his text forbids. It is not only that Butterfield himself was and remained a whig historian in many of his moods, but also that he helped draw up the decline of the whig typology and fixed its initial undoing largely before the First World War, a period when he was still a schoolboy. He did not cite Maitland, as so many have since, as the solvent of whiggery, but rather Glasgow's William Sharp McKechnie and his commentary on Magna Carta, published in 1905, which Butterfield thought destructive of the 'reading backwards' of history that he placed at the centre of whig misbehaviour.[7] On top of that, of course, Maitland's understated destruction of Stubbs's view of the parliament of 1305 had already led to extreme reactions among some – by no means all – constitutional historians, long before Richardson and Sayles began throwing their crockery at Stubbs in the 1930s and completed his rubbishing a quarter of a century later.[8] It seems exaggerated to us now that Brian Wormald, going up to Cambridge at the end of the 1920s, could be told that the first volume of Stubbs's *Constitutional*

Dutch Culture in the Golden Age (1988); *Citizens: a Chronicle of the French Revolution* (1989); *Landscape and Memory* (1996).

[4] David Starkey (1945–) has a wide audience for his television programmes on the Tudors; see also his *The Reign of Henry VIII: Personalities and Politics* (1985) and *Elizabeth: Apprenticeship* (2000).

[5] Niall Ferguson (1964–). Glasgow Academy and Magdalen College, Oxford. Research Fellowships, Hamburg and Cambridge, 1986–90. Fellow of Jesus College, Oxford, 1992–2000 and Professor of Political and Financial History there 2000–2. A variety of posts in the USA. Professor at Harvard from 2004. *The Pity of War* (1998), *The Cash Nexus* (2001), *Empire: How Britain Made the Modern World* (2003), etc.

[6] Lewis Namier, *The Structure of Politics at the Accession of George III* (2 vols., 1929); F. M. Powicke, *King Henry the Third and the Lord Edward* (2 vols., Oxford, 1947); J. E. Neale, *Elizabeth I and her Parliaments* (2 vols., 1953–7).

[7] W. S. McKechnie, *Magna Carta: a Commentary on the Great Charter of King John, with an Historical Introduction* (Glasgow, 1905). Butterfield thought McKechnie had successfully relativized discussion of the text and rendered it intelligible only when placed within the framework of feudal society; see Butterfield on *George III and the Historians* (1957), 195. Cf. his reflection after the Second World War: 'When I was young . . . the Whig-Protestant interpretation of history was already being undermined.' Butterfield, draft of 'Moral Judgment in History' (1947), later published in *History and Human Relations* (1951), 101–30, Butterfield MSS BUTT/122/1, p.13.

[8] H. G. Richardson and G. O. Sayles, *The Governance of Medieval England: from the Conquest to Magna Carta* (Edinburgh, 1963). Cf. James Campbell, *Stubbs and the English State* (Reading, 1989).

History was not merely unrecommended but positively forbidden reading to those preparing for the Tripos.[9] That was the atmosphere in which Butterfield attained maturity and the environment from which he would attack his false gods. Imagine how distant they must have appeared to him during his retirement in 1970 when an assiduous Dutch research student, P. B. M. Blaas, wrote to him about the doctoral thesis that he hoped would show how the whig school of history ran into difficulty in the 1890s and literally lost the plot by 1914. Those who came after, the thesis ran, fulfilled the function of mere continuators, 'seen from the whole direction and movement within the English historiography since Maitland, Round and other people . . .'[10] Encouraged in this view by Butterfield himself, Blaas went on to produce a formidable piece of scholarship that amounted to something rare and remarkable: an important Ph.D. thesis. When it appeared in print as a huge volume in 1978 under the title *Continuity and Anachronism*[11] the curve of whig historiography seemed firmly displayed and the overwhelming weight of evidence provided by Blaas left readers confident that the whigs were dead before a shot was fired in Flanders.

Blaas's achievement was prodigious but four contexts provided a natural limit to its effectiveness. First, Blaas tried to frame his narrative by taking the historiography of parliament as its determinant and the place of constitutional history in the curriculum as its governing location.[12] The problem with that concerns the degree to which a narrative about the history of parliament pre-dates significant changes in whig typologies as a whole, sometimes by several decades as we saw in the case of imperial historiography. Second, Blaas assumed that whig historiography had a natural relationship with Liberal politics, and thought that Liberal politics in England were undergoing vital structural change before 1914.[13] Both of those assumptions require invigilation. Third, he was dependent on the printed works of the historians under consideration. Since Blaas wrote, an immense amount of archival material has become available which enables us to see the problems

---

[9] Interview with B. H. G. Wormald. Helen Cam reinforced the message in 1948: 'I think that we are justified in advising the student to begin his study of Stubbs in 1066.' She cited advances in 'philological and archaeological researches' since Stubbs's death and his 'failure . . . to eliminate the strong impress of the influence of Maurer's dubious and irrelevant theory of the Mark'. Cam, 'Stubbs Seventy Years On', *Cambridge Historical Journal*, 9 (1948), 129–47 at 132.

[10] Blaas to Butterfield, 25 May 1970, Butterfield MSS BUTT/531.

[11] P. B. M. Blaas, *Continuity and Anachronism: Parliamentary and Constitutional Development in Whig Historiography and in the Anti-Whig Reaction between 1890 and 1930* (The Hague, 1978).

[12] Ibid., xii.   [13] Ibid., xii–xiv.

through unguarded private correspondence as well as the lapidary text. Fourth and most pressingly from the point of view of my investigation here, Blaas never quite turned his historians into people straddling thresholds, escaping models, holding their life and work together through experiences and combination rooms encountered in common, memories shared and recalled with meaning and relevance, personalities loved and books revered. He did not see the *canonical* nature of English historiography. Identifying intimations of change and the approach of a plausible future naturally weighs with the historian of historiography, else the subject will degenerate into a descriptive ramble. But ghosts are harder to see and we all walk with them: they help make our present what it is. There is not an historian alive, moreover, who can tolerate being described as part of a 'transitional' era or the mere continuator of superior scholars. If every age is immediate to God, every historian is immediate to his or her age and we owe the remarkable personalities of a post-whig sensibility the courtesy of thinking about how they related to their own age, not merely to its precursors or successors. Important though the couplets of a whig legacy are to understanding the force of the whig idea, that legacy cannot be left as a shopping list of characteristics. Its presence as the determinant of a past–present–future precious to those who experienced it needs stress and evocation.

Precursors and continuators

Precursors mattered within the twentieth-century past, all the same, and Professor Blaas was right to draw our attention to them. The new methods he discerns in J. H. Round, F. W. Maitland and A. F. Pollard contained the origins of much twentieth-century thinking in England and Maitland's phrases in particular ring down the decades like flicked crystal: 'we are moderns and our words and thoughts cannot but be modern'; 'the study of interactions and inter-dependencies [in history] is but just beginning . . .'[14] He had never known Stubbs – 'Stubbs was to me solely the writer of certain books' – and had only set eyes on him once.[15] He could move with the times in the 1890s without the drag of an acolyte. Retrospective observers as different as Butterfield and Stenton agreed that something important happened during that decade. For Stenton it lay in the new approaches of Round, Vinogradoff,

---

[14] Ibid., 66–7, 267, 269.
[15] F. W. Maitland to R. L. Poole, 29 Apr. 1901, in C. H. S. Fifoot (ed.), *The Letters of Frederic William Maitland* (Cambridge, 1965), 225.

Plummer and the early Liebermann. They stood at the beginning of a trend that he would later call, significantly, the 'modern tendency', which he reduced to two developments in some scribbled notes in 1944:

Modern tendency since 1900.
1 The study has become disinterested . . .
2 (connected with 1) The sanctity of the record. Carelessness of Vic historians.[16]

Butterfield as ever evaded so crisp (and revealing) a formulation but his long sentence breathes significance into the 1890s from a distance of eighty years. 'If anybody can sort out the multiple developments,' he wrote in 1969, '– and the many side-branchings into original paths – which result in one way and another from the ideas that were at issue in the 1890s, he will be able to make an unusually valuable contribution to the history of historiography.'[17] Beyond method and ideas lay new institutions and occasions appearing with the new century: the British Academy (1902); the Historical Association (1906); that over-celebrated inaugural of J. B. Bury's in 1903;[18] the more significant one from Charles Harding Firth in Oxford in the following year.[19] Behind it all lurked Berlin and Leipzig with their intimidating *Hilfswissenschaften* on whose undesirability Charles Oman discoursed so emphatically in his own inaugural lecture delivered in Firth's wake.[20] The twentieth-century dialogue between rival historical schools in Oxford and Cambridge, one in which the greatest teaching university confronted the aspirant research university, is already audible in these years with implications for whig comfort and sustainability. One knows instinctively that Maitland will think Firth the most distinguished Oxford product, as he did, just as one suspects that Gardiner would always have kept clear of the Fenland institution whose ethos, as he said, would 'knock [his] whole life's work into a cocked hat'.[21] Beyond those ancient walls an array of new and technical universities had their humanities side stocked with multi-tasking professors, few so significant for history as the former

---

[16] Holograph note untitled and undated [?1944], Stenton MSS 8/27/2.
[17] Herbert Butterfield, 'Trends in Scholarship in Modern History', *TRHS*, 5th series, 19 (1969), 159–84 at 178.
[18] J. B. Bury, *An Inaugural Lecture delivered in the Divinity School, Cambridge, on January 26, 1903* (Cambridge, 1903). Cf. his essay on 'Darwinism and History', in A. C. Seward (ed.), *Darwin and Modern Science: Centenary Essays* (Cambridge, 1909) and *The Idea of Progress: an Inquiry into its Origin and Growth* (1920).
[19] *A Plea for the Historical Teaching of History* (Oxford, 1904).
[20] Charles Oman, *The Study of History* (Oxford, 1906).
[21] Maitland to Henry Jackson, 13 Jul. 1902, in Fifoot, *Letters of Frederic William Maitland*, 323; S. R. Gardiner to Oscar Browning, 25 Feb. 1891, Browning MSS i/C.

Owens College, Manchester, now its own university, and the London colleges, especially University College during these years. Manchester and London meant Tout and Pollard, the one biography a prolonged intimation of a modernist future, the other innovative in snatches but not without its ghostly moments.

Following in the steps of Adolphus Ward (now Master of Peterhouse, Butterfield's future college), Tout rejected 'brilliancy' and 'picturesqueness' in historical work,[22] preferring the forensic skills of the undergraduate dissertation of which he was a pioneer. If we did not know, again, that he had five Ph.D. students by the outbreak of the First World War, we might well have guessed.[23] His analytical intelligence unpicked anachronism, particularly that of constitutional lawyers who treated chronology as a form of optional decoration, and found common cause with Round's dislike of whig complacencies. 'I have read your books to little purpose,' he assured Round in 1912, 'if I did not strongly agree with you that it is perfectly ridiculous and un-historical to apply the jargon of peerage lawyers of modern or post-Reformation times to the political system of England in the thirteenth century,'[24] a message he presumably impressed also on a pupil who would become the thirteenth century in the age of modernism, Maurice Powicke. Similarly, the country's best constitutional lawyer, looking for a collaborator in editing Edward II's Year Books, turned not to another lawyer but to one whom he described as a 'trained historical investigator'.[25] Had Albert Pollard accepted Maitland's overture perhaps his future work would have lost the bits of whiggery that remained. Certainly his enormous output in these pre-war years and his determination to give London its university *quartier* on the model of the Sorbonne placed Pollard at the centre of an important movement. He ran seminars on the German model, too, that became the precursors of the Thursday evening 'conferences' he instituted after the war. At the very beginning of the war, in October 1914, he wrote to his parents:

---

[22] Adolphus Ward reviewing Wolfgang Michael in the *English Historical Review* in July 1897. He compliments Michael for avoiding 'brilliancy or picturesqueness, of which, perhaps, we have had enough for the present generation's delight . . .' See Adolphus Ward, *Collected Papers: Historical, Literary, Travel and Miscellaneous* (4 vols., Cambridge, 1921), vol. II, 23–31 at 29.

[23] Tout to Pollard, 30 Oct. n.y. [?1911], Pollard MSS 860 box 48. '[A]ll on different subjects . . . a great handful.'

[24] Tout to J. H. Round, 21 Mar. 1912, Round MSS, 683 f.3.

[25] F. W. Maitland to Pollard, 30 Apr. 1903, Pollard MSS 860 box 47.

The 'circle' or History Club, into which my best seminar has developed, was attended by 20 members on Thursday. They included three officials from the Public Record Office and seven teachers of the University, as well as some independent historical writers. The idea is to form a link between people working at history in London.[26]

This was not a whig plan but rather part of the writing on the wall for the development of post-whig historical studies and it would be foolish to ignore it.

But the writing is smaller than may be apparent; nor does it all point the same way. To stand in 1914 and project forward in time the un-doubted developments of the past twenty years as though they were embryonic for the rest of the century is to apply that very whig method that is under review. It presents propositions resting on a couple of cases, moreover, as though they were universal. Charles Oman was not alone in mistrusting the Germans. When the young George Prothero, future professor at Edinburgh, returned from Bonn at the end of the 1870s, he had reported of his hosts

Too much tendency to stop at a collection of facts, to let the facts speak for themselves, or rather remain dumb . . . They don't seek enough to get at the great laws of history, development of nations, differences of national character, all that is greatest & widest, in fact what is really the teaching of history. They are the *gelehrt*, & despise popularizing. One wants a people with more imagination, with less caution, perhaps, to extract the essence from the material they collect, & that is what we ought to do in England . . .[27]

Extracting the essence would be done in the name of another ghost, of course, that of Leopold von Ranke who had stalked England for years in the body of William Stubbs, 'like himself a Conservative by tempera-ment', according to the editor of the *Revue historique*, 'who achieved a reputation by explaining the cause and necessity of change'.[28] The first volume of the *Constitutional History* may have become obsolete – James Tait of Manchester said so as early as 1908[29] – but it remained the stock on which everyone else grafted and Stubbs's ghost had only just begun his walks, looking for the host he would discover eventually in Butterfield's contemporary, Vivian Galbraith.[30] Freeman fared less well, admittedly, savaged in death as much as in life by Horace Round for being wrong

[26] Pollard to his parents, 11 Oct. 1914, Pollard MSS, box 4.
[27] G. W. Prothero to Oscar Browning, 25 Mar. n.y. [1879–82], Browning MSS i/Prothero.
[28] Charles Bémont, 'Bishop Stubbs', *Quarterly Review*, 202 (1905), 1–34 at 18.
[29] See his preface to Charles Petit-Dutaillis, *Studies and Notes Supplementary to Stubbs's Constitutional History: down to the Great Charter* (Manchester, 1908), vii–viii.
[30] V. H. Galbraith (1889–1976). Manchester University: pupil of Tout, Tait and Powicke. Then Oxford for a famous Third in Greats but followed by a First in Modern History.

in small things and by Oman for attempting large ones. The latter declared in 1906:

I did not hear Dr Stubbs's Inaugural Lecture – being then a small schoolboy – but I did hear that of his successor Freeman . . . an impassioned harangue in praise of what he called the 'Unity of History' . . . Freeman tried to illustrate it by delivering a series of lectures on the history of Sicily, which was to range from the earliest Greek and Carthaginian settlement of the island, past the Punic Wars, the Goths and Vandals and Moors, down to the days of the Norman Roger and Frederic of Hohenstaufen. But the lectures were never completed because no continuous audience could be found to attend them . . . It is a melancholy fact that the days are past in which it was possible for any one . . . to aim at being encyclopaedic.[31]

Nor did Freeman, like some, survive death. He pre-deceased his wife but she did not carry his candle as far as Alice Stopford Green carried *her* husband's, going on seemingly for ever, becoming president of the Historical Association and making sure that Jesus Quad bore a memorial tablet to her John Richard in 1909.[32]

Yet what of those younger critics of the whig tradition, how focused were they in their exorcisms? Butterfield points us to McKechnie, but although the latter's revisionism over Magna Carta in 1905 relativized to some extent a discussion previously seen in more absolute terms, there remains much in McKechnie that Stubbs would have welcomed, in particular the view of the *Constitutional History* as 'the starting-point of all historians and constitutional lawyers of the present generation'. McKechnie distanced himself at once from Edward Jenks's attack on the 'gigantic imposture' and 'venerable fraud' of Magna Carta, published in the previous year,[33] not least because 'traditional interpretations' have 'proved of supreme value in the battle for freedom', hardly a counter-whig proposition.[34] The greater constitutional scholar, Frederic William Maitland, meanwhile deserves an age, and more chapters than these, to

Assistant Keeper at Public Record Office, 1921–8; Reader in Diplomatic, succeeding R. L. Poole, and Tutorial Fellow of Balliol College, Oxford, 1928–37; Professor of History, Edinburgh, 1937–44; Director of the Institute of Historical Research, London, 1944–8; Regius Chair, Oxford, 1948–57. *Introduction to the Use of the Public Records* (1934); *Domesday Book: its Place in Administrative History* (1974).

[31] Oman, *Study of History*, 8–9

[32] Alice Stopford Green to Pollard, 17 May 1909, Pollard MSS 860 box 47.

[33] Edward Jenks, 'The Myth of Magna Carta', *Independent Review*, 4 (1904), 260–73. Cf. Jenks to Pollard, 14 July 1914: 'I noticed with pleasure in last Sunday's *Observer* that you had opened a campaign against that gigantic imposture Magna Carta; and, in view of the proposed celebration in London of that venerable fraud [in 1915], your action seems to me admirably timed.' Pollard MSS 860 box 47.

[34] McKechnie, *Magna Carta*, ix. '[I]ts moral influence has contributed to a marked advance of the national liberties' (148).

himself, but not all of their pages would demonstrate iconoclasm or even anti-whiggery. To speak of 'the general drift' of history, 'the stream of tendency', calls up memories of John Robert Seeley; but the phrases are taken from the pages of *Domesday Book and Beyond*.[35] To discover remarks on relating a known present to an unknown past, about the grown man who finds it easier to think the thoughts of the schoolboy than those of the baby recalls the anthropomorphism of Lecky; but they are found, too, in *Domesday Book and Beyond*.[36] His brilliant deconstructions of English law did not deconstruct its, for him, essential continuity; its texts could not only still be read but read backwards from the present in the way he had always recommended:

Hardly a rule now remains unaltered, and yet the body of law that now lies among us is the same body that Blackstone described in the eighteenth century, Coke in the seventeenth, Littleton in the fifteenth, Bracton in the thirteenth, Glanvill in the twelfth. This continuity, this identity, is very real to us if we know that for the last seven hundred years all the judgments of the courts at Westminister have been recorded, and that for the most part they can still be read.[37]

Equally, when we turn to Firth, the pioneer of post-whig, research-based history in Oxford, we find his early certainty that 'the ranks of the opposition are beginning to shake and waggle'[38] dimming into a depression about the hopelessness of his task that never lifted. And he himself was hardly a proto-Namier, not when he could look at a picture of Margaret Tudor and then remark to Pollard 'what a low type; she looks a thoroughly bad lot. I saw a woman very like her drunk in the Strand a few days ago.'[39] Tout, the most determined anti-whig, kept his austerities pure, but he did not hold a monopoly on how history might be done, even at Manchester, as his future colleague, Carless Davis reminded him as early as 1905. 'The difference between us seems to be in point of view,' he wrote. 'I am bitten with a taste for social, constitutional & intellectual history – the history of the community – and you I fancy attached [in his recent book] more importance to political events, the history of the nation.'[40] As for Pollard he won

---

[35] F. W. Maitland, *Domesday Book and Beyond: Three Essays in the Early History of England* (Cambridge, 1897), 9, 286.
[36] Ibid., 9. It should be conceded that these tendencies are far less marked, where one would expect them to be more strident, in Maitland's lectures published as *The Constitutional History of England* (Cambridge, 1908).
[37] F. W. Maitland, 'Outlines of English Legal History, 500–1600', in H. A. L. Fisher (ed.), *Collected Papers* (3 vols., Cambridge, 1911), 417–496 at 418.
[38] Firth to Tout, 22 Dec. 1907, Tout MSS 1/387/83.
[39] Firth to Pollard, 22 June 1902, Pollard MSS 860 box 47.
[40] Davis to Tout, 31 Dec. 1905, Tout MSS 1/264/3.

plaudits from anti-whigs for his revival of Tudor history and was seen by some as Maitland's successor as England's constitutional expert by 1914; but among Tories he carried still the taint of a repellent liberalism, and among even those who revered him he could be viewed as a 'gifted amateur' in the professionalizing atmosphere of war.[41]

The Great War brought its own ghosts, historical as well as personal. It encompassed the seven-hundredth anniversary of Magna Carta, the centenary of Waterloo and the Congress of Vienna, centenaries, too, of great Whig birthdays and books which would now fill the remainder of the century with a rolling programme of stocktaking and tokens of remembrance. Pollard the Institute-maker found himself writing about Hallam and Froude in the *Times Literary Supplement*, declaring both worthy of recall and Froude even of celebration.[42] Younger men escaped those ghosts but encountered others. On the Western Front a certain Sergeant R. H. Tawney wrote home to complain about the *Spectator*'s treatment of his generation. 'Our minds differ from yours', he said, 'both because they are more exposed to change, and because they are less changeable . . . [O]ur foreground may be different, but our background is the same. It is that of August 1914. We are your ghosts.'[43] He could have been writing of an historiographical era which he shared with his critics and of which he became his own, very different, representative. Modernists did not have to be brought up on the whigs to discover themselves unable to escape them in the eviscerated environment of inter-war England.

The issue of world war wants, again, its own treatment in the story of English historiography. Petit-Dutaillis had said before the war that enthusiasm had gone out of historians to be replaced by pessimism and insecurity;[44] but his anxieties lose all force before the shattering ones of

---

[41] In a discussion attended by Powicke in 1917, 'Pollard, in spite of his amazing ingenuity and readiness, seemed a gifted amateur beside these well-informed professionals.' Powicke to Tout, 19 Nov. 1917, Tout MSS 1/962/34.

[42] Hallam did not escape censure for his politics. 'His absorption of the doctrines of Whiggery atrophied his mind to any other aspect of the truth.' 'The Whig as Historian', *TLS*, 20 June 1918, 281–2 at 282. But he forgave Froude: 'I have no difficulty about writing on Froude because I long ago came to the conclusion that he had been unjustly abused as an historian of the sixteenth century. . .' Pollard to parents, 3 Mar. 1918, Pollard MSS box 5. Cf. 'Froude', *TLS*, 18 Apr. 1918: 'It is mere ignorance and prejudice to contend that in his research and treatment of its results Froude was consciously acting, not as Clio's votary but as a child of the father of lies' (178).

[43] Quoted in Storm Jameson, *Journey from the North* (2 vols., 1970), vol. II, 27.

[44] '[S]o many illusions have been dissipated . . . parliamentary institutions . . have more openly revealed . . . their inevitable littlenesses and . . . the formation of nationalism has turned Europe into an armed camp . . . history is written with less enthusiasm.' Petit-Dutaillis, introduction to French edition of Stubbs's *Constitutional History*, published in

1914–18. His fellow Frenchman Charles Bémont found the first post-war Congress of Historical Sciences – the famous one in Brussels that counted Pirenne, Febvre and Bloch among the audience – a bitter-sweet moment that combined normality and irreparable loss when he went there. 'J'ai rencontré . . . plusieurs de vos plus éminents compatriots,' he wrote to the elderly Horace Round that year: 'Poole, Tout, Vinogradoff.' But the thought took him back to London in 1913, the last Congress, and how, 'depuis cette époque, je n'avais pas mis le pied en Angleterre'. Four words and four only he put into English: 'The light that fails!'[45] One sees the depth of his despair in the closure of an entire chapter in the story of French history and its authors. His co-editor at the *Revue historique*, Christian Pfister, worked out in 1927 that, of the fifty three individuals who associated themselves with the foundation of the journal in 1876, 'aucun n'est plus vivant'.[46] The prospect of German scholars turning away from Britain also had its resonances in these sad years, from Karl Lamprecht of Leipzig, so long a friend of Adolpus Ward at Manchester, to Felix Liebermann, who had spent four years in Manchester studying the commerce of cotton before he became the independent scholar whose *Gesetze der Angelsachsen* became known as a monument to patient scholarship. Like Lamprecht, Liebermann turned his face away in 1914 and the third volume of the *Gesetze*, published in 1916, began to speak about the life-force of the German people. Round's compatriots certainly did not meet *him* at Brussels: the Germans were excluded on the grounds that their country was no longer part of the international community.[47] These painful atmospherics matter because they make their moment quite as vividly as Eliot's *Waste Land* or Strachey's *Eminent Victorians*. They confirm the degree to which historians could not avoid the war's shadow, whether in lamenting the death of Tout's favourite pupil, the historian of Chartism Mark Hovell, on the Western Front, or in finding some grim satisfaction in the thought that the scale of the experience might at least help change historians' preoccupations by inviting the products of conventional historical training finally to 'desert the Three Field System, the Manorial Court, or the King's Council and consider for the first time the more recent

1907; see his *Studies and Notes Supplementary to Stubbs' Constitutional History: down to the Great Charter* (Manchester, 1908), xiii.

[45] Charles Bémont to Round, 23 May 1923, Round MSS 621 f.26.
[46] Quoted in Charles-Olivier Carbonell, *Histoire et historiens: une mutation idéologique des historiens français 1865–1885* (Toulouse, 1976), xi.
[47] '. . . il ne fait pas partie de la société de nations.' Henri Pirenne to J. R. Tanner, 4 Feb. 1923, Tanner MSS CMH box 2.

foreign policy of their own country'.[48] These twin thrusts – on the one hand cultural despair in face of a dead civilization, on the other a determination to make history say something different for the post-war generation – worked between them to put whig susceptibilities between a rock and a hard place. Two of the opposed voices of modernism – Namier and Butterfield – felt something of that compression.

Lewis Namier, the elder by twelve years, needed no tuition in the fragility of civilization or the historical role of Prussians and Russians in cracking it beneath their boots. After he came to England as Ludwik Niemierowski from Poland in 1907 he took his geopolitical lessons mainly from Halford Mackinder at the LSE before moving to Balliol and the experience, frequently described, of anti-Semitism there. Neither conduced to a warm view of human nature and both kept the mind cosmopolitan: Namier was always likely to find the Balfour Declaration on the future of Palestine more significant than Lloyd George's ambitions or the daily news from the Front. And he was *in* the war, seeing it, though, from the perspective of eastern Europe as he worked in the propaganda and political intelligence departments of the Foreign Office where he ran into Arnold Toynbee. His pre-war visits to America on behalf of his father's business, his concern with empire as the great force of his age, above all his lack of sentimentality for ghosts of any kind, delivered him into the post-war era without the emotional commitments of so many of his contemporaries and with a natural hostility, never lost, to what he called 'flapdoodle'. It did not mean that he would automatically become a scourge of whiggery: there are those Europeans, like Geoffrey Elton (born in 1921) and Munia Postan (born indefinitely[49]), who become so affected by gratitude for a past they never had that they turn into honorary whigs. But in Namier one struggles to find such a mentality. His unwillingness to be thought of as a Zionist argues that he did not even want to be identified with an ambition for which he did feel considerable emotion. Whiggery he despised for its spongiform texture – he once rightly described it as a rubber ball, constantly changing its shape while remaining the same thing[50] – and it never ceased to offend

---

[48] Charles Webster, 'The Study of British Foreign Policy (Nineteenth Century)', *AHR*, 30 (1925), 728–37 at 728.

[49] Postan was famous for having always declared that he did not know when he was born because all the documents had been lost in the Bolshevik Revolution. Eric Hobsbawm once remarked that 'without corroboration you could not believe a word of what he said'. Hobsbawm, *Interesting Times: a Twentieth Century Life* (2002; paperback edn, 2003), 283–4.

[50] See Namier to Churchill, 6 Jan. 1934, in Julia Namier, *Lewis Namier* (Oxford, 1971), 228–9.

his sense of outraged complicity. Namier wrote always as spectator, notebook in hand, describing what the world brought before him with curiosity and intelligence but rarely with racing pulse, never with imprecision. Butterfield was quite, quite different.

Herbert Butterfield went up to Peterhouse, Cambridge with a County Major scholarship and West Riding vowels in October 1919. He took with him a sense of the cross-currents we have been thinking about: the conviction that a new era had dawned, the sense of great events taking place, but also a sense (he later wondered whether it was a northern, working-class sense) that only the Germany of the Kaiser had been defeated, not that of the real Germany defined by its literature and its music and its theology. Neither the sight of his tutor, Paul Vellacott, retching still from the gas of the trenches,[51] nor even the later outrages of the Nazi barbarians, would move him from this conviction. His Methodism, asserted until 1936 and influential beyond then, assisted his view of history as a search for moral meaning within reconciliation, and of the past as a place where God's intentions could sometimes reveal themselves, if the historian could divest himself of all traces of arrogance and take the longest perspective, the one that God would take. These elements of a complicated *Weltanschauung* took part of Butterfield towards an impatience with whig apologetics, in particular their facile rejection of certain points of view and their willingness to speak as though divinely inspired in their moral judgements. By far the greater tendency in Butterfield's mind pulled him, however, into a cautious sympathy with an historical canon that had insisted on narrative coverage of long periods and a Rankian search for essence in the human experience of the past. For all the strictures of *The Whig Interpretation of History*, Butterfield began from a position quite as likely to foster a whig mentality in future years as Namier's implied that he would always regard it as sulphur and brimstone. That is why these two participants in the historiography of these years give us avatars of something beyond themselves. They unconsciously map boundaries in the intellectual territory of a post-whig generation.

Of course, others from this generation map it too, and it is a broader persuasion that we are seeking. Richard Pares and Goronwy Edwards stand either side of Butterfield's birth in 1900 and join in this cameo as naturally as they later became co-editors of the *English Historical Review*,

---

[51] Paul Vellacott, CBE (1891–1954). Marlborough and Peterhouse, Cambridge. Gassed on Western Front; Brigade Major, General Staff (despatches and DSO); Fellow of Peterhouse, 1919; Tutor and Lecturer in History, 1920–34; Headmaster of Harrow, 1930–9; Master of Peterhouse, 1939–54.

occupying territory we might think of as Namierite in similar ways despite their radically different social class: Edwards, the son of a railway signalman in Salford who, like Lloyd George, became Welsh and thus made his way to Jesus College, Oxford, and remained there until called away to direct the Institute of Historical Research; Pares in some ways the pupil of his father, Bernard – Rowse later spoke of 'his father, the fanatic, coming out'[52]– but also of Winchester and Balliol, and whose period in Edinburgh feels always preparatory to returning to Oxford. A whig is harder to find in that generation, though the ecclesiastical historian Norman Sykes may be a candidate: no better born than Butterfield or Edwards – Heckmondwyke plays Oxenhope and Salford – and eventually the holder of the Dixie Chair in Cambridge, which put him in the line of Creighton, Gwatkin and J. P. Whitney. But travel just half a generation back and many men appear who were to survive the war and flourish in the 1920s and '30s – men who were brought up on the whigs or in reaction to them. Tout almost misses the cut, it is true: born in 1850 he retired in 1925. His colleague Ramsay Muir had been succeeded at Manchester in 1921 by H. W. C. Davis, who pointed the other way by bringing with him incongruous private money, aristocratic connexion and riding to hounds, but also many whig attitudes and a firm resistance to Firthian research. Pollard went on through the 1920s at UCL, possibly the last of a formidable generation brought up on that icon of proto-prosopography, Leslie Stephen's *Dictionary of National Biography*.[53] Powicke (Tout's most faithful pupil) remained a force in Oxford until after the Second World War, taking in his mental book-box, according to Richard Southern, Ranke, Hallam, Macaulay, Gairdner, Symonds, Burckhardt, Creighton, Sismondi and Roscoe. 'I am still living on the impressions which I got from this stuff,' he said.[54] Ernest Neale, Liverpudlian rather than Toutian, gave Manchester two years of the Tudors in the 1920s before moving to join Pollard in London.[55]

---

[52] A. L. Rowse, 'Richard Pares', *PBA*, 48 (1962), 345–56 at 349.

[53] A. P. Wadsworth recalled in his *Manchester Guardian* obituary of him in 1948: 'Pollard was probably one of the last survivors of that distinguished generation of historians, Firth, Round, Tout and others, who did their apprenticeship in contributing to the *Dictionary of National Biography*; he wrote for it no less than 500 articles and was assistant editor from 1893 to 1901.' Copy in Pollard MSS 860 box 48 *sub* Wadsworth.

[54] R. L. Southern, 'Sir Maurice Powicke', *PBA*, 50 (1964), 257–302 at 276.

[55] Sir John Ernest Neale (1890–1975). Liverpool University and UCL. Assistant at UCL 1919–25; Professor of Modern History, Manchester, 1925–7; Astor Chair in English History, London, 1927–56. Elizabethan scholar: *Queen Elizabeth* (1934); *The Age of Catherine de Medici* (1943); *The Elizabethan House of Commons* (1949); *Elizabeth I and her Parliaments* (2 vols., 1953–7).

John Holland Rose, another Owens College man,[56] held the Vere
Harmsworth Chair of Naval History in Cambridge until his retirement
in 1933. All of these names can come into play before one even mentions
the paragon of whig orthodoxy in G. M. Trevelyan, who published five
of his books during the inter-war period[57] without changing a single view
about the rightness of whig history and the imperative rightness of his
great-uncle. None of these names guaranteed the persistence or the
demise of whiggery, but they are some of the pins around which the
rival stories need to be woven.

In fact, one encounters a single story of ambiguity and confusion in
these years. It is easy to document the sense of 'moving on' from whig
typologies and habits: it could probably be done by invoking any of the
names we have been considering, even Trevelyan, who congratulated
Pollard on the seminars at his new Institute of Historical Research and
enjoyed the extinction of what he called 'the pedantries of 25 years
ago'.[58] Frank Merry Stenton thought it amusing to dwell on his rejection
of whigs in a lecture delivered around 1930. 'Having been compelled to
read the whole five volumes of the late Professor Freeman's history of the
Norman Conquest,' he declared, 'I certainly do not expect any one
outsider . . . to follow my example of his own free will.' And again: 'If
we must learn constitutional history, we avoid the great work of Dr
Stubbs, in which the details of medieval finance & law are frequently
interrupted by moral reflections in which a literary purpose is powerfully
present.'[59] Tout's sympathy for this position he could have assumed
from numerous published statements that talked about 'an enlargement
of the old view of the sphere of history' that was no longer, 'as Freeman
used to say "past politics" – that is, the history of the State. It concerns
itself with society as a whole.'[60] Privately Tout went further, telling
Round in 1922 that the political history of Edward III's reign needed
completely reworking: 'I have almost to make the frame', he said, 'before
I can fill in the administrative picture.'[61] Pollard's success with his

---

[56] 'I never knew before that Rose was one of your products.' Firth to Tout (postcard), 12
Mar. 1902, Tout MSS 1/367/69.
[57] *Lord Grey of the Reform Bill* (1920); *British History in the Nineteenth Century* (1922);
History of England (1926); *England under Queen Anne* (3 vols., 1930–4); *Grey of Falloden*
(1937).
[58] G. M. Trevelyan to Pollard, 29 Nov. 1920 and 28 May 1925, Pollard MSS 860 box 48.
[59] Untitled MS of lecture, n.d., Stenton MSS 8/14.
[60] 'The Manchester School of History', in Tout, *Collected Papers* (3 vols., 1932–4), vol. I,
85–9 at 85. The article was published in a *Manchester Guardian* supplement on history
and the universities in 1920.
[61] Tout to Round, 1 Aug. 1922, Round MSS 683 f.5.

Institute of Historical Research, founded in 1921, and Cambridge's decision, led by Harold Temperley and Holland Rose, to float its own historical journal in 1922,[62] complemented a mood of burgeoning professionalism and recourse to scientific method commented on by Peter Slee and Reba Soffer, and to which we shall ourselves need to recur, because these things had a direct effect in strengthening counter-whig assumptions. Butterfield himself suffered from neither professionalism nor, at this stage, science, though his monograph on Napoleonic diplomacy reflected Temperley's belief in 'technical history' which became an important category. Yet even without these assumptions he had no difficulty in trouncing his whigs in 1931. From his drafts and private writings in the 1930s we can draw fresher sentences warning of the danger of reading history backwards, which he took to be the seminal sin of whigs. 'It makes all the difference in the world', states one fragment, 'whether we already assume the present at the beginning of our study of history and keep it as a basis of reference or whether we wait and suspend judgement until we discover it at the end.'[63] Or about the irrelevance of politics to whig sensibilities. 'It is very strange that historians whom one should imagine to be Conservative, hankering after old ways and conscious of the spell of the past, have so often proved themselves Whig and have imposed upon the world a whig interpretation of history.'[64] For less penetrating critics, meanwhile, politics seemed far from irrelevant to their responses to the whig project. From the beginning of the 1930s a self-conscious political message came from the angry young men (and now women) of the Left who shared the young Eric Hobsbawm's contempt for a figure like Trevelyan, just as a focused conservative position saw heresy in whiggism for its neglect of transcendent national ideals.[65]

---

[62] Memo, by E. A. Benians (copy), 6 June 1922, and Firth to C. J. Longman (copy), 14 June 1922: both copies in G. N. Clark MSS 159. The list of financial guarantors for the new venture included Ward, Bury, Whitney, Holland Rose, Coulton, Gooch, Temperley and Vellacott.

[63] Undated fragment '. . . enjoy the benefit of a subsequent . . . ' 'Early Writing', Butterfield Miscellany.

[64] Single page fragment, undated. He goes on: 'Men who would have upheld the British rule in Ireland to the very last and who would have exhausted their ingenuity in defending the British domination over alien races, have been unable to say a good word for Christian rule over Italy and Bohemia. Men who opposed "Votes for Women" until the vote could be withheld no longer, have been unable to see that the opponents of the 1832 Reform Bill might be anything other than the corrupt defenders of profitable abuses.' Ibid.

[65] See chapter 7, pp. 176–82.

An account of simple *diminuendo* among whigs is therefore very appealing. Simplicities always are. Other simplicities could point us elsewhere, all the same. Just at the moment when historians are supposed to have set off on their modernist train towards new thinking in the 1920s, it becomes amusing to eavesdrop on an American student – Tom Mendenhall from Yale, later a professor at Wisconsin – writing home to say that he sees Mr Galbraith once a week 'and am starting right out with Stubbs to learn Medieval History'.[66] Similarly, C. R. L. Fletcher of Magdalen, whose Tory politics ought, on one diagnosis, to have made him an enemy of the whigs, sent Pollard off to the Ford Lectures armed with a whig spear in 1927:

Do go for Wolsey in your Fords: I am sure he was a bad man . . . and I don't think Creighton was a *good* man. Brewer was, but he was misled by his Churchmanship & misled Stubbs. I went to call on our B[isho]p at Cuddesdon the other day and saw dear old Stubby's grave in the beautiful Churchyard.[67]

History becomes easier to tame when we ignore such elegies. 'The whole place is full of ghosts,' said Herbert Fisher of Oxford in the following year;[68] but the ghosts are translucent in the record and one reads the texts through apparitions. Only the study of assumptions helps to illuminate the archive. Which is the more significant in an outburst of Temperley, for example: that Trevelyan would, if elected Regius Professor in Cambridge, do nothing 'to further the real study of history in its modern and preciser shape'; or his conviction that the election of Trevelyan to one of the most powerful positions in the profession was a foregone conclusion?[69] Which is the more permanent in Butterfield's historical psychology: that he criticized the whigs' treatment of technical history; or that he forgave them their sins, saw, in *The Englishman and his History* of 1944, that the sins were venial and realized (as he said in a fascinating letter to Friedrich von Hayek written during the second World War) that whig history had made life imitate art by turning those historical events that whigs wished to preserve into moments that

---

[66] Tom Mendenhall to Notestein, n.d., Notestein MSS 544/1/5/497.
[67] C. R. L. Fletcher to Pollard, 12 Sep. 1927, Pollard MSS 860 box 47. James Sherren Brewer (1809–79), Professor of History and English at King's College, London from 1865. A priest influenced by the Tractarians. Approached in 1856 to edit the *Letters and Papers, Foreign and Domestic, of Henry VIII*. The later volumes were completed by James Gairdner. Pollard's Ford Lectures were published as *Wolsey* (1929).
[68] Herbert Fisher to Lord Irwin (copy), 15 Mar. 1928, Fisher MSS 66 f.88.
[69] Temperley to Webster, 20 July 1927, Webster MSS 1/9/43. He and Webster saw themselves metaphorically as Firth's pupils; Temperley to Tout, 18 Jan. 1929, Tout MSS 1/1165/7.

actually *had* become decisive in the nation's destinies?[70] It is predictable, perhaps, that Trevelyan thought the years after the First World War needed 'the resurrection of great men [now] entirely dead or hazy to this generation'[71] but it seems less so that a pioneer of the new social and economic history such as George Unwin could confess that he learned all his social history from J. R. Green and Macaulay, or that David Knowles could argue as late as 1969 that everybody ought to read Macaulay every four or five years.[72] And what of the message of those Marxist and *marxisant* critics of the whig historical canon? Are there not senses in which their own creations after the Second World War replicated rather than replaced whig historical method in charting linear narratives of progress interrupted by necessary and cathartic regression?

One need not dwell on debating points. It is demonstrable that precisely at the time when whig historians were supposed to be receiving their *coup de grâce* from one direction, they were bouncing up in a different place remarkably unhurt. The thirties of the twentieth century brought new appreciations of Froude, in the wake of Waldo Dunn's study,[73] and of Macaulay (Arthur Bryant's *Macaulay* of 1932 sent Trevelyan into ecstasies).[74] It appeared in evaluations such as the American Wilbur Abbott's judgement holding out the hope in 1935 that 'picturesque' history was on its way back into national life.[75] The acknowledgement could remain unspoken in method and presumption, as in Stenton's feeling that continuity should always be assumed in history unless evidence overwhelmingly suggested disruption.[76] It could lie on the bookshelf in books half-forgotten but half-remembered. As late as 1938 Powicke still could not throw off unease about all that early reading:

[70] Butterfield to Hayek, 31 July 1944, Butterfield MSS BUTT/1(i).

[71] G. M. Trevelyan to J. R. M. Butler, 17 Nov. 1924, Butler MSS E4.

[72] Unwin to unknown correspondent, n.d. [1916], quoted in R. H. Tawney's memoir printed in Unwin, *Studies in Economic History: the Collected Papers of G. Unwin* edited by R. H. Tawney (1927), lxvii; M. D. Knowles, 'Tendencies of Scholarship in Medieval History, 1868–1968', *TRHS*, 19 (1969), 139–57 at 144.

[73] Waldo H. Dunn, *Froude & Carlyle: a Study of the Froude–Carlyle Controversy* (1930).

[74] Trevelyan to Bryant, 20 July 1932, Bryant MSS E3.

[75] 'Unless all signs fail, the so-called "picturesque" school of historical writing is coming back into favor . . .' He saw a time when Froude, Motley and Parkman would reappear and even thought that Macaulay's famous third chapter was 'still a model for all "social" historians'. Wilbur C. Abbott, 'T. B. Macaulay: Historian', in Abbott, *Adventures in Reputation: an Essay on Some 'New' History and Historians* (Cambridge, MA, 1935), 1–27 at 1 and 4.

[76] Stenton, in controversy with F. J. Haverfield over Roman London in 1914: 'it seems to me that continuous life, in however degraded a form, most easily explains what one sees when there are a few definite facts to work upon'. Stenton to Haverfield (copy), 8 Dec. 1914, Stenton MSS 8/14.

That the period of the glorious Revolution was not exactly as I found it [in Macaulay's history] was inconceivable. The writing was so confident, so object-ive, so sure. Where has that glamour gone? What is this dark, inscrutable history that remains, like a great mountain, left cold and stark after the glory of the setting sun has died away?[77]

Perhaps so painful a landscape struck the Christian socialist Helen Cam less pessimistically. Writing from her own dark, inscrutable moun-tain in 1942, she nevertheless felt it important to connect Pollard's Tudorism to Stubbs's whig picture in thinking about representative institutions of the middle ages, and to connect both perceptions to the Atlantic Charter with all the confidence, objectivity and certainty of a Macaulay or Freeman.[78]

An exaggerated death

This dialogue of advance and regression, change and stasis, could and should appear in any history of historiography in England after 1945 as well as before. But the point of this introductory exposition is not to describe a century's writing but rather to suggest a case; and perhaps enough has been said already to license the outline of one. Our governing image of whig historiography, one fostered, as we have seen, by Butterfield himself and Blaas in a more recent generation, depends on drawing a line across the end of the nineteenth century and depicting a state of affairs coloured in the tones of before-then-after, worse-then-better. We would do well to recall with Durkheim that when societies worship, they tend to worship themselves. The image to which we are heir flatters the vanity of modernism by proclaiming its role as a terminus and its platform as a place where all passengers must change.[79] I prefer to retain the railway metaphor but to reorganize it in order to make some sense of the ghosts and intimations that surround the station and its timetables. A more plausible image of the moving whig paradigm is one that uncouples its various pieces of rolling stock and conceives not of a single train but of several moving in parallel, one now easing into the lead while another falters and stalls, to be reanimated by the night shift

---

[77] F. M. Powicke, *History, Freedom and Religion* (Durham, 1938), 13.
[78] H. M. Cam, *Liberties and Communities in Medieval England: Collected Studies in Local Administration and Topography* (Cambridge, 1944), xi, xiv.
[79] Thus David Knowles in 1942, amid endless propaganda about the war, could recognize only 'a tendency among English historians *of the past* to study all public men from a purely national standpoint, and in relation to political and constitutional development'. 'Some Aspects of the Career of Archbishop Pecham', *EHR*, 57 (1942), 1–18 at 1 (emphasis added).

and appear the day after tomorrow, miles down the line, forgotten by everyone. The picture has the virtue of moving parts, which for a British audience argues that the railway language should cease, and it omits all notion of destination. It offers the opportunity to think about the power of, say, moral judgement in history at a point in the narrative at which one may have decided that whig constitutionalism has lost power and come to a halt. It allows for an acceleration in story-telling even if Macaulay's way of doing it no longer commands an audience. It lets us discover whigs refurbishing their arguments about peace and war in a new Pullman car even when we know that their vintage carriages have long since gone out of commission.

Surely, comes the retort, no one seriously wants to argue that whig history survived Auschwitz, the Cold War, the H-bomb, the first major-ity socialist government in Britain, Suez, decolonization, the New Left, a parliamentary Liberal party reduced to the size of a football team and a Lady who was not for turning? Or an intellectual location that belonged more to Bertrand Russell, Alfred Ayer and logical positivism than it did to the comfortable last days of British Idealism that helped make the world a whig place? Or a spiritual location that replaced the Erastianism of Davidson and Lang with a sense of commitment and fissiparousness in the face of global threats from abroad, relative deprivations at home and an aggressive, cynical materialism that saw in Hitler no sign of God's moving finger? These are serious questions. The historiography reflects them, often confirming far more than denying that the world had changed irrevocably. There was that new mood of *Weltgeschichte*, for example, that issued in a string of collaborative, multi-volume ventures that saw power relations transformed and a new Europe caught in their crossfire.[80] More sedately, there was a new plan for the *Cambridge Modern History*. G. N. Clark and Herbert Butterfield put their names to the printed prospectus a week before Hitler shot himself. All the planned volumes from before the war had to go. '[T]he accepted idea of general history has changed,' they said. 'In the first place some branches of the subject will require fuller and more continuous treatment, especially economic and social matters and the history of literature, thought and religion.'[81] It would no longer tell the story of the nation state, the story that whigs knew best and where they felt most at home. If general history no longer looked as it once had, neither did

[80] On the British side of this persuasion see Michael Bentley, 'The Singularities of British *Weltgeschichte*', in B. Stuchkey and P. Wende (eds.), *Writing World History 1800–2000* (Oxford, 2003), 173–96.

[81] Printed, unpaginated report on the *CMH*, 23 Apr. 1945; copy in the Clark MSS, 164.

the particular. G. N. Clark lamented to an elderly Pollard during the war 'how even the very great seem to be departmentalized in their knowledge';[82] and historiography would carry the mark of that deepening 'departmentalization' through the post-war decades marked by the professional monograph produced by full-time university lecturers and professors, with perhaps only Hugh Trevor-Roper's riding to hounds bridging the breach with the past. No wonder that Butterfield had come by 1947 to think parts of John Richard Green 'curious and silly'.[83] Even Powicke, open to much post-whig suggestion before the war, had hardened his arteries, at least in the matter of method. *King Henry the Third and the Lord Edward* (1947) took pleasure in its own lushness as a text but had counter-whig moments: 'To track down every nerve in the body politic and locate each impulse, as though they carried some secret message, is as futile as to read into the rivulets which compose the upmost waters of the Thames a foresight of the wharves and shipping in the spacious estuary.'[84] Whiggery had been *about* reading the rivulets of time and discerning the estuary where the waters became a nation's life-blood.

Before closing the mind to a continuing whig presence, however, recall Namier's rubber ball. The Butterfield who disparaged Trevelyan's worries about teaching wrong history, the same man who had decided by 1947 that Acton had a palsy of the brain and who announced in 1956 that all the real revisionism of his century had consisted in 'reversals of a Whig or Whig-Protestant interpretation', was the same historian who spent much of the 1940s bemoaning the virulence with which whig notions of moral judgement in history survived into the post-war era and the 1950s trying to put the essentials of whiggery back into the eighteenth century despite Namier's efforts to repel them.[85] The Christopher Hill who wanted to see rewritten an entire agenda of English history in the seventeenth century nevertheless complained to the Parisians – he could hardly say it in Oxford – that the interpretation of Godfrey Davies's 'volume de la classique *Histoire d'Angleterre d'Oxford*

---

[82] G. N. Clark to Pollard, 30 Oct. 1941, Pollard MSS 860 box 47.
[83] For an earlier example see David C. Douglas in the *TLS*, 9 Mar. 1933: 'Green's story of English origins is based . . . upon a legend. The nineteenth century crowds in upon the sixth, and Simon de Montfort in the thirteenth speaks with the voice of Gladstone.' *Time and the Hour: Some Collected Papers of David C. Douglas* (1977), 41–9 at 44.
[84] *King Henry the Third and the Lord Edward*, vol. I, 340.
[85] Untitled draft, 'I suppose it is true to say. . .' (1947), 'Early Writing', Butterfield Miscellany; 'Moral Judgement in History', draft, n.d., Butterfield MSS BUTT/122/1; 'Clio in Council', *TLS*, 6 Jan. 1956. He was still concerned in 1952 that '[t]he story of a thousand years comes to be seen . . . as a gradual progress towards modern liberty.' Herbert Butterfield, *Liberty and the Modern World* (1952), 33.

. . . est toujours celle qui fut proposée pour la première fois par S. R. Gardiner . . .'[86] Firth, according to Maurice Ashley in 1957, did not have Gardiner's prejudices and should be brought back within the the fold of respectability.[87] Andrew Browning wanted to bring Macaulay inside again two years later, indeed the whole of 'that much-maligned group of individuals known as the Whig historians'.[88] Hallam, earliest and most primitive of the entire tradition, had become 'a pioneer of *Kulturgeschichte*' by 1967.[89] As the anniversaries rolled by, so the carriage wheels turned again and ghostly passengers resumed their journey.

Nor was it a matter merely of polite, centenary tributes. Helen Cam meant far more than that in her widely read and remarked reassessment of Stubbs in the *Cambridge Historical Journal* in 1948, a piece that brought so animated a letter from H. G. Richardson that they seemingly did not correspond again for three years.[90] No centenary prompted V. H. Galbraith's emphatic judgement as late as 1968 that 'Stubbs is still the *best* history of the English Middle Ages', together with his usual private urbanities about contemporaries who failed to understand the fact, particularly Richardson and Sayles who, he declared, were gradually going off their heads.[91] Even if they weren't, there was no getting round the place of Stubbs still in curricula, both in the universities and in school in the 1960s. When J. W. Stubbs visited Charterhouse in 1962 he reported back to Goronwy Edwards that 'I was asked by the Librarian if I knew of any source from which the School could get a second copy of my grandfather's Constitutional History, as their only copy is in constant use with a queue rapidly forming for it.'[92] There is a permanence about school libraries against which all revisonism beats in vain. Or go back to Macaulay. His centenary in 1959 had nothing to do with the letter

---

[86] Christopher Hill, 'L'oeuvre des historiens marxistes anglais sur l'histoire du XVIe et du XVII siècles', *La Pensée*, 28 (1950), 51–62 at 51.

[87] Maurice Ashley, 'Sir Charles Firth: a Tribute and Reassessement', *History Today*, 7 (1957), 251–63 at 255.

[88] Andrew Browning, 'Lord Macaulay: 1800–59', *Historical Journal*, 2 (1959), 149–60 at 155. Cf. David Knowles's remark in 1960 that Macaulay's *History* should still be seen as 'the first model of a social history of England'. *Lord Macaulay* (Cambridge, 1960), 11.

[89] Peter Clark, 'Henry Hallam Remembered', *Quarterly Review*, 305 (1967), 410–19 at 418.

[90] Richardson was Stubbs's fiercest critic and believed Maitland had put paid to him. '[T]he assertion that Stubbs was more learned than Maitland strikes me as a mere Galbraithian ineptitude.' Richardson to Cam, 4 Apr. 1949, Cam MSS 2/2/14.

[91] Galbraith to Goronwy Edwards, 20 Jan. 1968, Edwards MSS 203 f.101. In their *Governance of Medieval England*, the offending pair had written of Stubbs that 'in the mountain of chaff the wheat is now of little account, and the chaff is fit only to be thrown away'. Quoted in James Campbell, *Stubbs and the English State* (Reading, 1989), 3.

[92] J. W. Stubbs to Edwards, 12 July 1962, Edwards MSS 203 f.73.

defending him that Mark Thomson of Liverpool University had written to Butterfield nine years earlier after the latter had sent him a new edition of the *Whig Interpretation* and it ought to have its place on the notice-boards of all modernists.

I think . . . you are a bit hard on the Whigs, whoever they may be. With all their faults, they surely have taught us much. I presume you could reckon Macaulay a Whig and suppose you disagree with much that he says. But do you write him off as worthless? I have read his History several times and have felt I got a lot out of each reading. You may say that this damns me or that Macaulay's merits, if any, are incidental, while his point of view is unhistorical. But do not his merits depend on his point of view? . . . [I]f Macaulay is worthless, why is he still read? . . . If the Whig view had no merits it would be forgotten; in fact you would not have written the attack that has provoked this letter.[93]

That queasy feeling, the sensation that there must be something *in* whig history, is a view I recall repeated by a senior colleague in another provincial university well into the 1970s.[94] For a caustic depressive, the days of 'nasty Elton and such' were more than enough to encourage emigration. 'How much better the days of Trevelyan, great man!'[95] And for a committed optimist such as the Liberal George Watson, the mystery lay only in the validity of whig history having ever been challenged. He sounded shrill about this in 1986, shriller still in 1989, and was urging us to reclaim the whig version of the past in 2002.[96]

But then the postmodern world has in some ways encouraged the rubber ball to resume its bouncing in the direction of history as meaning, story-telling, communicating with a wide general audience. It also despises 'grand narratives', of course, most of all 'master narratives' of the kind that the Victorian whigs had offered. All the same, the stock of the hyper-modernist Namier plummeted after 1980 as that of the post-whig critic Butterfield rose, though he did not live to see it. It did not rise because of *The Whig Interpretation of History*, which now seemed a modernist period piece. It happened because those looking for a humanist historiography saw something sympathetic in a man who had

---

[93] Mark Thomson to Butterfield, 29 Oct. 1950, Butterfield MSS 531/T83. R. S. Rait of Glasgow claimed in 1928 to have read Macaulay's *History* five times in the past five years. 'I can appreciate him not only as an historian but also as a Whig.' Rait to H. A. L. Fisher, 12 Dec. 1928, Fisher MSS 66 f.170.

[94] Professor K. H. D. Haley of Sheffield University was given to saying that he had 'always thought there was a lot in it'. Private knowledge.

[95] A. L. Rowse to J. H. Plumb, n.d., Plumb MSS.

[96] George Watson, 'The War against the Whigs: Butterfield's Victory . . . and Defeat', *Encounter*, 66, (1986), 19–25; 'The Whig Interpretation of History', in Watson, *The Certainty of Literature* (1989), 165–184; 'Take Back the Past', *European Review*, 10 (2002), 459–67.

pleaded for retaining stories that traversed time and focused on personalities. Perhaps that atmosphere also helped Butterfield's enemy, J. H. Plumb, and more particularly so some of his pupils, especially Simon Schama, David Cannadine and Linda Colley, whom no one could describe fairly as whig but no one successfully evaluate outside a whig genealogy running back through Plumb's teacher, Trevelyan, to those days of Edwardian England with which we began. This does not argue circularity so much as plurality within an historiographical tradition that too often is deemed monoglot. It does not argue linear evolution so much as random persistence. It acknowledges the genuine excitement of the century's many intimations of the new future to which we must now turn, but seeks to retain sight of ghosts that constantly called back a more traditional way of resuscitating the past. In the modernist age historians found space and time for several types of ambiguity. They carried them into their studies of English constitutional development and the history of parliament, into the history of the church and religion, into new emphases on the economic and the social, into the nature of international history amid world war and totalitarianism, into their procedures and methods of research, into their understanding of how the enterprise of historiography itself ought to be conceived. In recalling the excitements of their vision, it behoves a later generation to remember the ghosts they could not see.

Part II

Modernist investments

5   New historians, new histories

For all their haunting by ghosts from the past, the generations who followed the whigs believed themselves to be involved in an important process of modernization. The First World War, just as much as European intellectual influence after 1890 or the sociology of 'professionalization', played a critical role in confirming this notion. A post-war age, the argument ran, demanded a post-whig understanding of what had created it. Sometimes this meant that the ideologies gaining strength across Europe required historical acknowledgement. Sometimes it indicated the importance of new methodologies geared to a scientific age. But it also incorporated a natural progression towards a social history that would make more sense of a fast-moving popular culture, and a serious economic history that would place the depressed post-war years in context. It may not be completely arbitrary that the Economic History Society came into being in the same year as the General Strike, any more than that Eileen Power's swing from monastic history to the study of medieval economic and social history should have taken place in a post-war atmosphere within which the first generation of professional female historians in England cut their teeth. 'Normalcy' would not have attracted the new modernists even had they not rejected it on grounds of literacy.[1] Death and disruption brought their own imperative to make a new historical world, one more 'relevant' to present needs and perspectives. We have seen, however, that a *trompe l'oeil* within the vision of later generations has masked the degree to which those perspectives did not supplant older ones but rather formed contrasting images alongside them. This fundamental continuity becomes clear when we turn away from 'new' history to those areas of scholarship that had been stressed before the Great War. Older traditions of historical writing, perhaps in particular the history of parliament, received a fresh injection of attention

---

[1] The word came, of course, from the unlettered intellect of President Warren Harding, but won currency as a neologism in Britain. Political 'correctness' has done the same, despite Lord Dacre's persistent (and predictable) preference for 'correctitude'.

from historians who saw themselves quite as distant from whig complacencies and teleologies as their radical counterparts who now followed
the paths of social and economic enquiry.

No one should read the historians of the inter-war period, for all their
ambivalences, without sensing that here was a new generation with its
own questions and prejudices and insights. Maitland, their spiritual
ancestor, had himself disdained flimsy social histories – 'a few lightly
written paragraphs on "the manners and customs of the period" . . . but
they must not be very long nor very serious'[2] – yet even he had not
envisaged the depth of contempt that this generation would summon in
their critique of romantic platitudes or appeals to some intangible *Zeitgeist*. To the new historians, moreover, one should add a new audience,
one sensitive to realism and the groundedness of documentation, but
also showing a taste for a fresher history of the people as well as their
governors. 'That tide has been gathering force in the last thirty years,'
Coulton said at the beginning of his investigation of medieval religion;
'the man in the street does now ask more and more insistently for
something deeper and wider than mere political history. Moreover increasing numbers of thoughtful readers are now willing to spend time
and money in support of the social historian who will give them documents as well as theories.'[3] It was the same with the political authors
echoing the new world of Notestein's celebrated Raleigh Lecture of 1924
or Vivian Galbraith's publication of a chronicle that revolutionized the
study of medieval parliaments in 1927, or of course Lewis Namier's two-
volume destruction of whig parliamentary mythologies in 1929.[4] Economic or social or political or (increasingly) local historical writing felt
the impress of a generation that had survived the death of the Great
Powers and reflected a past that was less present-dominated in spirit
than the celebrations and rationalizations of the whigs, but which went
beyond them in modernization by producing an often-implicit critique
of contemporary culture.

Economic and social histories had long enjoyed some intertwining in
their content and method of approach. The two adjectives often occur
together, indeed, from the end of the nineteenth century but did not

---

[2] F. W. Maitland, 'English Legal History', in *The Collected Papers of Frederic Maitland*,
edited by H. A. L. Fisher (3 vols., Cambridge, 1911), vol. II, 3.

[3] G. G. Coulton, *Five Centuries of Religion* (4 vols., 1923–50), vol. I, xxxii.

[4] Wallace Notestein, 'The Winning of the Initiative by the House of Commons', *PBA*, 11
(1924–5), 125–75; V. H. Galbraith (ed.), *The Anonimalle Chronicle 1333–1381 from a MS
written at St Mary's Abbey, York* (Manchester, 1927); Lewis Namier, *The Structure of
Politics at the Accession of George III* (2 vols., 1929).

become inseparable in a William'n'Mary sort of way until the 1960s when they merged as the title of departments in the universities and other institutions of higher education.[5] They announced a style of history that would supposedly find a new way into the past and initiate historical projects that would appeal to reborn historians of the post-war world. The style might appeal especially to the newest of the new: the women whose names come into English historiography with such force and distinction after 1918. Despite the opening of limited educational provision for females since the 1870s, women had experienced almost insurmountable problems in taking up academic careers in history.[6] We hear occasional mention in the pre-war correspondence of 'Miss Norgate'[7] or 'Miss Bateson'[8] or 'Miss Skeel'[9] among medievalists, but the instinct lingers that they were regarded, for all their evident distinction, as worthy fillers for positions if one could not find a good man. In the inter-war years this situation altered, hardly as a cultural norm – one senior English professor lamented female historians as 'trouble' as late as the 1980s[10] – but simply as an accomplished fact. Shortlists for chairs began to look different. In women's institutions the names mentioned in dispatches became first-rank names. Elizabeth Levett may have been appointed 'without any enthusiasm' by the selectors at Westfield College in 1929, but it may be more significant that she succeeded so established a scholar as Caroline Skeel and that the list had contained, according to

---

[5] N. B. Harte, 'Trends in Publications on the Economic and Social History of Great Britain and Ireland, 1925–74', *EcHR*, 2nd series, 30 (1977), 20–41 at 21. See also T. C. Barker 'The Beginnings of the Economic History Society' in *EcHR*, 2nd series, 30 (1977), 1–15.

[6] See for the background Bonnie Smith, 'The Contribution of Women to Modern Historiography in Great Britain, France and the United States 1750–1940', *AHR*, 89 (1984), 709–32, and *The Gender of History: Men, Women and Historical Practice* (Cambridge, MA, 1998).

[7] Kate Norgate (1853–1935). Father a London bookseller and later partner in Williams and Norgate. Protégée of J. R. Green. Books on twelfth- and thirteenth-century England. Took the side of Freeman when he was savaged by J. H. Round. Honorary Fellow of Somerville College, Oxford, 1929.

[8] Mary Bateson (1865–1906). Prominently connected: father Master of St John's College, Cambridge, and brother the biologist William Bateson. First Class certificate – degrees were not available in Cambridge for women until 1948 – in both parts of the Historical Tripos. Fellow of Newnham College, regular contributor to *EHR*. Would have been an editor of the *Cambridge Medieval History* but died aged forty-one.

[9] Caroline Skeel (1872–1951). Born in London of Welsh descent. First Class in History at Girton College, Cambridge, then Westfield College in London for rest of a professional career truncated by severe depression. Retired 1907; returned 1911; Reader 1919; Chair 1925; retired for good 1929. Considerable private money, much of it left to Westfield.

[10] Clues: history of dismissive, often ungrounded judgements; not in England when announcing this one. Yorkshire roots.

Richard Lodge, '3 goodish women'.[11] For the first time in English historiography, and not only in female circles, women became prominent in bibliographies of English history, and posterity looks back on these years as belonging as much to Helen Cam, Eileen Power, Joan Thirsk, Lillian Knowles, Lucy Sutherland or Lillian Penson as it does to Stenton, Tout, Powicke, Namier, Temperley or Butterfield. Women sometimes involved themselves, moreover, in the newer fields of study, no one more so than Eileen Power,[12] who by 1922 was ready to reject treating the reigns of Edward III and Richard II as political narratives when offered them by the Cambridge Medieval History because she had now become more interested in economic and social history.[13] Her studies in Paris, her move to the LSE, her involvement with Tawney, Charles Webster and her future husband, Munia Postan,[14] all encouraged her towards the intellectual width and radicalism which led to her history of the medieval wool trade that became seminal for economic historians. That she was a woman and a product of Girton College, Cambridge, she never forgot, and that awareness played an important part in forming her intellectual taste and interests.[15]

Danger lies, all the same, in exporting this model of female motivation to the generations of women who were to play an important role in English historiography before 1960. For every Power there was a Cam (the first female professor at Harvard) or a Penson (the first female vice-chancellor in England) or a Sutherland running an Oxford College – historians who worked within an existing paradigm of scholarship and even represented its supposedly 'masculine' facets such as imperialism

[11] Richard Lodge to D. B. Horn, 22 Feb. and 5 Mar. 1929, Horn MSS Gen 766/1. Helen Cam 'interviewed better', runs this very male account, but 'the women' were prejudiced against her.

[12] Eileen Power (1889–1940). Born in Altrincham, daughter of fraudulent stockbroker. Girton College, Cambridge; eventually directed historical studies there (1913–21). London School of Economics from 1921 for rest of career. Professor of Economic History, 1931. Medieval People (1924); her Ford Lectures on the wool trade were published posthumously in 1941.

[13] Power to J. R. Tanner, 10 July, n.y. [?1922], Tanner MSS, CMH box 2. For the background to the progress of the Cambridge Medieval History in the 1920s, see Peter Linehan, 'The Making of the Cambridge Medieval History', Spec., 57 (1982), 463–94.

[14] (Sir) Michael ('Munia') Postan (1899–1981). Born Bessarabia. England from 1920. LSE, eventually Eileen Power's research assistant. University College, 1927–31, LSE again, 1931–5, Cambridge from 1935; Chair of Economic History, 1938. Edited Economic History Review, 1934–60, and Cambridge Economic History of Europe. British War Production (1952); An Economic History of Western Europe 1945–1964 (1967).

[15] For a development of this perspective see Maxine Berg, A Woman in History: Eileen Power 1889–1940 (Cambridge, 1996).

(Margery Perham,[16] Lillian Penson,[17] Lucy Sutherland[18]) or Tory political economy with an imperial face (Lillian Knowles[19]). They did not take 'the more conventional and "male" route':[20] they simply decided that they were as good as or better than any male and that they would compete with men on their own terms and win. Paradoxically, their achievement is *diminished* by the later feminist critics who came intending to praise rather than to bury. What strikes one so forcibly is often how small a role their femininity played in forming the ambitions of these formidable modernist women. They were not forced into studying the history of the countryside or of medieval trade because that was the only niche they could find in a grey-suited power structure. They did not choose constitutional or imperial history out of a desire to conform to a male world. Was it not Helen Cam who, blocked by an officious doorman trying to keep 'ladies' out of an academic forum, swept him out of the way with the memorable retort: 'I'm not a lady, I'm a professor'? But behind the violence to their sense of themselves lies a deeper concern. It may well be the case that Eileen Power drew on feminine insights to move beyond Maitland and Vinogradoff in order to 'write about the lives of [social] groups directly, and not as reflected through the evolution of legal codes'.[21] Regarding her reaction as typical may, however, distract later readers from noticing how many social and economic historians of these years, male and female, did not begin from there because they correctly saw themselves, not in contradistinction to the historians of law, but as their most direct legatees.

[16] (Dame) Margery Perham (1895–1982). Read history at St Hugh's College, Oxford. Lectured at University of Sheffield during and after the Great War. Lost her faith there, leading to nervous breakdown. Returned to St Hugh's (1924) and taught imperial history. Africa from 1928. Several books on her experiences. Returned to Oxford (1935) as research lecturer in colonial administration. Returned to Christianity in later life. Reith Lectures on *The Colonial Reckoning* (1961).

[17] (Dame) Lillian Penson (1896–1963). University of London throughout her academic career from student to Vice-Chancellor. Chair of Modern History at Bedford College, 1930. Vice-Chancellor, 1948. Interests in foreign policy, on which she worked with Temperley, in the nineteenth and twentieth centuries.

[18] (Dame) Lucy Sutherland (1903–80). Born in Australia, but brought up in South Africa. Oxford from 1924. Taught by Maud Clarke; very close to Lewis Namier and Richard Pares. Board of Trade during the Second World War. Principal of Lady Margaret Hall, Oxford, from 1945. Abandoned Presbyterianism for Anglicanism. Much work for *History of Parliament*. Best-known study *The East India Company in Eighteenth-Century Politics* (1962).

[19] Lillian Knowles (1870–1926). Cornish background. Taught by Cunningham at Cambridge. First class certificates in history and law. Reader in Economic History, London, 1907; Chair 1921. *The Industrial and Commercial Revolutions in Great Britain during the Nineteenth Century* (1921); *The Economic Development of the Overseas Empire* (1924); *Economic Development in the Nineteenth Century* (1932).

[20] Berg, *A Woman in History*, 63.   [21] Ibid., 113.

Helen Cam made the point herself when she came to collect some of Maitland's papers for publication in 1957. An edition already existed, but Cam believed that H. A. L. Fisher had omitted some of the most important parts of Maitland's work and contributed thereby to misinforming 'a generation that has entered into his labours without recognizing its debt'.[22] Not only had Maitland seen his constitutional history as resting ultimately on social foundations in the manner of Stubbs,[23] but he had also pointed to law as the way forward in trying to reach the very social and economic history that the new moods among historians had identified as the next step, precisely because 'the way to this is barred by law, for speaking broadly we may say that only in legal documents and under legal forms are the social and economic arrangements of remote times made visible to us'.[24] Time and again Maitland had shown how a legal transaction that had left a trace in the record could bleed social history if pressure were applied at the right point. It was 'lamentable', Cam thought, that later observers persisted in their view that he was just a 'constitutional historian'.[25] Vinogradoff suffered similarly from his 'legal' pigeon-hole. True, he would become Professor of Jurisprudence at Oxford, but the young scholar's analysis of Folkland in a celebrated article of 1893, with its insistence that the traditional distinction between Folkland and Bookland had to be abandoned, not only led Stubbs to make his only major change to the text of the *Constitutional History* but became a signal turning-point in thinking about medieval landholding in general.[26] Nor need one remain with these earlier generations to make the point. A later constitutional historian such as J. R. Tanner gave the

---

[22] Helen Cam (ed.), *Historical Essays* (1957), ix. Fisher had asserted in his introduction to Maitland's *Collected Papers* that 'wherever an article . . . contains a new grain of historical knowledge or reveals Maitland's original thought upon some problem of law or history', it had been included (vol. I, v). But Cam countered that 'more than half' of her own selection had been omitted by Fisher. Cam (ed.), *Historical Essays*, vii.

[23] William Stubbs, *The Constitutional History of England in its Origin and Development*, (3 vols., 1873–8), ch. 31, §454 vol. III, 520 refers to 'the social history which underlies the political history'. As late as 1969, David Knowles felt comfortable with his description of Stubbs's '*Constitutional* (and, we may add, socio-political) *History of England* . . .' 'Some Trends in Scholarship 1868–1968 in the Field of Medieval History', *TRHS*, 5th series, 19 (1969),139–57 at 143.

[24] Maitland, 'English Legal History', in Fisher (ed.), *Collected Papers*, vol. II, 3. Cf. Maitland's complaint elsewhere over 'the traditional violation of the study of English law from every other study' in 'Why the History of English Law is not Written', ibid., vol. I, 480–97 at 487.

[25] Cam, *Historical Essays*, ix.

[26] Stubbs altered the 1896 edition of the *Constitutional History* to take account of Vinogradoff's observations: see Helen Cam, 'Stubbs', *CHJ*, 9 (1948), 129–47 at 132. For the article in question see Paul Vinogradoff, 'Folkland', *EHR*, 8 (1893), 1–17. The research squashed the view that folkland was held by the common people without a title-deed and

lie to any accusation that his style of history ignored economic issues. Just as Stubbs had to think about taxation as an important element in his discussion, particularly once wool revenues played so central a part in the discussion of the financial stability of the later medieval monarchy, so Tanner saw in the 1920s that the tax-base of seventeenth-century England suffered from under-assessment and that the economic balance-sheet of James I's court had to be given primary weight in his difficulties.[27]

Because such authors had drawn on economic history when it suited their preponderant concerns in explaining political and constitutional history, they had inevitably down-graded it to a subordinate status in their accounts.[28] For a hard-nosed economist such as Alfred Marshall the situation of economic history remained a scandal as the nineteenth century closed, with no 'tolerable account', in particular, 'of the economic development of England during the last century and a half'. It was a 'disgrace to the land'.[29] Even after the war one can find jeremiads about the absence of serious work, as when Tawney[30] over-egged his own account of economic history by alleging in his London inaugural lecture in 1932 that 'the economic forces behind the English constitutional struggles continued to be almost ignored by historians till the

bookland by a written instrument – 'a fancy which has been the will o'the wisp of Anglo-Saxon history' (17). Vinogradoff's own view had become traditional when T. F. T. Plucknett revisited the issue in 1935. He confirmed the sense that folkland should be seen as 'ordinary unprivileged land and the normal type of property'. 'Bookland and Folkland', *EcHR*, 6 (1935), 64–72 at 72.

[27] See J. R. Tanner, *Constitutional Conflicts* (1928), 7–9. Even Eileen Power, normally scathing about constitutional historians, complimented Tanner on the interest of his work.

[28] 'Broadly speaking', Helen Cam wrote in her evaluation of Stubbs in 1948, 'one could say that the most marked contrast between Stubbs' approach to early English history and that of a modern historian is his almost complete disregard of economic considerations . . .' 'Stubbs', 132. She may have felt the same about Seebohm, though he did at least describe himself as 'a student of Economic History'. See John Burrow, '"The Village Community", and the Uses of History in Late-Nineteenth-Century England', in Neil McKendrick (ed.), *Historical Perspectives: Studies in English Thought and Society in Honour of J. H. Plumb* (1974), 255–84 at 274.

[29] Alfred Marshall to Acton, 13 Nov. n.y. [1897], quoted in Herbert Butterfield, 'Some Trends in Modern Scholarship in the Field of Modern History', *TRHS*, 5th series, 19 (1969), 159–84 at 173.

[30] R. H. Tawney (1880–1962). Born in Calcutta to notable Sanskrit scholar in the Indian education service. Rugby and Balliol College, Oxford. Anglican socialist with a passion for social justice. Toynbee Hall in Whitechapel and WEA. Married William Beveridge's youngest sister. Wounded on first day of the Somme battle in July 1916. After the war public positions in adult education policy. Appointed to LSE in 1920. Labour party politics in the 1920s: unsuccessful candidate. Professor of Economic History, 1931. *The Agrarian Problem in the Sixteenth Century* (1912); *The Acquisitive Society* (1921); *Religion and the Rise of Capitalism* (1926).

theme was taken up in our own day by Russian scholars'.[31] But those
who built the tradition of economic history in England in the later
Victorian period – men such as the elder Arnold Toynbee and William
Cunningham – did not have the advantage of knowing the works of
Weber or Sombart and could not bring the force of recent theoretical
criticism to their subject with the power of the post-war generation; so
their contributions seemed already dated to young students caught up in
a wave of Marxist enthusiasm that would last until after the Second
World War.[32] Tawney was relentless in his pursuit of the legal mind as an
obstacle to real economic history, and especially for the damage it had
done to the entire question of land utilization (as opposed to questions of
title) which had left its mark as 'undoubtedly one of the weakest sides of
agrarian history', a subject that had begun to come into its own after
1939.[33] Compared with Postan, who saw himself as not merely the voice
but the physical embodiment and legacy of the Bolshevik Revolution,
Tawney's dismissals did not go nearly far enough; he taught that the
veneration once accorded to Vinogradoff should be accorded no more,
as Peter Gatrell learned after asking Postan a harmless question in 1980:

V. stood wholly outside the controversy (within Marxism). He was a liberal in
politics . . . I certainly know of no writings of his to reveal a detailed knowledge
or interest in village collectivism – references to the 'mir' or 'zudruga' in his
writings are very casual. He was of course interested in various aspects of peasant
agriculture in the West (not in Russia) . . . I suspect that most of his [papers]
concern legal history and belong more to the German than the Russian academic
tradition.[34]

So the 'legal' accusation cast a long shadow. As always, however, we find,
too, a less committed modernist point of view, even in the later days of
the persuasion among men and women who look back to a creative and
literary paradigm now under threat or perhaps to the very legal history
that Postan excoriated. When David Chambers and Gordon Mingay
were working together on a book that became central to economic and
social history in the 1960s, Chambers wrote to his collaborator:

One question I would perhaps like to have answered sometime . . . is what
proportion of land was held on copyhold? When [Jack] Fisher [of the London
School of Economics] was up talking to our students [at Nottingham] some time
ago he seemed to have some peculiar ideas about tenure [in the sixteenth and

[31] R. H. Tawney, 'The Study of Economic History', *Economica*, 13 (1935), 1–21 at 3.
[32] We shall return to the ideological environment and the response of historians in chapter 7.
[33] R. H. Tawney to W. G. Hoskins, 11 Apr. 1945, Hoskins MSS box 11.
[34] M. M. Postan to Peter Gatrell (copy), 13 June 1980, Cambridge UL Add MSS 8961/I/
55.

seventeenth centuries]: letting and subletting so that it was difficult to find who the tenant really was. He made the whole subject much more complicated than I had imagined it to be . . .[35]

Perhaps the 'legal' historians had something to say to the new economic history after all.

They could hardly expect much of a hearing in the self-conscious inter-war years when the new discipline of economic history took shape in England. Everyone knew the antecedents: the German school of economic historians from the 1860s, Thorold Roger's *Economic Interpretation of History* (1887), Toynbee's lectures on the Industrial Revolution, delivered in 1881–2, not to mention Cunningham and Marshall. It had all been so much in the air that Trevelyan misremembered the Cambridge of the 1890s as suffused with economic history during a decade when there was talk of organic change within society and endless 'development' in the manner of Comte and Spencer and Darwin.[36] But this post-war mood had a different feel. Cunningham himself said at the end of his life in 1919 that so much economic history now came off the presses that he could not keep up with it.[37] And what came off the presses had a different kind of hand behind it: less an archdeacon's than that of a northern schoolboy made good. Different images remained in the memory and it is not hard to discern their place in a boy like John Clapham who, years later, would still describe himself as 'a man born in Lancashire (with Pendle Hill as my boyhood's notion of a distant mountain when the smoke of industry would let me see it) of a Yorkshire father born in the house that Charlotte Bronte made into Fieldhead . . .'[38] How different must King's College, Cambridge have seemed, how infuriating to have to suffer the patronage and obstruction of the preposterous Oscar Browning. But Clapham's determination to abandon constitutional history for the world of economic forces never left him and in 1919 the Cambridge *Reporter* advertises his lectures in all three terms with assistance and supplement from the unknown 'Mr Fay' of Christ's College.[39] Two years later, the London School of Economics decided to launch its own journal in order to provide an outlet for a prolific faculty

---

[35] J. D. Chambers to G. E. Mingay (copy), 25 Jan. 1962, Chambers MSS C1. See Chambers and Mingay, *The Agricultural Revolution* (1966).

[36] For Trevelyan see Harte, 'Trends', 38. The 'development' theme of the 1890s was picked up by Butterfield in his own review of historiographical trends: Butterfield, 'Some Trends in Modern Scholarship', 174.

[37] Harte, 'Trends', 38.

[38] John Clapham to Wallace Notestein, ?1938, Notestein MSS 544/1/2/149.

[39] *Cambridge University Reporter*, 9 Oct. 1919. J. H., later Sir John, Clapham went on to become the first Professor of Economic History in Cambridge and the senior economic historian of his generation. *The Economic Development of France and Germany 1815–1914*

and research students who worked in social science, including contributions to economic history; and within a few more years *Economica* had established itself as a pivotal periodical that printed, for example, the inaugural lectures of both Tawney and Power – the latter's with its call on all *social* historians to mimic both the new scientism and the intellectual astringency of traditional political history and to reconceive their field as 'a structural analysis of society, a line of approach to historical investigation which requires as rigorous a mental discipline and as scientific a methodology as any of the longer established branches of history'.[40] Meanwhile, the strange, isolated and self-financing economic historian from Sheffield's commercial community, Ephraim Lipson, had played a major part in stimulating the formation in 1926 of an Economic History Society, which proceeded to found another new journal whose importance to twentieth-century historiography would prove paramount. One has only to glance at the initial editorial board of the new *Economic History Review* to sense the power it could bring to bear on its subject matter. Behind the co-editors Tawney and Lipson stood English names like those of Elizabeth Levett, Eileen Power and Arthur Redford, but also an American in N. S. B. Gras and significant foreign correspondents in Pirenne, Sée and Kosminsky. How tentative a venture it must have seemed at the time we can infer from Clapham's absence; how confused it was in its theoretical orientation from a recollection of Julia Mann who played so large a part in managing the early periodical. Interviewed by Theodore Barker in 1977, she racked her brains to answer his questions about how the new economic historians saw their subject and where they thought they were going.

I don't believe they ever asked themselves these questions. I think they thought of themselves as developing a branch of history which hadn't been very much developed hitherto . . . I certainly never asked myself where I was going and I can't remember anybody ever saying to me where is the subject going to or what is its object or anything like that, any more than one would have asked in those days what is the object of history in general.[41]

All the same, the next twenty years would bring this journal to the heart of English academic history until the advent of *Past and Present* in 1952 opened new channels with definite theoretical content.

(Cambridge, 1921); *An Economic History of Modern Britain* (3 vols., Cambridge, 1938). C. R. Fay (1884–1961). King's College, London and LSE. Fellow of Christ's College, Cambridge, 1908–22; Professor of Economic History, Toronto, 1922–30; Reader in Economic History, Cambridge from 1930. *The Corn Laws and Social England* (1932); *Imperial Economy* (1934), etc.

[40] Eileen Power, 'On Medieval History as a Social Study', *Economica*, new series, 1 (1934), 13–29 at 14.

[41] Barker, 'Beginnings', 15.

If the infrastructure available to economic historians developed impressively in the inter-war years, then its advance after the Second World War has to be seen as exponential. It made most impact in the provincial universities which established chairs and departments to prosecute what had come to be seen as social science history. Negley Harte counted thirty chairs in economic history in 1970 with nearly two hundred specialist teachers of the subject in the universities – a considerable distance from Lillian Knowles's appointment as the first full-time lecturer in economic history, at LSE in 1904.[42] Cambridge had lost Clapham from its lecture list by 1956 but the new names are arresting in range and quality: Moses Finley on the economic history of the ancient world, Postan on medieval economic history, Charles Wilson on the early modern perspectives, Sidney Checkland and David Joslin on the later periods with Frank Thistlethwaite on American economic history, plus a special subject from Peter Matthias on the expansion of the British economy in the first half of the nineteenth century.[43] Such scholars no longer had any fear of isolation. Indeed through the heyday of economic history between about 1960 and the mid-1970s there developed a sense of superiority and exclusiveness reinforced by later claims to distinctiveness of the Economic and Social Research Council. The new elite gathered to itself the first-name familiarities of a confident coterie that saw itself at the centre of a network of academic power and funding. David at Nottingham would drop a note to Harry at Birmingham who might run it past Nora or Theo at the LSE or perhaps see what one of the two Sidneys thought about it.[44]

With confidence, moreover, came a certain rigidity combined with an opinion about traditional historians delivered *de haut en bas*. When Munia Postan came in the 1960s to revise Clapham's *Cambridge Economic History of Europe*, which had been planned and partly published during the war, he declared much of it unrevisable: only a 'wholly new edition' that would bring the venture up to date by 'modernizing some chapters and substituting wholly new chapters for those considered impossible to modernize' would meet the new demands of economic history.[45] It was England's Braudellian moment and if no one on the northern side of the English Channel had yet said that the historian of

---

[42] N. B. Harte, 'Introduction: the Making of Economic History', in Harte, *The Study of Economic History* (1971), xi–xxxix at xi, xxv.

[43] *Cambridge University Reporter*, 4 Oct. 1956.

[44] J. D. Chambers, W. H. B. Court, E. M. Carus-Wilson, T. C. Barker, Sidney Pollard, S. G. Checkland.

[45] Preface to 2nd edition of *The Cambridge Economic History of Europe* (1966–), vol. I, unpaginated.

the future would be a computer programmer or he would be nothing, Peter Laslett had at least said that 'numerical study must soon become important to everyone seriously interested in social change'.[46] The enthusiasm pressed particularly on demographic study with its new imperative, embodied from the 1970s in the Cambridge Group for the History of Population and Social Structure, to seek family-reconstitution techniques of greater sophistication for the analysis of parish and other records. For a sample of the sort of recommendation that now had to be copied into the researcher's notebook, read the following prescription from 1966. It helps to take a deep breath first.

> . . . if the combined number of births and deaths is fewer than 50 per thousand, there is some presupposition in favour of omission [in the parish register] . . . Therefore, if a parish shows fewer than about 45 annual entries of baptism and burials per 1,000 of the population, the figures need close scrutiny. But of course we may not know what the population was. In that case it is useful to take the 1801 census as a rough guide, and to assume that the population doubled between 1700 and 1800. If we then connect the points by a straight line . . . we may have a start for our check. Take a parish of 1,000 people in 1801. We assume there were 500 in 1700, and therefore on our model 800 in 1760. If in that year there were 10 burials and 14 baptisms, we have a combined rate of 25/800 or 30 per thousand, or 33 per thousand with a correction of ten per cent.[47]

Here is the glad, confident morning of late modernism with its evangelism for a history built on models and resting on assumptions about what can be known from quantificatory analysis of sources that are in fact, *malgré lui*, locked in our present and vary from the plausible to the dubious to the hilarious. It marks the final resting place of a history that deals in scientific truth-claims and speaks, seemingly, for a modernized and professionalized discipline that believes itself to have evolved a manual of practice.

We have already seen enough complication in post-whig historiography to suspect that this impression of simple triumph demands critical scrutiny. For economic and social historians, as for all the other kinds under review here, whig elements persisted and loosened what might have become a scientistic strait jacket. Of course, it is easy to point to a G. M. Trevelyan and his lush social histories that make the past a series of romantic poetics: he had hated the scientific enterprise from the start.

---

[46] Peter Laslett, 'Introduction: the Numerical Study of English Society', in E. A. Wrigley (ed.), *An Introduction to English Historical Demography from the Sixteenth to the Nineteenth Century* (1966), 1–13 at 6. The ill-fated remark on computer programming is attributed to Emmanuel Le Roy Ladurie.

[47] D. E. C. Eversley, 'Exploitation of Anglican Parish Registers by Aggregative Analysis', in Wrigley, *Introduction to English Historical Demography*, 44–95 at 55.

Or one might think of an Arthur Bryant or a C. V. Wedgwood with their commitment to a populist story-telling. This style of thinking leads, however, into an unsatisfactory model of its own – the idea that professional, serious history became modernist in its approaches and that narrative histories became the province of a few well-meaning, widely read but fundamentally amateur authors. In fact 'soft' history and the whig tendencies on which it rested often penetrated further into the professional establishment than this model implies. Few economic historians between the wars equalled Tawney's contempt for the weak-kneed ramblings of nineteenth-century whiggery. Yet in his own inaugural in 1932 we read that historical materials must be seen as 'specimens cast from a continuous life of which past and present . . . are different aspects', that 'all history is the history of the present', that the historian comes to realize, 'and sometimes realises too late, that what [s/he] supposed to be the past is in reality the present'.[48] Tawney had, it is true, a life-long belief in history as a human and humanizing discipline and he may therefore be taken to be easy game in searching for post-whig susceptibilities. Consider a harder case in Gordon Mingay who could hardly be accused of soft-centredness in thinking about economic history. Reading a manuscript of his collaborator J. D. Chambers in 1960, he advised a correction nevertheless that could have been recommended by Seeley. 'I do think', he said, 'the whole account of the growth of the banking system would be more readily followed if students were aware of *the structure and principles towards which experience was tending.*'[49] Unspoken assumptions of this kind lurked beneath the surface of much discussion that covered its nakedness with statistics and produced an implicit narrative of tendency that a sharp observer might catch sight of from time to time, but of whose nature authors remained unconscious in their determination to insist that their figures were yielding a shape rather than the other way round. Those who remained critical about their figures tended to remain, in England at least, sceptical about their possibilities. American enthusiasm for quantitative revelation, on the other hand, knew few bounds from the second half of the 1950s as the so-called New Economic History became a vogue. When two early converts, Eugene Genovese and Stanley Engerman, wrote to Munia Postan in 1970 to find out how the mission was going in England, they received a disappointing reply from one who prided himself on according a scientific basis to his history. He had pupils who worked on serfdom, he said (the enquiry had concerned slavery), but none of

---

[48] R. H. Tawney, 'The Study of Economic History', *Economica*, 13 (1933), 1–21 at 9–10.
[49] Mingay to Chambers, 23 Jan. 1960, Chambers MSS C5. (Emphasis added.)

them could be described as a quantitative historian. His conclusion was gloriously understated. 'In general you may find the attitudes of this country to so-called "quantitive" history are not unmixed.'[50]

They had never been other than mixed, even when quantification had still been a twinkle in the programmer's eye. One reason for this lay in the English understanding of social history and its relation to economic process. By the 1930s serious historians who had not felt compelled by the Marxist analysis emanating from Moscow – and most of it remained untranslated for another decade – found French models of understanding exciting in their new *Annaliste* form; and the call within that understanding for an *integrated* history that synthesized economic, social and geographic elements ran easily into a tradition of humanistic social commentary such as the Hammonds and others had produced before the Great War.[51] These instincts acted as a brake on unreconstructed scientism within economic history and, whether historians discussed the impact of the Black Death or the standard of living of the common people during the Industrial Revolution or the consequences of enclosure of common lands or the seriousness of unemployment as a phenomenon, a concern with liberal humanism visibly affected the positions taken. Economic historians moved away from economics, understood as the analysis of process and mathematical modelling of explanation, towards a synthetic history that did something different and something *better* in its own vision. 'Believe it or not,' David Chambers told Asa Briggs in 1961, 'our economists frequently leave this University with no knowledge of history of any kind, not even of their own discipline. They are excellent technicians but have no roots in the soil which they have cultivated so sedulously on the surface.'[52] Soil and roots: they formed the environment for the true historical study that must be a 'human and personal account as well as a mere economic analysis'.[53] Another of Chambers's correspondents, the economic historian Herbert Hallam, wanted to use a language of internal and external realities to encompass the same distinction, 'if only because the best economic historians are beginning to see [in 1958] the major factors in economic history which

---

[50] Postan to E. D. Genovese and S. L. Engerman (copy), 26 Dec. 1970, Cam UL Add MSS 8961/I/55.

[51] J. L. and Barbara Hammond, *The Village Labourer, 1760–1832: a Study in the Government of England before the Reform Bill* (1911); *The Town Labourer, 1760–1832: the New Civilization* (1917); *The Skilled Labourer, 1760–1832* (1919). See commentaries by Peter Clarke, *Liberals and Social Democrats* (Cambridge, 1978) and Stewart Weaver, *The Hammonds: a Marriage in History* (Stanford, CA, 1997).

[52] Chambers to A. Briggs (copy), 20 June 1961, Chambers MSS C1.

[53] Chambers to T. S. Ashton (copy), 20 June 1961, Chambers MSS C1.

factors are not really economic at all. Economic history is beginning an escape from the clutches of the economist and to take its rightful place as the *external* aspect of social history . . .'[54]

A blend of economic and social insights formed a powerful ingredient in English history as it was analysed between 1930 and 1970. If we leave to one side the Marxist concern with an urban proletariat, the theme that would reach its apogee in Edward Thompson's *Making of the English Working Class* in 1963 and to which we shall return in considering the place of ideology within English historiography, then it becomes interesting how much exploration took place into the nature of the countryside and the function of land – its productive forces and its social relations – as a determinant of English history. Town and village made their mark to be sure – an ever greater one as local history acquired new credentials in the generations of W. G. Hoskins[55] and Maurice Beresford[56] – but class relations in the countryside, particularly those surrounding the English nobility between 1300 and 1485 and the 'gentry' during 'Tawney's century' between 1540 and 1640, focused the attention of many historians in the inter-war and immediate post-war years. These concerns then fed into a wider understanding of 'agrarian history' that eventually attracted its own vast, serial history[57] to stand alongside the *Oxford History of England*, the *Cambridge History of the British Empire* and the *Cambridge Economic History of Europe*. Blinded by the sheer sparkle of E. P. Thompson's brilliant, wild and evanescent epic, historians of the 1970s and 1980s would often miss the sense in which the other Thompson created a more permanent work in his simultaneous study of *English Landed Society in the Nineteenth Century* (1963), which brought together themes captured by McFarlane and Tawney and gave them a further, modernist twist.[58]

[54] H. Hallam to Chambers, 22 Dec. 1958, Chambers MSS C5.
[55] W. G. Hoskins (1908–92). Baker's son from Exeter. Degree from that university and then mostly involved with the University of Leicester. Board of Trade during the war; then back to Leicester where the Anglo-Saxonist Frances Attenborough was instrumental in founding an English Local History Department in 1948. Reader in Economic History, Oxford, 1951–65; back to Leicester as Hatton Professor of English History. Resigned famously 'in despair' in 1968 to live in Devon. *The Making of the English Landscape* (1955). Much broadcasting and popularization.
[56] M. W. Beresford (1920–). Double First from Jesus College, Cambridge, then always Leeds. Chair of Economic History, 1959–85. *The Lost Villages of England* (1954); *Medieval England: an Aerial Survey* (1958); *New Towns of the Middle Ages* (1967).
[57] Joan Thirsk (ed.), *The Agrarian History of England and Wales* (8 vols., Cambridge, 1967–2000).
[58] F. M. L. Thompson, *English Landed Society in the Nineteenth Century* (London and Toronto, 1963). Cf. Miles Taylor's penetrating remarks on the significance of this Thompson's achievement in 'The Beginnings of Modern British Social History?', *History Workshop Journal*, 43 (1997), 155–76.

Bruce McFarlane did not need much twisting because his advanced modernism *avant la lettre* made him sound remarkably contemporary, even in the early work that earned him so many admirers in Oxford. In retrospect, among the postmodern generations, he has become a figure of fun. He is the man who never wrote anything himself but instead rubbished all those who did. Stories decorating the theme can still be heard: man enters McFarlane's study where he has been 'writing' all morning; discovers hero still hunched over his desk; looks over McFarlane's shoulder and finds that the sheet of paper contains one word at the beginning of the first line; it has been deleted. In fact, of course, the stories are themselves rubbish. No reader of McFarlane's astonishing letters, superb literature but also abounding in historical intelligence, could fail to see the force and industry of a driven scholar. He wrote more than most historians ever write. But he did not publish what he wrote. Rather, his days went into transcriptions from the record office collections of manuscripts, endless, patient accretion at once prompted and bounded by endless, corrosive *thought*. His thinking took its direction from the traditional concerns of Stubbsian history, but it rejected very quickly the 'Lancastrian experiment' and turned to a brief brush with Marxism in the search for a model of class relations in later medieval England.[59] He moved away from both a political history that told a whig story of noble emergence and an economic critique that starved law out of the explanation. His Ford Lectures of 1953, unpublished for a further two decades, combined strands of explanation for the transition of the English nobility into the caste it resembled by the advent of the Tudors and it made the case for a class that was *sui generis* within the noble ranks of Europe. He made his case most overtly in a paper to the International Congress of Historical Sciences in Vienna in 1965 which identified the power of entail to transform the tendency of an entire social formation:

a nobility of a type peculiar to England, having little in common with the French *noblesse* and the German *Adel*, first came into existence and established itself in that position of dominance in English society which it was to retain and exploit for several centuries to come. The essential changes had already occurred by 1485; they had hardly begun in 1300.[60]

---

[59] See his unpublished paper on 'Crown and Parliament in the Early Middle Ages', printed in K. B. McFarlane, *The Nobility of Later Medieval England* (Oxford, 1973), annex, 279–98.

[60] K. B . McFarlane, 'The English Nobility in the Later Middle Ages', in *Nobility*, 268–78 at 268. He goes on to make inheritance in tail male the central mechanism of this process: see 273–4.

His mission lay in dissolving facile generalizations that wanted to see economic and social change – and the political power that rested on it – as explicable through an alleged process of rise and fall.

R. H. Tawney sought to encourage precisely that conclusion and he spent the years after 1940 insisting on an economic explanation for the English Civil War that had its roots in aristocratic collapse and a rising gentry. His insistence had roots of its own that ran back at least to 1931 and the publication of Bloch's *Caractères originaux*,[61] which Tawney reviewed in 1933, and to Bloch's visit to the LSE in the following year.[62] The *Annaliste* concern with deep structure and Bloch's illumination of the working of pre-industrial society made its mark on Tawney and he made reference to Bloch in the famous essays of 1941 that whipped up the 'storm over the gentry' immortalized by J. H. Hexter many years later.[63] This formed one end of his thinking. Another came from the young Habbakuk whose early article on English landowners *after* the Civil War helped provide a problematic and a contrast with what Tawney thought would prove the key to the previous century.[64] His ammunition for these ideas flew from both barrels simultaneously in 1941: an essay on 'The Rise of the Gentry' in the *Economic History Review* and a Raleigh Lecture for the British Academy on Harrington's *Oceana* as a text illustrating and confirming the rise.[65] Quite what he expected from these pieces now lies beyond reconstruction.[66] The date plainly tells a story. He had been through some desperate years with the loss of his beloved Eileen Power to Postan in 1937, which must have cast a pall over Mecklenburg Square; then her brilliant success in the Ford Lectures in 1939 followed by an unbearable early death in the following year. War gripped him no less tangibly and the sense of great events growing from deep roots may have urged him further in the direction of

---

[61] Marc Bloch, *Les caractères originaux de l'histoire rurale française* (Oslo, 1931).

[62] For some context see Berg, *A Woman in History*, 210ff.

[63] J. H. Hexter, 'The Storm over the Gentry', in Hexter, *Reappraisals in History* (1961), 117–61.

[64] H. J. Habbakuk, 'English Landownership 1680–1740', *EcHR*, 10 (1940), 1–17. This piece argued that great landowners returned to the English scene and increased rather than declined; it offered by implication reinforcement for Tawney's view that the period before the Civil War had witnessed some aristocratic extinction and the rise of new men. Tawney referred to it in his essay on Harrington and it should stand beside H. E. Chesney, 'The Transference of Lands in England 1640–60', *TRHS*, 4th series 15 (1932), 181–210, which Tawney acknowledged in 'The Rise of the Gentry 1558–1640', *EcHR*, 11 (1941), 1–38 at 12.

[65] Tawney, 'The Rise of the Gentry'; 'Harrington's Interpretation of his Age', *PBA*, 27 (1941), 210–23.

[66] His main expositor, Ross Terrill, retreated as an act of policy from treating the historiography: see his *Socialism as Fellowship: R. H. Tawney and his Times* (1974), 13.

cosmic explanation. Probably he threw himself into writing to put grim things behind him, but he must also have hoped for some kind of response from so concentrated a barrage of argument. He certainly did not expect what followed. The story has been told so fully and vividly by Hexter and others that it will not stand another rehearsal; besides, it hardly makes for elevating reading.[67] Academic historians have rarely displayed such small-minded bitchiness as they inserted into the collection of replies and ripostes and counter-ripostes over the next decade. Hugh Trevor-Roper went in with the cudgel, drawing the famous biblical remark from Tawney that an 'erring colleague is not an Amalekite to be smitten hip and thigh'.[68] Then he turned his attention to Lawrence Stone – 'I am going to liquidate Stone,' he wrote cheerfully to Wallace Notestein[69] – and produced another wave of accusation and rebuttal. Tawney lamely continued to look for material that would revive his case, asking a young researcher, for example, whether he had found anything useful on rising rents,[70] but his academic reputation never recovered in the lacerating atmosphere of post-war modernism of which Trevor-Roper became an icon. It all rumbled on none the less. As late as 1962, when Richard Southern made an attempt at *longue durée* by thinking about the place of Henry I in English history, he still took his story forward to Tawney and the gentry, to the bewildered amusement of McFarlane.[71] Five years later, however, Gordon Batho's contribution to the new *Agrarian History*[72] offered a chapter on 'Landlords in England' which passed over the gentry controversy in near-silence, implying that even this memory had passed a threshold towards oblivion.

[67] Apart from Hexter's essay, there are descriptions of the acrimony that consumed the next ten years in Lawrence Stone, *The Causes of the English Revolution 1629–1642* (1972) and William Palmer, *Engagement with the Past: the Lives and Works of the World War II Generation of Historians* (Lexington, KY, 2001). One undergraduate observer, Julian Mitchell, later recalled that it seemed like a war over the future of England rather than its past. 'I'm not sure we weren't right.' 'Mitchell The Myth and the Man', in A. L. Beier, D. Cannadine and J. M. Rosenheim (eds.), *The First Modern Society: Essays in English History in Honour of Lawrence Stone* (Cambridge, 1989), 3–7 at 6.

[68] Heard by Lawrence Stone and quoted in Palmer, *Engagement with the Past*, 207. Cf. I Samuel 15:7, 'And Saul smote the Amalekites from Havilah'; and Judges 15:8, 'And he smote [the Philistines] hip and thigh with a great slaughter.'

[69] Hugh Trevor-Roper to Notestein, 4 Jan. 1951, Notestein MSS 544/1/8/747

[70] Tawney to W. G. Hoskins, 18 June 1943, Hoskins MSS box 11. Cf. a similar letter at the end of the year: 'From evidence elsewhere, I have no doubt that pressure on the land was an important factor in the rise of industrialism' (16 Dec. 1943, ibid.).

[71] Richard Southern, 'The Place of Henry I in English History', *PBA*, 48 (1962), 127–69. See McFarlane's remarks in McFarlane to Rees Davies, 19 Mar. 1964: 'It was as if he wanted to show that the medievalists of the twelfth century were with it, it being Namier, Tawney, Trevor-Roper and Neale!' *Letters to Friends, 1940–1966* (Oxford, 1997), 21.

[72] See Thirsk, *Agrarian History*, vol. IV, 1–12 and 161–255; and vol. VII, 298–388.

That multi-volume agrarian history deserves its own place in the history of a modernist economic and social history. It owed its conception to the Department of Local History at the University of Leicester which had been established at the instigation of an Anglo-Saxonist, F. L. Attenborough, and placed under the leadership of another medievalist, H. P. R. Finberg, though it eventually emerged into public awareness through the writing and broadcasting of the highly prolific W. G. Hoskins. The centre of energy and direction for the *History* came from a different historian, however, in the remarkable but self-effacing woman whose influence in the hinterland between economic, social and local history has never received due acknowledgement. By the side of Helen Cam and Eileen Power, the name of Joan Thirsk may seem weaker in resonance, but the fault lies with those among whom it resonates, for her achievement was enormous.[73] When the scheme for a systematic agrarian history came under consideration at Leicester in 1956 she held an unsatisfactory Fellowship there and had little power to organize the venture under Finberg's control. As with all such projects, on the other hand, planning bore little relation to production and none at all to schedules. Finberg eventually retired to work at his own volume in the project (AD 43–1042) and Thirsk took over direction of the entire series. She brought out her own volume (1500–1640) as the first published instalment of the *History* in 1967; and all the later volumes, apart possibly from Hallam's on the high middle ages, carried her imprimatur. Her introduction to volume IV ran to 112 pages on 'The Farming Regions of England', a theme that an expert on Lincolnshire would wish to drive through the enterprise as a whole in order to move the subject on from a few stereotypical perspectives. Historians needed to see England and Wales as a complex patchwork of characteristics, 'and not to regard the Midlands or Middlesex as the mirror of the kingdom . . . East Anglia's corn growers were not the nation, nor were the common fields of the East Midlands the only landscape.' They needed to dig down to 'the infinite variety of social forms and economic activity that lie beneath their generalizations'.[74] Her chapters on 'Farming Techniques' and 'Enclosing and Engrossing' did precisely that, and other contributors were encouraged to seek local instances that confounded the comfortable certainties of the textbook. The editors she brought into the later

---

[73] (Irene) Joan Thirsk (1922–). Camden School for Girls and Westfield College, London. Senior Research Fellow in Agrarian History, Leicester, 1951–65; Reader in Economic History and Fellow of St Hilda's College, Oxford, 1965–83.
[74] Joan Thirsk, introduction to *Agrarian History*, vol. IV, xxxvi–xxxvii.

volumes, such as Edward Miller[75] on the later middle ages and Gordon Mingay on the crucial century after 1750, responded in the same way; they too had temperamental commitments to particularism – with the result, in Mingay's case, that his 1,200 pages of text, including 183 pages of statistical appendix, became a modernist monument. Thirsk oversaw the entire programme and wrote introductions to the volumes that reflected her immense learning. Her referee ran little risk of hyperbole in describing her as 'more original and better read than almost any agrarian historian in this country that I know'.[76]

Local history reflected and reinforced this sense of particularism in the post-war years and became a respectable style of forensic history in the 1960s. This, too, was new. Localism itself had existed ever since people found fascination in their own town or city; it had a relationship with the antiquarianism that became such a force in the eighteenth century.[77] But overwhelmingly that form of enquiry had preoccupied amateur enthusiasts – the local rector, perhaps, or retired army officer or local lord of the manor. It produced stories and anecdotes intended to give a stranger an impression of place with quotations from local worthies. None of this fitted what Finberg and Hoskins wanted to do. Nor did it meet the standards of the slowly evolving *Victoria County History*, whose early volumes had contained much fluff with an occasional article from an Oxford graduate needing work, but which now self-consciously sought a higher level of scholarship. These moods fertilized one another – Finberg's certainty that local history now amounted to 'the most advanced form of historical study', Chambers' idea that historians now had the materials for a real local history of the Midlands that one could offer to undergraduates. 'The basic reading material', he told John Roskell, 'would of course be [the] county history of the counties concerned, supplemented on particular aspects by the work of Joan Thirsk (Lincolnshire), W. G. Hoskins (Leicestershire) and myself (Nottinghamshire).'[78] County particularism also enjoyed an Indian summer in the 'county' studies of the 1960s and '70s that hoped to

[75] Edward Miller (1915–2000). Son of a Northumbrian shepherd. St John's College, Cambridge: double starred First; later Fellow of St John's College and University Lecturer. Professor of Medieval History at Sheffield, 1965–71; Master of Fitzwilliam College, Cambridge, 1971–81. *The Abbey and Bishopric of Ely* (1951) deservedly became seminal among economic historians.

[76] Almost certainly Postan: ?Postan to Finberg (incomplete copy), 24 Nov. 1963, Finberg MSS D/FIN/8.

[77] The famous introduction by a master is Arnaldo Momigliano, 'Ancient History and the Antiquarian', in Momigliano, *Studies in Historiography* (1966), 1–39.

[78] H. P. R. Finberg to W. J. Gardner (copy), 12 Nov. 1957, Finberg MSS D/FIN/7; Chambers to John Roskell (copy), 17 Apr. 1961, Chambers MSS C1.

reorient seventeenth-century history by exposing the ligaments that supposedly joined local and national government.[79] Left to itself the tendency, together with others that we have been considering, might have produced the kind of modernism which Postan thought desirable and which he eulogized in his *summa* of economic and social history for a well-known symposium on history in the *Times Literary Supplement* in 1956. He pointed to the gulf between his idea of the subject and 'the *terra firma* of conventional narrative history'.

The main difference . . . is in the choice of problems. Nowadays economic historians choose them not from among the familiar events and personalities of history, but from the hypotheses of social sciences. The relation between aggregate output of agriculture and the productivity of new land, the 'terms of trade' between agriculture and industry, the effects of supply of bullion and of population trends on the movements of prices, the part which technical change played in the evolution of industry – these are a fair sample of the topics which now occupy the medieval economic historians. What agitates the modernists are problems like relative contributions of birth rates and death rates to long-term trends of population, the validity of the Marxian hypothesis of expropriation of peasant landholders as a pre-requisite of the Industrial Revolution, the influence of the rate of interest on the supply of capital, the behaviour of business men in different phases of industrial development, the responsiveness of labour to the economic stimuli of wages.[80]

This was not uplifting and Postan was not uplifted. He wrote in a mood of depression because he saw few signs in 1956 that the precondition for what he thought of as progress, the coming together of the social sciences and historical writing, lay even on the horizon. His vision had the status of an impious hope.

It failed to materialize for reasons that have already become familiar. Modernism became a predominant persuasion in England but it never became a hegemonic one, able to legislate all other ways of doing history out of existence. Not only did traditional forms of historical writing continue, albeit increasingly outside the academy, but those inside who espoused some of the tendencies of modernist utopia rarely approved of them all. Joan Thirsk had little truck with amateurism and the romantic clap-trap of so much rural history. She remained a pupil of Tawney, all the

---

[79] Among many example see Alan Everitt, *The Community of Kent and the Great Rebellion* (Leicester, 1966); Anthony Fletcher, *A County Community in Peace and War* (1975); J. S. Morrill, *Cheshire 1630–60: County Government and Society during the English Revolution* (Oxford, 1974); Clive Holmes, *Seventeenth-Century Lincolnshire* (Lincoln, 1980).

[80] M. M. Postan, 'Economic and Social History', *TLS*, 6 Jan. 1956. The symposium was instigated by the Master of Postan's own College, Herbert Butterfield, and reached a wide audience. Postan reprinted his piece in his *Fact and Relevance: Essays on Historical Method* (Cambridge, 1971), 65–71. The quotation here can be found at 69–70.

same, seeking always the *visual* in her prose, deploying impressionistic travel histories as readily as hard data, and joining up economic themes with the wider social history on which she believed understanding of the past rested. Just as Eileen Power had seen her sheep – literally, out of the window, when writing her Ford Lectures on the wool trade – as symbols of a medieval freedom denied to agrarian settlement, so Thirsk continued the theme of pasture in the early modern period as 'the most fertile seedbeds for Puritanism and dissent'.[81] They had all moved on since Lord Ernle's expansive canvas of *English Farming* written before the First World War and his whig remarks after it.[82] But they did not forget that it was over 'agrarian matters' that Seebohm had made his epoch[83] and that a place remained for the human, the imaginative and the judgemental in the new economic and social history.

Nor did the new historians live by bread alone. If histories of land and subsistence, labourers and wages, towns and their escalating populations, attracted many of the new generation after 1918, so did a recast political history. In considering the place of constitutionalism in post-whig historiography we dwelt on parliament as a persistent and continuing concern.[84] The men and women who committed themselves to that study believed themselves quite as novel and searching in their historical work as those who took to the hills for their sheep or the towns for their trade unions. New historians who had been taught by Firth in Oxford or Tout in Manchester needed no persuading that their mentors had taken history forward in powerful ways for all the seeming conventionality of their subject matter. If they learned from Firth the importance of the seventeenth-century constitution, they also learned that it would not do to treat it as Macaulay had done and that the concept of 'research' demanded attention. The most radical of his pupils would not be compelled to apologize for their inaugural lecture as Firth had been made to do for his suggestion that all was not well with the Oxford history faculty.[85] None of Tout's many pupils, likewise, ever forgot the power of his capacity to innovate and inspire towards new territory; the work of

---

[81] Eileen Power had argued in *The Wool Trade in Early-Medieval History* (1941) that the 'small virgates and large pastures of the Danelaw go with freedom' (6–7) and she had remarked on the relation between her subject and social class (e.g. 121–3). Cf. Thirsk in the *Agrarian History*, vol. IV, 111–12.

[82] Lord Ernle, *English Farming Past and Present* (1912); Ernle, *Land and its People* (1925). Ernle was R. E. Prothero and is not to be confused with his professorial elder brother, G. W., later Sir George Prothero.

[83] Maitland to Edwin Ashworth, 12 Nov. 1900, in C. H. S. Fifoot (ed.),*The Letters of Frederic William Maitland* (1965), 277.

[84] See chapter 1 pp. 29ff.

[85] C. H. Firth, *A Plea for the Historical Teaching of History* (Oxford, 1904).

a Powicke or a Galbraith would have looked very different without the impulse of that energy.

Or, away from Tout, think of Stenton[86] – one of the most powerful modernizers of the century who nevertheless embodied so many of the ambivalences of the genre: a Victorian caught out of time, yet also a man determined to advance the historical study of his Anglo-Saxons beyond anything dreamt of by Stubbs; a synthesizer of all that was 'known',[87] yet a mind constantly working at the frontier; a *soi-disant* social historian who simultaneously wanted to offer a new picture of the English polity in what he took to be the earliest years of its formation; a proponent of modernist method who produced from it images of an England lush in its romanticism and solid in its continuities with pre-Norman experience. It all began with coins – buying them, collecting them, arranging them – and for a distinguished numismatist like Philip Grierson the determination of Stenton to advance the understanding of early English society through its coinage counted among his major achievements. Then came place-names, the foundation of Stenton's professional work and a lifetime's commitment through the English Place-Name Society. He collected place-names as he collected coins because they did the same thing, presenting the past before one's eyes so that it could be envisioned as tangibly as one might feel the weight of silver in the hand. Literary history had to go because it lacked this solid base which 're-search' would amplify. Detail would show in its sheer multiplicity the reality of historical knowledge and ultimately make it possible to produce an incontrovertible section of the past. That, of course, was the objective of Stenton's masterpiece, *Anglo-Saxon England* (1943), which gave the wartime public a picture of its progenitors so overwhelming in its evidence and elegance that it would hold the centre of pre-Norman studies for more than a generation.[88] Yet it was never the modernist document that Stenton had imagined himself to be creating over the past decade; and that is why, paradoxically, it proved so successful.

---

[86] Frank Merry Stenton (1880–1967). Son of Southwell solicitor. Unconventional schooling, then scholarship to Keble College, Oxford. *Victoria County History* and some teaching. From 1907 Reading University (College) where he remained for the rest of his career. Vice-Chancellor from 1946. Married Doris Parsons in 1919 and she became, as Doris Stenton, a major scholar in her own right. *The First Century of English Feudalism, 1066–1166* (1932); *Anglo-Saxon England* (Oxford, 1943).

[87] James Campbell convincingly stresses this element of Stenton's work in 'Stenton's *Anglo-Saxon England* with Special Reference to the Earlier Period', in Donald Matthew (ed.), *Stenton's* Anglo-Saxon England *Fifty Years On* (Reading, 1994), 49–60.

[88] Simon Keynes reviews that changing influence in his important essay on 'Anglo-Saxon England after *Anglo-Saxon England*', in Matthew, *Stenton's* Anglo-Saxon England, 83–110.

Modernizers could take away from the text an unanswerable array of specifics: geographical masteries, archaeological confirmations, knowledge so pestled and mortared that it could scatter across every page. But much remained to inspire whigs and generalists from Trevelyan to Bryant, not only because the book brought Stenton's genuine intellectual elegance and sharpness of prose to the volume, but because it had a political message that was not modern at all. Stenton had in effect built a bridge between the new social history informed by the scientism of historical and archaeological analysis, and a view of political development that turned Anglo-Saxon England into a sophisticated and centralizing nation state *avant la lettre* of Stubbs's constitutional history. Where once medievalists had seen fog before 1066, they now saw a landscape remarkably familiar to them as the author of *The First Century of English Feudalism* pushed its lessons backwards towards the Witenagemot in the absence of a parliament.

The re-Tudoring of modern England by Pollard and Neale, meanwhile, called up a long-held tradition in its focus on the Tudor parliament; but what *they* did with it – and the consequences for a Stubbsian chronology and trajectory – went far beyond tradition. It announced itself self-consciously as a new history written for the new age. Of course, the balance sheet of whiggery and modernism within all this writing shows entries in each column, just as it does for Stenton: it does not indicate a bodily shift of investment from one column to another. For every Pollard or Elton trying in their respective generations to make whiggery go away, there appeared popular accounts of patriotism, improvement and unfolding freedoms to point up contrast and remind the reader that no man is a desiccated calculating machine. It would become the complaint of a later era that the modernists had come close to killing history through their professional snobberies, their fascination with the technical and arcane, their preferencing of the forensic over the imaginative. At no time, however, was the opposite persuasion absent from the bookshelves and the public lecture hall. Authors from G. M. Trevelyan to Arthur Bryant to Veronica Wedgwood kept alive a whig commitment to *audience* and the need to communicate if history were to live. All the same, it remains the case that the new historians who sought to push forward political history as much as its newer variants stamped their impress on a generation and created new base-lines for the appraisal of historical accomplishment.

Decrying those achievements comes easily, especially when the speed of continental development is brought into the picture. Strasbourg boasted its iconoclastic *Annales* from 1929. What could England offer in the same year? Lewis Namier's *Structure of Politics at the Accession of*

George III and Butterfield's *Peace Tactics of Napoleon* – neither apparently a manifesto for revolution. Yet appearances deceive. Namier had begun a shock-wave in political history whose strength would still shake scholars fifty years later. From a university chair in Tout's Manchester and then from an underground burrow in London with his colleagues on the *History of Parliament* project, Namier set about remaking the eighteenth century with an intelligence, range and aggression that provoked discussion among historians as far away from that century as Richard Southern, meditating about the nature of England's twelfth-century monarchy, or Ronald Syme, deep in his thoughts about the Roman republic.[89] Butterfield's monograph could make no such claim. He had produced a competent piece of diplomatic history under the impress of Harold Temperley, his former supervisor at Peterhouse, Cambridge. But it was the last such monograph he ever wrote, and the *Structure of Politics* threw a man who was Namier's equal in intelligence and superior in human grasp into a lifetime's opposition, not to Namier necessarily, but to all that he stood for in taking political history – perhaps all history – in the wrong direction. Their respective contributions merit a note here among the new historians of their age. But they also require a chapter to themselves, not because they wrote about the eighteenth century, though both did, not even because the eighteenth century became peculiarly influential in the thinking of modern historians, which it undoubtedly did, but rather because they brought into question the very basis of the historical enterprise and raised issues far beyond their immediate concerns. One of Butterfield's closest friends and colleagues, Brian Wormald, sent him a thoughtful memorandum in 1963 recommending the rebuilding of the seventeenth century on the grounds that 'important *general* considerations . . . have to be faced and that scrutiny of the evidence alone cannot help us'.[90] That is why the eighteenth century had come to matter so much and why its template became formative for other periods: it had turned by the 1960s into a forum for making historical presupposition, and modernist confidence, explicit.

---

[89] Southern found Henry I replete with the motives Namier had made familiar in his studies of the eighteenth-century political elite. 'No king has been a more devoted Namierite than he.' Southern, 'The Place of Henry I in English History', 130. For Syme, see pp. 207–8.
[90] Memo by B. H. G. Wormald, n.d. [Mar. 1963], Butterfield MSS BUTT 531/W486.

6   The new eighteenth century

Why did they study the eighteenth century? It is a question rarely asked of the modernists who committed their lives to it, not even of their most famous personalities, Namier[1] and Butterfield,[2] but behind it lies their world and the prefigurings of their historical thought. The nineteenth-century historians, Adolphus and Lecky apart, had raked their fire far more over the seventeenth and later the sixteenth century when they were not redesigning the medieval state. Perhaps the eighteenth century could only come into focus when whig history itself became sufficiently self-questioning to reflect critically on its own period of supreme self-satisfaction, and its exponents are therefore part of a generational instinct; but that thought probably puts the cart before the horse. Historians tend to adjust their sights only after someone or something compels them to revisit and reflect. It seems clear that some process of this kind had already developed momentum before the First World War. Yet it is less clear who began it and why; and we may have to think, in answering the question, about movements not only in English historiography but also elsewhere. Whatever the reason, the historiography of the

---

[1] (Sir) Lewis Namier, originally Niemirowski (1888–1960), born to landed Polish parents. England from 1907. LSE, then Balliol College, Oxford. Foreign Office during Great War. Oxford again but then left to make money in order to provide time for writing. Professor of Modern History at Manchester from 1931, but most of his time taken up after the war in his involvement with the *History of Parliament*, though he died with his own volume unfinished. *The Structure of Politics at the Accession of George* III (2 vols., 1929); *England in the Age of the American Revolution* (1930); many books reflecting on European history especially in the age of the dictators, including *Diplomatic Prelude* (1948), *Europe in Decay* (1950) and *In the Nazi Era* (1952).

[2] (Sir) Herbert Butterfield (1900–79). Son of a clerk in a West Riding mill. Keighley Trade and Grammar School, then Peterhouse, Cambridge, where he remained for the rest of his life, first as Fellow, then as Master (1955–68). Professor of Modern History, Cambridge, 1944–63; Regius Chair 1963–8. *The Whig Interpretation of History* (1931) and *Christianity and History* (1949) his best-known books. The eighteenth-century work is best displayed in *George III, Lord North and the People* (1949) and *George III and the Historians* (1957).

eighteenth century became imbricated to a unique degree in the teaching of its substantive history during the twentieth. Constitutional history perhaps supplied a strand of the argument, at least to the extent of providing a framework within which the discussion of law, liberty and tyranny – a discussion that became frenzied in the age of Butterfield and Namier – could find some of its reference points. It is not that Erskine May, Walter Bagehot and Albert Dicey themselves recast the bases of eighteenth-century history.[3] Their concern with the limits of authority and the questions they raised over the theoretical postulates of Blackstone and Burke nevertheless found their way into the texture of historical argument in the next generation and sentiments like these from Kenneth Pickthorn – no whig – in 1925 as he brooded on the significance of the Younger Pitt's coming to power in 1784 as a *constitutional* issue:

> The Whig doctrine – that the Government of England should be directed by a Party Cabinet, headed by a Prime Minister who could rely on the votes of more than half of the House of Commons, and that the King should reign – but in no way govern – had gained definition and driving-power in the struggle against George III's attempt to revive the influence of the Crown. That doctrine was now flouted by the dismissal of Fox and North, and still more by Pitt's persistence in office in spite of a hostile Lower House; yet his ministry was to prove the decisive process in converting the doctrine into the effective rule of the constitution.[4]

Ireland, too, played its subversive part. The years when Home Rule emerged as an ambition threw the mind back to Grattan and the coming of the Act of Union at the very end of the eighteenth century. They were the same years during which eight vast volumes flowed from the pen of a great Irishman, William Edward Hartpole Lecky, whose *History of England* expended two of its volumes on Ireland and cast much of the other six in an audible brogue. Lecky's whiggery, magnificent more than furtive, established the eighteenth century as a morality tale with a structure that would become hard to erase in the twentieth century. The early part of the eighteenth could be dispensed with: it displayed what Lecky called a 'singular monotony'.[5] Then we have Walpole with

---

[3] T. Erskine May, *The Constitutional History of England since the Accession of George III* (2 vols., 1861); Walter Bagehot, *The English Constitution* (1867); A. V. Dicey, *Introduction to the Study of the Law of the Constitution* (1885); Dicey, *Lectures on the Relationship between Law and Public Opinion in England during the Nineteenth Century* (1905).

[4] Kenneth Pickthorn, *Some Historical Principles of the Constitution* (1925), 65. Sir Kenneth Pickthorn (1892–1975). Trinity College, Cambridge, but then a lifetime's association with Corpus Christi College in its high Tory period. Conservative MP and junior minister. Apart from *Some Historical Principles*, he wrote the two volumes of *Early Tudor Government* (1934).

[5] W. E. H. Lecky, *The History of England in the Eighteenth Century* (8 vols., 1878–90), vol. I, 316.

his 'coarse and cynical banter', the snake on whose neck real Whigs would need to tread. 'Like many men of low morals and of coarse and prosaic nature,' writes Lecky, 'he was altogether incapable of appreciating as an element of political calculation the force which moral sentiments exercise upon mankind, and this incapacity was one of the great causes of his fall.'[6] The fall produces party chaos and faction, broken only by the glory of Pitt the Elder – 'no minister had a greater power of making a sluggish people brave, or a slavish people free, or a discontented people loyal' – whose power to redeem the nation ultimately fails in the face of George III's 'sullen and rancorous nature' that quickened his plans to re-establish personal rule, plans that culminate in his refusal to turn to Pitt, now Earl of Chatham, when the French, rotten as always, turned against us in 1778. Lecky was beside himself. 'This episode appears to me the most criminal in the whole reign of George III, and in my own judgment it is as criminal as any of those acts which led Charles I to the scaffold.'[7] But George no better understood the wages of sin than had Walpole. In 1769, a year 'very memorable in political history', says Lecky,[8] the formation of the Society of the Supporters of the Bill of Rights brought the people into politics – the beginning of the end for tyranny, the first move in the development of proper political parties and the era of real reform with 1832 just visible on the horizon.

This persistent story firmed the foundation of much twentieth-century writing, sometimes by extension, sometimes by modulation. The people, embodied in a conception of popular radicalism, preoccupied social democrats such as the Hammonds and the Webbs; and the story of burgeoning success in the radicals' pressure from without reached seminal status in G. S. Veitch's account of *The Genesis of Parliamentary Reform* in 1913, with its acknowledgement of the early eighteenth century as a 'dead season', surprising no doubt to Dr Sacheverell and the Jacobites, and its assertion that later eighteenth-century political arrangements were 'indefensible and call[ing] aloud for readjustment'.[9] Likewise, the early studies of Britain's industrial evolution called attention

---

[6] Ibid., vol. I, 373.   [7] Ibid., vol. IV, 82–3.
[8] Ibid., vol. III, 174. His authorities seem to be Erskine May and H. T. Buckle.
[9] G. S. Veitch, *The Genesis of Parliamentary Reform* (1913), 23, 352. In his introduction to the 1965 reprint of this volume, Ian Christie argued that the analysis was thought to be so formidable that no one confronted the subject for the next twenty years (p. vii). Another catalyst for the Hammond generation had been studies of eighteenth-century personalities written by authors such as John Morley, Leslie Stephen and the young G. M. Trevelyan. It was his father's study of Charles James Fox, published in 1880, that attracted Lawrence Hammond to the eighteenth century for the first time; see Stuart Weaver, *The Hammonds: a Marriage in History* (Stanford, CA, 1997), 72.

to the relationship between economic dynamics and their political expression. But much the most powerful contributors to the awakening of eighteenth-century awareness among historians were two individuals: Thomas Pelham-Holles, Duke of Newcastle, and William Pitt, Earl of Chatham. Newcastle contributed in death far more than in life by bequeathing one of the greatest archives to survive into the modern era. Pitt made his mark by becoming a cardboard construction that had been, like so much else in the 1890s, made in Germany.

Look anywhere in the English political historiography relating to the eighteenth century and references to Albert von Ruville will abound. Freiburg, rather than Oxford or Cambridge or the spacious town houses familiar to Lecky and Leslie Stephen, was the home of the Graf von Chatham. He appeared in 1905, this particular ghost, looking very like Frederick the Great as seen by a Prussian Junker in the era of Bismarck.[10] And indeed it had been the Seven Years War and the breakdown of relations between England and Frederick that had formed Ruville's original questions which he then prosecuted through the Newcastle Manuscripts in the British Museum. 'Da trat mir denn die glänzende Erscheinung des Mannes vor Augen, der in den entscheidenden Jahren mit kräftiger Hand die Zügel des britischen Staates geführt . . . hatte';[11] and Ruville was hooked. '[H]e is the great historical personage, the powerful minister, who at a dangerous crisis led England to victory, and also helped by his success to give a new direction to German developments.'[12] Ruville's construction also gave fresh direction to German historiography of England, especially in Wolfgang Michael's *Englische Geschichte*,[13] which attempted to revive the age of Walpole, but also directed English writing (joining hands with Lecky) in encouraging a view of Pitt as the human bulwark against faction and party who had been done down by an unscrupulous monarch, a view that reached its apogee in the young Basil Williams's two-volume life of Pitt, published in 1913, which in turn conditioned his much better-known inter-war volume of the Oxford history with its tell-tale title, *The Whig Supremacy*.[14] Most of all, however, the thrust of this reading from Ruville

---

[10] Albert von Ruville, *William Pitt, Graf von Chatham* (3 vols., Berlin and Munich, 1905). An English translation appeared two years later with an introduction by H. E. Egerton, whom we met when discussing the empire, who deemed it odd that it took a German to write the first serious life of Pitt based on manuscript material (Introduction, v).

[11] Ruville, *Graf von Chatham*, vol. I, 3–4.

[12] Albert von Ruville, *William Pitt, Earl of Chatham* (3, vols., 1907), vol. III, xxi–ii, 347.

[13] Wolfgang Michael, *Englische Geschichte im 18ten. Jahrhundert* (Hamburg, 1896).

[14] Both of these volumes ran into the impending war. A. F. B. Williams, *The Life of William Pitt, Earl of Chatham* appeared in 1913. A cheaper wartime edition came out in August

confirmed the objectives of D. A. Winstanley's *Lord Chatham and the Whig Opposition* (1912), in which George III's darkness deepened. Of Pitt, Frederick the Great had been right to announce that England had brought forth a man.[15] In the king it had brought forth not a mouse but a rat. In his undoing of Chatham after 1766 George III initiated a narrative of national decline. 'Within those years the destinies of the nation were determined,' said Winstanley, 'and the work of the Revolution [of 1689] nullified.'[16]

Now the work of challenging this shape in the history of the eighteenth-century constitution and its politics did not concern only Namier and Butterfield and it did not begin with them. Harold Temperley, Butterfield's future research supervisor at Peterhouse, revised in the pre-war years the eighteenth-century prehistory of the cabinet, for example.[17] But significant revision did not begin in England at all before the 1920s, nor yet in Germany, but rather (of all implausible places) up the Mississippi. Few historians anywhere had heard of Clarence Walworth Alvord. Only when his two volumes on *The Mississippi Valley in British Politics* came off the press in Cleveland, Ohio, in 1917 did it become apparent that a virtual unknown had cheerfully denied what everybody had been saying for the past thirty years about eighteenth-century parties, principles, Whigs, Tories and the loss of America. He followed convention in regard to Pitt the Elder as a solvent of party in 1766. But he placed his images in a territory far from conventional and redolent of what Namier would astound the world with twelve years later. 'Too frequently', runs his argument, 'American historians have read back the conditions of the succeeding century in order to explain [pre-revolutionary] politics, and having classified men and their measures as Whig and Tory have rested satisfied. A more careful analysis does not reveal any such division . . . Of principles there is almost no sign.'[18]

1915, however, and lent greater weight to the epigraph of the legendary war-leader printed on the title page: 'Lord Chatham was a great, illustrious, faulty human being, whose character, like all the noblest works of human composition, should be determined by its excellences, not by its defects.' Cf. Williams, *The Whig Supremacy* (Oxford, 1939).

[15] D. A. Winstanley, *Lord Chatham and the Whig Opposition* (1912), 27.

[16] Ibid., v. '[T]he austere policy of George III had rendered the Bill of Rights and the Act of Settlement . . . almost constitutionally valueless. Parliament, which had previously been the puppet of the whig nobility, now became the slave of a court. By preying upon the weakness of mankind, and cynically indifferent to the morality of public life, George III had conquered where better and more scrupulous men might have failed . . .' (16).

[17] See John D. Fair, *Harold Temperley: a Scholar and Romantic in the Public Realm* (Newark, DE, 1992), 86–9; cf. Harold Temperley, 'The Inner and Outer Cabinet and the Privy Council 1679–1783', *EHR*, 28 (1912), 682–99.

[18] Clarence W. Alvord, *The Mississippi Valley in British Politics: a Study of the Trade, Land Speculation and Experiments in Imperialism Culminating in the American Revolution* (2 vols.,

Not only did this view reshape what Namier would later call England in the age of the American revolution, but it also carried important implications for the whole narrative of party. 'True party government was finally evolved out of the prevailing political disorder of the time', but for Alvord 'its culmination falls well within the nineteenth century. The latter half of the eighteenth century knew it not.'[19] These were significant allegations and they helped frame the concerns that both Butterfield and Namier were to demonstrate throughout their lives as professional historians. They do not, however, explain why both of them became concerned with the eighteenth century in the first place.

Lewis Namier's case is the simpler. Two contexts governed his development during the years of his education in England: the prevalent climate of imperial opportunity with its accompanying visions or fantasies of imperial federation, on the one hand, and his visits to America before 1914 on the other.[20] The themes coalesced in an essay submitted for the Beit Prize in Oxford in 1912. Its title, 'Proposals for Imperial Federation before 1887', makes it sufficiently clear that he did not see himself necessarily as an eighteenth-century historian; but the interest in America meant that he never got any further in his narrative than the American revolution. Nor did the American theme end there. In 1913 Charles M. Andrews[21] said to Namier that the American school of revolution-historians had said nothing worthwhile on the British side of the argument.[22] This became what Namier himself called his 'main work' on the eighteenth century and it was from that broader trunk that the branches of study in relation to parliamentary and electoral history ultimately spread. It did so for reasons identified in a private letter to Philip Kerr (later Lord Lothian) in the year that *Government and Parliament at the Accession of George III* [23]– the original title – was to appear.

Cleveland, OH, 1917), vol. I, 15. Alvord's significance is well attested in B. W. Hill, *British Parliamentary Parties 1742–1832: from the Fall of Walpole to the First Reform Act* (1985), 4, as is that of W. R. Laprade, an important American commentator on the developing historiography of the eighteenth century through his connexion with the new Chicago periodical, the *Journal of Modern History*. See, for example, his review of the literature thus far in Laprade, 'The Present State of the History of England in the Eighteenth Century', *Journal of Modern History*, 4 (1932), 581–603, and his monograph on *Public Opinion and Politics in Eighteenth-Century England, to the Fall of Walpole* (New York, 1936).

[19] Alvord, *Mississippi Valley*, vol. I, 43.
[20] See Julia Namier, *Lewis Namier: a Biography* (1971), 107–14.
[21] Charles M. Andrews (1863–1943): author of invaluable guides to archival material in London, Oxford and Cambridge that became foundational for American research students coming to England. Farnham Professor of American History at Yale, 1910–31; President of the American Historical Association, 1924.
[22] Namier to Philip Kerr (copy), 11 Aug. 1926, Namier MSS 1/1a/1.
[23] Of course the two volumes that appeared in 1929 came out instead as *The Structure of Politics at the Accession of George III*.

First, said Namier, Britain could not cope with the American difficulty because 'the British Parliament was (as it still remains) a territorial and not a tribal institution and that therefore its authority could not extend to members of the race permanently settled in other territories'. And, second, that the 'tribal sovereignty of the Crown, now the bond of the Empire, was as yet impossible' because 'in the eighteenth century the King . . . could not be separated from the British Parliament'.[24] The consequences of this imperative in Namier's interests and his failure to follow it through as a comprehensive programme are familiar. There was going to be what he called 'a kind of "static" review of the situation in 1761 which was supposed to function, incidentally, like the first volume of Halévy's history of nineteenth-century Britain';[25] then there would come, again in his words, two volumes offering 'a running account of the British Parliament 1761–1783' and broken at 1770.[26] Though the latter volumes never happened, Namier retained his concentration, in these eighteenth-century studies, on a period from 1740 to 1783, years that he saw evocatively as two dams built across the stream of time that would enable him to analyse the trapped waters.[27]

But of course there was also a temperamental affinity with the minute examination of specifics that gratified a powerful logical mind that frequently faltered conceptually and hardly existed imaginatively except among the pillow's nightmares. This by itself would have brought some subversion to a whig story. On top of that, however, we need surely to graft Namier's need to turn eighteenth-century people into copies of himself and make a society that reflected the cool, sometimes cruel acknowledgement of human frailty that was part of his personality and the distance between ideas and their well-springs that he learned as much at the tables of the English intelligentsia as on the couches of Viennese psychiatrists. A. L. Rowse, sharper about people he knew than about the historical periods he described, saw this tendency in Namier as a '[c]omplete & utter disillusionment with human beings, despair at human prospects. He didn't attach much importance to what humans *think* – neither do I. Most of their political concepts, like their economic, are just rationalisations of their interests.'[28] This carapace of cynicism, together with an over-assimilated Englishness in suit and umbrella, gave the impression of an aspirant country gentleman but with a Polish twist.

[24] Namier to Kerr (copy), 6 Feb. 1929, Namier MSS 1/1a/1.
[25] Elie Halévy, *A History of the English People in the Nineteenth Century* (5 vols., 1924–34 ; 6th edn, Harmondsworth, 1939).
[26] Namier to Whitney H. Shepardson (copy), 4 Nov. 1926, Namier MSS.
[27] See Julia Namier, *Lewis Namier*, 187.
[28] A. L. Rowse to J. H. Plumb, 30 Mar. 1967, Plumb MSS.

It concealed, however, an 'aching, bruised, slightly-fearful inner life', in Plumb's evocative phrase.[29] J. L. Talmon saw deeper than Rowse in finding the proposition that Namier did not believe in ideas badly framed for it was far more complicated than that.

In a certain sense Namier was in fact obsessed by the question of the role of ideas in history to the point of its having a tragic meaning to him . . . Far from denying the potency of political and social ideologies, he was frightened by their power to disturb, and he was inclined to regard them as the neurotic symptoms of a society, as traumatic visitations.[30]

The eighteenth century kept traumatic visitations away in those serene, flat portraits of prosperous self-satisfaction. And the more Namier painted them, the more they smiled back from the canvas as men like himself and reinforced their bond with him.

On whom, though, did Butterfield smile in the 1920s? The case seems both more complex and more elusive: complex because Herbert Butterfield had a deeper engagement with the universe than did Namier, elusive because there survives virtually no documentation from this period to help make the pieces fit. His early influences do not depict an eighteenth-century man, apart from his fascination with John Wesley and perhaps Sir Walter Scott, with whom he had a juvenile and short-lived acquaintance. Pointing to Temperley as his guide hardly helps much:[31] by the time Butterfield became his research student, Temperley's interests lay in the first half of the nineteenth century and, in so far as he pushed Butterfield anywhere, he pushed him towards Napoleon and the first monograph on the peace negotiations of 1806–7.[32] In later years Temperley's over-bearing and often crude mind frankly irritated Butterfield. We have his prize essay on the historical novel which has a purple page about the eighteenth-century streets in York,[33] which may suggest that imagination came before analysis in his

---

[29] J. H. Plumb, 'Sir Lewis Namier', in Plumb, *The Making of an Historian: Collected Essays* (2 vols., Brighton, 1988), 10–19 at 19.

[30] J. L. Talman, 'The Ordeal of Sir Lewis Namier: the Man, the Historian, the Jew', *Commentary* (Feb. 1962). Copy enclosed in Talmon to Lucy Sutherland, 29 Oct. 1962, Sutherland MSS box 9.

[31] John D. Fair sees Temperley behind many of Butterfield's decisions. I find this implausible. See his biography of *Harold Temperley: a Scholar and Romantic in the Public Realm* (1992).

[32] Herbert Butterfield, *The Peace Tactics of Napoleon* (1929).

[33] Herbert Butterfield, *The Historical Novel* (Cambridge, 1923). '[I]f we wish, say, to see the vivid life of three hundred years ago stirring in the crooked streets and topsy-turvy houses that converge upon York Minster, we must charge our history with some of the human things that are irrecoverable, we must reinforce history by our imagination'(18; see also 22–3).

dix-huitième moments. If so, analysis was not long in coming and it came in reaction to what others said rather than through proposals of his own. Namier's two books of 1929 and 1930 he almost certainly admired but he may have found his teeth set slightly on edge at the implied value-structure imposed on eighteenth-century people. Compare one remark we do have, not on Namier but on G. M. Trevelyan and in relation to *England under Queen Anne* which had begun to appear in 1930.[34] It is an untitled, single-page reflection in the middle of an early notebook:

> Trevelyan seems to idealise – or too easily to forgive – the morality and profligacy of the 18th century. This is not because he really approved of such ways of life: this would have been inconsistent with his temperament and his traditions; but it is the result of a particularly facile historian's use of printed memoirs and correspondence – the cumulative effect of his choice of the 'spicy' anecdotes and surprising examples. For the same reason the 18th century world which he described was perhaps not so profligate or immoral as it might seem from a hurried reading of his book.[35]

Here we have Namier in negative: a rejection of, rather than complicity in, an assumed morality or lack of one that has been imposed retroactively.

This may be a clue. It seems congruent with Butterfield's intellectual development in these years to suggest that he turned to the eighteenth century in the same spirit and for the same reasons that he began his attack on *The Whig Interpretation of History* in 1931, and that is out of a concern with the procedures informing historical writing in his generation. It was not simply that he found the conclusions to which they led occasionally rebarbative, but that he saw within the working-out of these interpretations about the later eighteenth century ways in which the entire enquiry of modern history could come under threat. And that lies at the heart of an otherwise bewildering conundrum over which Frank O'Gorman has expressed an understandable sense of mystery when one looks back on it: why did it seem so exciting, important and controversial in the 1950s and '60s to work out whether George III was a tyrant or not?[36] Butterfield offered a kind of answer – one that I want to develop – in an entry in his Commonplace Book after the Second World War. 'I should expect', he said, 'any developments in the study of George III's [reign] to be interesting not merely in points of narrative but rather in

---

[34] G. M. Trevelyan, *England under Queen Anne* (3 vols., 1930–4). For the context of this book, see David Cannadine, *G. M. Trevelyan: a Life in History* (1992), 114–19.

[35] Herbert Butterfield, 'The Printing of Records . . .', Early Writing, Miscellany.

[36] Author's interview with Professor O'Gorman.

what I should call the general set-up.'[37] He did not expect, perhaps, that a controversy over that set-up would produce one of the bitterest divisions in English historiography in the twentieth century and one that commented on the survival of a whig paradigm as much as its extirpation.

None of this seemed evident when Lewis Namier returned to England from Vienna at the end of 1923 and visited the fount of eighteenth-century politics, the Newcastle Manuscripts, in the British Museum. The experience 're-awakened his excitement over eighteenth-century problems', according to Julia Namier,[38] and led to the two great books on eighteenth-century politics in 1929 and 1930 and then on to his appointment at Manchester, where E. F. Jacob finally beat down the opposition of the Faculty to filling the Modern History Chair when they were still resentful of the over-mighty subjects they had encountered in Tout and Powicke.[39] That he stood on the shoulders of others in reshaping the eighteenth century we have already noticed, and to that discussion one could add the work of Fortescue on the correspondence of George III, an edition that Namier would excoriate and correct, and Romney Sedgwick's printing of significant sections of the correspond-ence between the king and Lord Bute.[40] Butterfield's stimuli were different, though he must have written undergraduate essays on the eighteenth century for Temperley. He began a journey in the direction of Namier, rather than away from him, through his research on Euro-pean foreign policy in the years surrounding Tilsit: a volume that appeared in the same year as Namier's *Structure of Politics*. This work suggested the superficiality of vast interpretative frameworks and the importance of what he came to call 'technical history', a subject to which we shall return.[41] Implications followed from that – whatever whig history claimed to be, it was not a manual of technique – and they had some point put on them in 1930 and 1931, partly through an encounter with Namier's crushing scholarship, partly perhaps through a more enjoyable encounter with the century's two best-selling and most mem-orable historical scholars, Sellar and Yeatman, whose *1066 and All That*

---

[37] Commonplace Book, n.d., Butterfield MSS BUTT/122/4.
[38] Julia Namier, *Lewis Namier*, 181.
[39] Norman Sykes to Claude Jenkins, 28 June 1930, Jenkins MSS 1634 f.232.
[40] *George III, King of England: Correspondence from 1760 to December 1783; printed from the original papers in the Royal Archives at Windsor Castle, arranged and edited by the Hon. Sir J. Fortescue* (6 vols., 1927–8); *Some Materials towards Memoirs of the reign of King George II; edited by R. Sedgwick* (1931); *George III, King of England: Letters to Lord Bute, 1756–66; edited with an introduction by R. Sedgwick* (1939).
[41] See chapter 8, pp. 214–15.

first appeared in 1930, proclaiming the universe to be English and Whig. Mainly and essentially, however, Butterfield entered into a continuing dialogue with the figure who obsessed him for most of his life, Lord Acton, who frequently emerges from behind the curtain in Butterfield's works. Unlike Namier, Butterfield condensed his concerns about loose readings of modern British history into a 25,000-word essay, not on the eighteenth century in particular but on the Whig paradigm in general. Or at least that is how it looked. In fact the language about Protestant triumphalism in *The Whig Interpretation of History* concealed more emphatic rejections of Catholic judgementalism; and Butterfield's aggression about drawing the past into the present extended only to the question of preventing substandard historical technique rather than to a frontal assault on what Whigs believed about the continuities of national identity and the importance of making the past a civilizing agent. As Butterfield later expostulated, he had always been a whig and he remained one.

Truth to tell, both Namier and Butterfield ran their eighteenth centuries in the same direction at this stage of their dialogue, a conclusion we readily miss by reading the debate backwards from its more entrenched and heated moments in the 1950s and 1960s. Yes, Butterfield doubtless worried even then about X-ray plates taking the place of sensitive portraiture, about Namier's 'static' history replacing the depiction of change over time. Yes, Namier's acidic temperament would have found Butterfield's essay on *The Historical Novel* a painful and irrelevant intervention. But polarities of this kind seem closer together when situated in a wider perspective. One of these authors would later appeal to the importance in historical accounts of 'providential joints' where the narrative switches tracks; but that author was Namier, not Butterfield.[42] One of them would proclaim that 'without the "structure of politics" we cannot properly narrate the story of George III', but the proclamation came from Butterfield, not Namier.[43] Only after a world war, and then only partially, did the dismantlings of both writers and a second generation of pupils take them in opposite directions. So whether or not John Cannon was right to have suggested in his Wiles Lectures two decades

---

[42] Julia Namier, *Lewis Namier*, 170. It is true that Namier meant by these something less inspired than Butterfield's visions of providential intervention. He meant the occurrence of chance events unforeseen by anyone that make all actors in the situation alter their plans. Namier's own spiritual life in his later years should not be dismissed, however. His baptism into the Church of England in 1947 with its commitment to 'rock-bottom things' may have contributed to his undoubted pain over some of the positions taken by pupils and admirers. Ibid., 269–70.
[43] Herbert Butterfield, 'Clio in Council', *TLS*, 6 Jan. 1956.

ago that 'since the early 1930s . . . the work of Namier and Butterfield landed like a cluster of mortar bombs on the traditional Whig/Liberal interpretation of eighteenth-century England',[44] he was certainly right to see his soldiers training the same mortar on a common target.

Perhaps a chink of light opened between them in Namier's Ford Lectures on 'King, Cabinet and Parliament in the Early Years of George III' delivered in Oxford in the Hilary Term of 1934. Butterfield remained in the dark about them apart from second-hand reports: his appointment diaries give no suggestion that he went to Oxford to hear the lectures and they were not published until after Namier's death, when John Brooke and Lucy Sutherland produced an abbreviated version.[45] His reasons for not publishing were probably, and paradoxically, very similar to those explaining Butterfield's reluctance to publish his work on Charles James Fox. Namier, it is true, became overtaken by other commitments, but looking back from 1951 he felt sure that he had been wise to wait, as he told Jack Plumb. 'I am jolly glad that I delayed so long publishing my Ford Lectures,' he reported; 'now with your finds and work, those of J. B. Owen for the Pelham period, and Aspinall,[46] for the period following mine, I shall be able to produce something far better and more complete than I could have done then.'[47] The lectures, then, were not a finished view, but they announced the death of Temperley's narrative about the origins of the cabinet, which Butterfield must have absorbed as an undergraduate, saw off Dicey on the eighteenth-century constitution, and contested the idea that George III perpetrated some form of royal revanchism.[48] As for party formation, Namier swept it under the royal carpet in an American metaphor that Butterfield might have admired but not approved. 'For America is, in certain ways, a

---

[44] John Cannon, *Aristocratic Century: the Peerage of Eighteenth-Century England* (Cambridge, 1984), viii.
[45] These are printed in Sir Lewis Namier, *Crossroads of Power: Essays on Eighteenth-Century England* (1961), 73–117. The lectures had been dictated to a temporary secretary which may account for their impermanence. Completely missing was one dealing with eighteenth-century bureaucracy; it proved beyond reconstruction except through the notes of John Owen and Christopher Hill: see correspondence between Lucy Sutherland, John Brooke and J. B. Owen, Sutherland MSS box 9.
[46] Arthur Aspinall (1901–72). Professor of Modern History, University of Reading. Prolific author including *Lord Brougham and the Whig Party* (1927), *The Early English Trade Unions* (1949) and *The Cabinet Council 1783–1835* (1952), but best known for extensive editing of correspondence and diaries, especially those of George III and George IV, and as co-editor of Aspinall and E. A. Smith (eds.), *English Historical Documents 1783–1832* (1959).
[47] Namier to Plumb, 26 Nov. 1951, Plumb MSS.
[48] Lewis Namier, 'The Ford Lectures', in Namier, *Crossroads of Power*, 73–117 at 77–8, 81–6, 97.

refrigerator in which British ideas and institutions are preserved long
after they have been forgotten in this country. In 1760 the King of Great
Britain was the actual head of the Executive, as the President of the
United States is today.'[49]

Butterfield already held a more expansive view of what an executive
might amount to and he sensed the negotiations and compromises in
which that executive must practically have become embroiled. He was a
long way distant from the thesis announced many years later in *George
III, Lord North and the People*, but an article in 1937 already homed in on
1779 as a crux, already saw Ireland as one of its contexts and revealed a
deep immersion in the Robinson Manuscripts. That archival work
formed one of at least three elements in a broadening understanding of
what party was about and what impact the American war had made on
it. A second element doubtless emerged in his teaching. Unlike Namier,
for whom undergraduates frequently seemed a species of pond life,
Butterfield listened hard to what their essays said and he pressed them
no less firmly for further information about the entire period of George's
reign. The failure of an historian to read history forwards rather than in
reverse became one of his central criticisms of the Namier approach for,
as he argued in his inaugural lecture as Professor of Modern History at
Cambridge in 1944, if the historian 'goes forward to the nineteenth
century from the eighteenth, (instead of looking back to it from the
present time), many of the angles will be placed more appropriately,
many of the lines will run in a different way'.[50] Parties plainly did exist in
the nineteenth century and they came from somewhere. And, third,
Hitler's war itself, and the long prelude of Nazism before it, lent little
support to a view of past politics that excluded the masses or one that
implied serene control from above at times of profound national crisis.
The conviction endured that more remained to be said than Namier had
announced in 1929 and 1930.

Much mutual misunderstanding between Butterfield and Namier
stemmed from neither of them having written the books they had
intended to write. Had Namier constructed *The Rise of Party* in time to
head off Butterfield's attack on him for failing to see the rise, and had he
not allowed much of his own case to be put by pupils and acolytes rather
than in considered expressions of his own, the fate of the late eighteenth
century between the end of the Second World War and the 1960s
might well have taken on a different aspect. As it was, heavy duties in

---

[49] Ibid., 78.
[50] H. Butterfield, *The Study of Modern History* (Cambridge, 1944), 30.

Manchester kept his head below the parapet until 1938 when, like any self-conscious supporter of the Jewish people, he had other things on his mind; and the war years produced defences of western civilization against the evils of the Third Reich[51] rather than a monograph on the 1760s. Butterfield, too, had his encounters with the cosmos during those charged years; but in his case they provided reflections that underpinned a series of instincts about the working of politics after 1760 that would come to fruition in his book on the later years of the North ministry and the place of the people – more realistically the Yorkshire Association – in sealing its fate. The appearance of that volume in 1949 probably carried the twentieth century in the grain of its argument, despite Butterfield's methodological recommendations of a few years before. Does it not bear the mark of 1945 when a war government got its come-uppance at the hands of the people? Lord North hardly played Churchill, but his supposed mauling by Butterfield's new forces of public opinion may have shown the beginnings of a party system that even a Churchill, especially a Churchill, could not subdue. '[T]he years 1779–80 see an unusual stirring of the waters as extra-parliamentary opinion not only finds a voice but discovers what *as yet* are irregular means of making itself effective at the very seat of government.'[52] There it is – the revealing 'as yet' that puts the train on its track and gives the story a whig engine.

Not among the best of Butterfield's books, *George III, Lord North and the People* strained to put the people back into Namier's arguments, but by using a focus and sources that Namier himself might have used, rather than breaking new ground entirely in the way that John Brewer, for example, would attempt a quarter of a century later.[53] The Yorkshire Association undoubtedly mattered in late eighteenth-century radicalism and Butterfield had no difficulty in persuading a reader to take it seriously. Yet even his own language sounded hyperbolic:

[Christopher Wyvill] and his collaborators launched upon the country, and set fairly and squarely on its course, the most important of the movements that have made the modern world. The Yorkshire Association bridges the gulf between Middlesex radicalism – Wilkite, undiscriminating, and half-disreputable – and the national movement of parliamentary reform. It assists the transition from eighteenth-century parties based on 'connection' to the modern kind of party

---

[51] Lewis Namier, *In the Margin of History* (1939); *Conflicts: Studies in Contemporary History* (1942); *Diplomatic Prelude* (1948); *In the Nazi Era* (1952); *Europe in Decay: a Study in Disintegration 1936–40* (1950).

[52] Butterfield, *George III, Lord North and the People*, 379.

[53] John Brewer, *Party, Ideology and Popular Politics at the Accession of George III* (1976). Butterfield's diaries show several meetings with Brewer, though he does not appear among the acknowledgements.

which is a matter of issues and principles . . . Below this surface drama [of king and aristocracy] is a movement long, slow and deep . . . We must conceive it not as a conflict but as a tide – one which throughout the country is bringing wider classes of Englishmen to intellectual awareness and a realization of the part they might play in politics.[54]

To these substantial claims he added a further, more strident one. Had North's ministry not responded to the crisis in the country in 1779 and 1780, the result would have proved cataclysmic to national stability. 'Our "French Revolution" ', runs the spectacular sentence, 'is in fact that of 1780 – the revolution that we escaped.'[55]

A problem faced by all such claims is the ease of their undoing. Let any historian of modern Britain assert that powerful contemporaries in whatever period stood in fear of their lives from revolution and it becomes a simple matter to show that many, often most of them, slept soundly in their beds. Butterfield wanted to show something far more subtle; but he hung the argument around a rather contrived series of happenings which happened not to frighten either the king or his advisers. Namier himself threw half a punch against this idea in his Romanes Lecture of 1952, in which he warned against the dangers of making the eighteenth century do service for the nineteenth; he found, he said, 'no trace of a party system'[56] in the earlier years of George III. The attempt of Robert Walcott to make the early years of the century look Namierite had already faltered and come under systematic attack, but J. H. Plumb believed that the post-1760 contentions remained beyond quibble in the light of Namier's lecture. Reading the text in advance of its delivery, Plumb was moved to speak like a voice of modernism about the 'old school' and their withering before the simple truth:

The lecture is a magnificent and authoritative statement which will become the basic theorem for eighteenth-century parliamentary politics. We may produce minor variations on a decade here or there but your analysis of party is the historical truth, and it can never be better said. The old school will have no answer to this. Do you think I might burn a copy of the 'Second Tory Party' in the Market Place whilst you are delivering the lecture in the Sheldonian?[57]

The *coup de grâce* came the following year, from a Namierite of sorts, certainly, but also and damagingly from one of the century's best historical minds and a man whose worst enemy could not describe as fanatical

---

[54] Butterfield, *George III, Lord North and the People*, 8–9, 282 (quotations reversed).
[55] Ibid., vi.
[56] Lewis Namier, 'Monarchy and the Party System', in Namier, *Crossroads of Power*, 231.
[57] Plumb to Namier (draft), n.d. [1952], Plumb MSS. The Sheldonian Theatre in Oxford is used for formal lectures of this kind. Keith Feiling, *The Second Tory Party, 1714–82* (1938), was Plumb's proposed tinder.

or disproportionate. Indeed the Ford Lectures of Richard Pares[58] marked in effect a majestic summation of the argument so far between a Namierism that had already showed its capacity for a thin and reedy intellectuality, on the one hand, and a developing critique that wanted to put ideas and passions, narrative and agency back into versions of the second half of the eighteenth century, on the other. Pares was brutally clear in his dismissal of Butterfield's opinions, both here and in his review of *George III, Lord North and the People* in the *English Historical Review*.[59] Many of the whig legends, which Butterfield seemed closer to recommending than uprooting, were put quietly to rest. George III had not been trying to implement Bolingbroke's Patriot King. He had not tried to implement anything. He was a rather sweet bumbler in Pares's memorable phrases: 'the spiritual ancestor of Colonel Blimp', 'a conscientious bull in a china shop'.[60] Equally, however, Pares left the eighteenth century full of significant political language which a modern student might helpfully consider. The recognition that contemporaries did not intend to talk about party, he appeared to be arguing, did not defend effectively against the case that it lurked inadvertently among the labels and persistent allegations that bedevil relationships within a changing community. There was still room here for the operation of Butterfield's instincts.

Even in 1953, however, there were signs of sclerosis in this developing argument that now would become misaligned, personal and bitter. The establishment of the *History of Parliament* project in 1951 set in cement something that Butterfield despised: Namierism would now arrive ready-mixed by the lorry-load. The idea for a parliamentary history had begun in the 1930s, as we saw in chapter 1, through the efforts of an eccentric parliamentarian, Josiah Wedgwood, who worked at the early volumes of such a history, financed by private money. The war put an end to the enterprise in the form that he had devised. But in 1951 the government agreed to return to his project by providing funding for the next twenty years, and in July Frank Stenton announced the new initiative at the Anglo-American Conference of Historians in London. In

---

[58] Richard Pares (1902–58). Son of Sir Bernard Pares (1867–1949), historian of Russia. Winchester, Balliol College, Oxford, and All Souls. Board of Trade during Second World War. Later contracted crippling illness that shortened his life. *War and Trade in the West Indies, 1739–63* (1936); *King George III and the Politicians* (Oxford, 1953).

[59] 'I do not share Professor Butterfield's belief that the growth of parliamentary reform associations in 1780 constituted a dangerous crisis or a revolution *manquée*; at least, there is hardly any evidence that it worried the king or Lord North.' Richard Pares, *King George III and the Politicians*, 199. Cf. *EHR*, 65 (1951), 526–9.

[60] Pares, *George III and the Politicians*, 67, 69, 71.

deciding to follow the path of 'prosopography' by providing mini-biographies of every member of parliament, the project became the apotheosis of state-sponsored modernism by taking 'analysis' (the modernist buzz-word) quite literally and applying its dictionary definition: 'the resolution or breaking up of anything complex into its simple elements'. Four main decisions gave the venture its shape: there would be biographies of MPs; there would not be biographies of peers – McFarlane's sticking point; there would be short periods of around forty years for each volume; and Wedgwood's unsatisfactory early volumes would have to be replaced. By 1953 work was underway on the first commissions. J. E. Neale had agreed to take on 1558–1603 and Namier had committed himself to doing 1754–1790. Bindoff[61] agreed to come in behind Neale and edit the early Tudor volume; and Namier persuaded two men he trusted to treat the periods either side of his own: Sedgwick for 1714–1754 and Aspinall for 1790–1820. The editorial board later came to 'tentative arrangements' with McFarlane, Roskell and Plumb, though only Roskell remained on board. Namier believed that the pixilated picture provided by hundreds of biographies would prove valuable as a work of sociology.[62] His confidence perhaps suggested a view of sociology from which most sociologists would want to dissent. No matter: he threw himself into the work and spent more and more of his time in London energized by the task. It killed him. Notwithstanding the labour and support of others around him – John Brooke, Lucy Sutherland and many others – the weight of the job would have broken any man. By 1958 he had begun to accuse everybody of letting him down with only 1,320 biographies written and 646 to go. 'It is pretty hard,' he whimpered to Sutherland.[63] It became harder still, of course, once the inevitable hospital stay came in August of that year with so many portraits still to write. He never saw the end, needless to say, and had been dead for a year before John Brooke brought the tally to a close in the summer of 1961.

Butterfield knew nothing of all this. His view did not concern Namier, for whom he always felt a real admiration, but the principle of the enterprise, with its stress on unpublished archives and its reduction of people's lives and souls to a list of material aspirations. His patience

---

[61] S. T. Bindoff (1908–80), son of a pub landlord in Sussex. University College, London; studied under the Dutch historian Pieter Geyl and later joined staff at UCL. Married Pollard's research assistant, Marjorie Blatcher. First Professor of History at Queen Mary College, London where he remained. 'A career remarkable chiefly for its uneventfulness' (Bindoff, quoted in *Oxford DNB*). Edited *History of Parliament* for the period 1509–58. One well-known book, *Tudor England* (Harmondsworth, 1950).

[62] Namier to Lucy Sutherland, 30 June 1958, Sutherland MSS box 9.   [63] Ibid.

snapped in the year of Suez[64] when, now Master of Peterhouse and tied down away from archives, he watched authors whom he regarded as second-rate jerry-building on Namierite foundations. Even an acute and knowledgeable commentator on these years would probably fail to spot the paragraph, if the text were set as a gobbet exercise, that finally made Butterfield see various shades of red and black. It lies embedded in John Brooke's seemingly inoffensive book on the Chatham administration published in 1956. 'To win mass support', the passage began,

parties must enshrine principles or represent interests, both of which are threatened or need to be advocated or defended. These conditions did not exist in the eighteenth century. There were no constitutional or religious issues to cause deep rifts in the nation as in the previous century . . . The unenfranchised classes, not yet herded into towns, were hardly aware that political action might be a remedy for their grievances, economic rather than political in their nature. There was no mass electorate and no need for party programmes. The story of party in the eighteenth century centres in Parliament rather than in the constituencies.[65]

It would later become Brooke's understandable complaint that not once but on four separate occasions this book suffered violence in print at Butterfield's hands. 'I can think of no young historian publishing a first book', he groaned, 'who has had to face such repeated criticisms from so distinguished a scholar.'[66] In fact he did not know the half of it. Butterfield had conceived a powerful animus against an intellectual position of which he took Brooke to supply a representative; and he found great difficulty in preventing personal enmity from riding on the back of it.[67] Fears arose also for the future of J. B. Owen, Namier's pupil, in the same year if his book[68] were to come Butterfield's way. Asked by Namier to review it for the *English Historical Review*, Plumb prudently decided, since *EHR* was an Oxford journal and therefore safe, to do it for the *Cambridge Historical Journal* and thus 'prevent it falling into undesirable hands'.[69] A second edition of *The Structure of Politics* in 1957 did

---

[64] Suez actually found its way into his forthcoming study of *George III and the Historians*, when he questioned whether the crisis (and by extension eighteenth-century crises) was simply about keeping out the Labour party or getting out the Tories: Butterfield, *George III and the Historians* (1957), 209.

[65] John Brooke, *The Chatham Administration 1766–8* (1956), 220. Cf. Pares in 1953: 'Party history in the eighteenth century is the study of men's: their friendships, their connections, their ambitions, their interests.' Pares, *George III and the Politicians*, 234.

[66] John Brooke, 'Namier and his Critics', *Encounter*, 24 (1965), 47–9, at 48.

[67] It needs saying that this enmity was later put to rest. Brooke visited Butterfield in 1965 and found him 'very friendly and we got on famously and I think we may have buried the hatchet'. Brooke to Lucy Sutherland, 27 Nov. 1965, Sutherland MSS box 11.

[68] J. B. Owen, *The Rise of the Pelhams* (1957).

[69] Plumb to Namier (copy), 27 Jan. 1956. The Cambridge enmity can be overdone as easily as the Oxford sympathy. Julia Namier's draft biography, reporting that Namier

nothing, meanwhile, to soften the lines of debate with the Prince of Darkness. When Namier came to Cambridge to receive an honorary degree in April 1957, Butterfield refused to have him at the Lodge,[70] fortified no doubt by the knowledge that Namier would rather sleep rough than with the Master of Peterhouse, but also by the article that had appeared or was about to appear in that month's *Encounter* which brought the entire discussion to a logical conclusion and, really for the first time, saw Butterfield's views declared with precision and *à outrance*.

'George III and the Namier School' was an article with none of Butterfield's normal emollience: it dealt with the Namier School in that school's own register. It contained two major stipulations: that Namier and his followers did not understand the depth of political sensibility in eighteenth-century England, and that they perversely employed a method designed to prevent them from discovering it. The first allegation concerned levels of awareness. Namier and his 'squadron' – Butterfield's favourite description in these years – looked only at contemporary conceptions of faction after 1760; but behind these short horizons lay territory little changed from the generation before and where party had flourished. As in their X-ray plates of 1761, Namierites located the body but lost the clothes in what Butterfield derided as a 'purely positivist attempt to describe party in the nude'. What else could you expect from people who thought ideas did not matter? After all, 'a great proportion of the history of party lies in the realm of thought'.[71] It also lay in change over time and time was what Namierites did not consider. 'It is not permissible', Butterfield wrote, 'to imagine that the England of 1760 is unique in the sense that *just here* the study of "structure" must replace other forms of history – *just here* the "narrative" method has been rendered obsolete.'[72] In June it was Romney Sedgwick's turn to be roasted in the *Cambridge Review*, despite his being 'accompanied by the roar of a disciplined squadron',[73] but only as prolegomenon to what

---

had, in old age, met a 'riot of abuse' at a seminar in Keble College, Oxford, occasioned embarrassment and denial among the faithful and she removed the incident from the printed version. Lucy Sutherland to John Bromley (copy) and reply, 16 Oct. and 25 Oct. 1970, Sutherland MSS box 9.

[70] Butterfield to Vice-Chancellor (copy), 11 Apr. 1957, Butterfield MSS BUTT 76/2. Namier was put up by Noel Annan who had recently become Provost of King's at the remarkable age of thirty-nine. See Julia Namier, *Lewis Namier*, 313.

[71] Herbert Butterfield, 'George III and the Namier School', *Encounter* (April 1957), 70–6 at 75.

[72] Ibid., 72.

[73] Letter for publication from Butterfield to editor of *Cambridge Review*, 8 June 1957, Butterfield MSS BUTT 76/2; it was slightly altered in the published form.

Butterfield himself called 'a full dress attack'[74] in his forthcoming book on *George III and the Historians*. In this, much his most powerful book on the eighteenth century, dismissed in an American review of recent literature as 'an essentially polemical work that contrives to combine much ill-tempered and irrelevant criticism with some perceptive suggestions',[75] Butterfield subjected not the history but the historiography to the penetration of time's arrow and showed how whig history had turned into *soi-disant* 'modern history', with success but at a price. Whig historians 'took ideological pretensions too much at their face value', a plausible accusation; but 'the modern school tend[ed] to drain the intellectual content out of the things that politicians do', with dereliction both to historical plausibility and to the role of history as a civilizing form of study. Certainly, whig historians proved cavalier about their sources and did not have access in their day to the wealth of manuscript evidence now available. One must not merely utilize such evidence, however, but also recognize its limitations and prescriptions. 'A man who wished to write the history of my College,' wrote the Master of Peterhouse, 'and tried to confine himself to the documents in the College Treasury, might too easily imagine that we were a body concerned only with the administration of money, buildings and other property.' In just the same way Namierites lost the larger picture in their endless transcriptions of private letters. He could admit, again, that the whigs' faith in the higher morality of English statesmanship had more charm than persuasion. Was the Namierite picture not itself equally superficial? 'Men do not support the government merely because they enjoy profits and places,' Butterfield insisted. 'Human beings are the carriers of ideas as well as the repositories of vested interests.'[76]

But Butterfield's case rested on more than method: it stood as a reminder that, if whig ideology had its negative moments, so did what he called 'Tory prejudice'.[77] Namier himself had already receded from some of his more reductive assertions and those sympathetic to Butterfield thought that more withdrawals would follow, not least

---

[74] Butterfield to Ross J. S. Hoffman, 29 May 1957, Butterfield MSS BUTT 76/2.

[75] J. Jean Hecht, 'The Reign of George III in Recent Historiography: a Bibliographical Essay', *Bulletin of the New York Public Library*, 70 (1966), 279–304 at 283. Among the Namierite squadron attacked by Butterfield, Hecht counted, apart from Namier himself, Pares, Brooke and Ian Christie, with Betty Kemp and Archibald Foord as escorts (282).

[76] Butterfield, *George III and the Historians*, 205, 210, 212. The squadrons inevitably surrounded him in this text. The Namier School was 'the most powerfully organized squadron in our historical world', 'a formidable squadron for any critic to have to face'. Ibid., 10, 203.

[77] Herbert Butterfield, 'George III and the Constitution', *History*, 43 (1958), 14–33 at 15.

because the Namierites sometimes saw their kind of history as a proleg-omenon to Butterfield's – a way of clearing away the scrub, as it were, so that more delicate plants could thrive. Dudley Edwards (not one of Dublin's more delicate plants) thought this way and sent an encouraging note from UCD at the beginning of 1958:

> For the Namiers, the bald sequence of events, duly analysed, should precede the higher history of Butterfield and Labrousse . . . Namierism is unlikely, in the long run, not to accept the reality of myth. Thereafter, admission to Namierism Inc. will necessitate passing an exam in Butterfieldism.[78]

Four years later, as though to echo the theme, an article appeared on George III with the startling subtitle 'a new Whig interpretation', com-pleting the *bouleversement* with a reflection that 'when all necessary deductions are made, and all anachronisms avoided, there still remains a Whig interpretation which rests upon objective facts and serious valu-ation of their meaning . . .' Butterfield's contentions about the signifi-cance of Bute and the plans of the king, it went on, 'cannot be brushed aside as non-existent, any more than as illegitimate'.[79]

These points and the tissue of argument that supported them unques-tionably told on the Namierite camp. Had Namier lived – he died in 1960 – there is no doubt that a full rebuttal would have come. Butterfield was meanwhile magnanimous: his radio obituary of Namier astonished Julia Namier in its level of praise.[80] Her husband's supporters found charity harder and won the argument by leaving Butterfield's name out of all their texts and indexes, a ploy maintained today more through ignorance than strategy. They had their god and god had written big books from the archives. Where were Butterfield's? The point was a painful one and was not lost on Butterfield himself during the nineteen years remaining to him after Namier's death. He had his reasons: histor-ians always do. The Vice-Chancellorship of Cambridge University left him exhausted and unwell in 1961; he had the college to run until his retirement in 1968; he fell seriously ill in 1971; he no longer had the strength and energy to carry his project forward. None the less *his* unwritten book – the second one in this story – gave away some of his ground. If he had ever written that life of Charles James Fox that he was supposed to have been working on since before the war, he could have shown, not merely asserted, the place of ideas and a blindness to

---

[78] R. Dudley Edwards to Butterfield, 9 Jan. 1958, Butterfield MSS 531/E9.
[79] W. R. Fryer, 'King George III, his Political Character and Conduct, 1760–84: a New Whig Interpretation', *Renaissance and Modern Studies*, 6 (1962), 68–101 at 69, 84.
[80] Julia Namier to Lucy Sutherland, 9 Apr. 1961, Sutherland MSS box 9.

self-interest in one of the period's most important players and demonstrated that a command of primary material could illuminate ideas and principles and not merely conceal them. Namier himself had said, after all, that a formidable reason for not writing *The Rise of Party* was that he would have to confront 'that bounder Fox'.[81] Critics asked why Butterfield did not confront him and make him central to a different narrative of late eighteenth-century Britain. Denis Brogan, who always thought Butterfield a prig despite the pleasantries printed in the latter's *Festschrift*, believed that a Methodist teetotaller could not find it in himself to spend years in the company of one of the century's most immoral rakehells.[82] More cynical observers simply took the view that Butterfield had never done the work and that, like his abandoned life of Harold Temperley, it was little more than a figment of ambition. But there is a coda to the story and it bears telling.

When the Butterfields' retirement cottage at Sawston was to be sold a few years ago, Peter Butterfield found some odds and ends and asked whether I would like to look at them before they disappeared. There were a few files and packets and, in the middle of the table, a large, dusty boxfile on the front of which Peter's father had written the single word 'Fox'. It was immediately apparent that any biographical project must live in this box and I bore it away. It contained no text: to that extent Butterfield's critics won the day. It did not contain the hundreds of record cards I wondered about. It held instead thousands – literally thousands – of paper dockets, most of them covered in the familiar tiny hand that Butterfield deployed in his note-taking, almost all of them quotations from primary sources illustrating the context of Fox from his early life (which had already been bundled for use) right up to 1792. Elastic bands enclosed the records of individual years in date order, sometimes with subject organization, sometimes not, sometimes (as with 1792) surrounding individual months of the narrative. Speaking with thirty years' experience of turning material of this kind into connected text, I think I can report that this single box contains a very large book, though one that would still have required considerable further research, not least in the archives that Butterfield tended always to shun. Why, then, did he hold back? A clue exists in a remarkable private letter Butterfield wrote to a former research student, now Professor Frank O'Gorman, in 1966. 'I personally always like to wait till other people

---

[81] A. J. P. Taylor, remarking on what Namier had said when Taylor asked why he had never written the book: review of Steven Watson's volume of the *Oxford History of England*, *Observer*, 2 Oct. 1960.
[82] Private communication from Professor Hugh Brogan, 13 Aug. 2002.

have published their books first,' he wrote. '[P]eople always condemn me for not having produced my proposed life of Fox ten or twenty years ago but I always think what a fool I should have been if I had done that.'[83] As always, he did not explain or elaborate. One way of glossing this remark, however, is suggested by the narrative we have been considering. Perhaps Namierism and 'the modern school' with its fighter-squadrons had to shoot one another down before Butterfield could feel the moment ripe. Or, in a different metaphor, perhaps, like a cataract on the eye of historiography, the evil had to harden before it could be lifted and sight restored.

For the moment soft tissue remained and Butterfield's own death in 1979 passed without that restoration of wider and deeper vision that he had made his mission. Namierism did attenuate all the same and take new forms. Even as early as 1957 Richard Pares suggested that he, for one, had become an ex-squadron leader when he vetoed a potential successor as editor of the *English Historical Review* on the ground that 'he is a devout member of the Namier School, and I feel some hesitation about handing over the Review to a member of any of the gangs – whether the Namier gang or the Trevor-Roper gang'.[84] Distinguished historians of the eighteenth century remained devoted to Namier's memory across two, even three generations – Romney Sedgwick (who had 'come so much under Namier's influence' that there was 'no hope of his ever shaking himself free from it'[85]), Lucy Sutherland,[86] Ian Christie, John Cannon and, in a third generation, the rising Jonathan Clark, who arrested the normally unshockable Geoffrey Elton by announcing in conversation that he was the new Namier.[87] On the Butterfield side of the argument, it seems that he won firm and significant supporters in his own research students, especially from John Elliott, John Pocock and Frank O'Gorman, and ammunition for his case from the generation of John Brewer and Linda Colley, while simultaneously becoming seen more and more as the progenitor of the very historical Toryism he had opposed, not least through a series of appointments to Fellowships in

---

[83] Private communication. I am most grateful for Professor O'Gorman's permission to cite this letter.
[84] Pares to Goronwy Edwards, 17 Dec. 1957, Edwards MSS 213.
[85] Denys Winstanley to J. R. M. Butler, 10 Feb. 1940, Butler MSS A1/147.
[86] William Roger Louis sees her applying Namier's 'conceptual framework' in her analysis of the politics and finances of the East India Company: see his introduction to the *Oxford History of the British Empire* (5 vols., 1998–9), vol. v, 34. Cf. Lucy Sutherland, *The East India Company in Eighteenth Century Politics* (Oxford, 1952).
[87] G. R. Elton in conversation with the author. It should be said that Elton remained a loyal supporter of Professor Clark's work both in public and in private.

Peterhouse such as those of Edward Norman, Maurice Cowling and John Vincent – all of whom, incidentally, would find the Tory-Namierite label inaccurate if not offensive.[88]

But our initial question concerned more than matters of academic lineage. It related to the relationship between these old and new constructions of the eighteenth century and the supposed demise of a whig paradigm of historical writing in the face of modernist criticism. Where does the story leave that question? What it seems to suggest is that Namier and his squadrons did indeed engage on the destruction of several aspects of whig legend, in particular the centrality of ideas and public language as explanatory instruments in history, the reliability and usefulness of secondary accounts of past happenings, and the place of grand narrative in constructing plausible descriptions of detailed, often chaotic and sometimes ill-natured manoeuvres by fallible human beings. All of these things had their lethal side, but perhaps most deadly of all was Namier's call for 'static' history. In the rejection of time itself, whiggery's entire impetus drained away because, out of the temporal journeys made by the agents under consideration, whig historians had built trajectory and plot. It was not simply that Namierites made available plots unattractive to whig sensibilities but that they eradicated the need, at least at one level, for plot itself. The tale, such as it was, was emphatically not one told by idiots, but the whole signified something close to nothing. It did so still more obnoxiously if one began with the view that history had to be conceived as a humanizing subject that laid the foundations among young people for an appreciation of citizenship and its obligations. Butterfield stood among those who wanted to see the study of eighteenth-century history function as a form of 'political education'.[89] To accomplish that objective it had to show statesmen to be better than crooks and wastrels, and to provide a story whose denouements would reveal improvement even when leadership had proved lacking. This did not make Butterfield a whig in any simple sense: his historical reputation rested, after all, on a rejection of any supposed 'technical history' that rested on whig prescriptions. But he remained a half-whig in a more complicated sense, 'poised precariously', as he once wrote in his private journal, 'between the whig interpretation and the Namierite interpretation'.[90] As he grew older, poised or not, Butterfield

---

[88] Stress on this aspect of the Butterfield legacy is placed by Richard Brent in his article on 'Butterfield's Tories: High Politics and the Writing of Modern British Political History', *HJ*, 30 (1987), 943–54; and Reba Soffer, 'The Conservative Historical Imagination in the Twentieth Century', *A*, 28 (1996), 1–17.
[89] Butterfield, *George III and the Historians*, 205.   [90] Journal, 7 Apr. 1963.

felt that the technical history of the eighteenth century was not enough and that preventing bad forms of it held less importance for the world than ensuring that history in Acton's sense as an illumination of the soul – stories of change and development across time – retained its vitality and purpose. Frank O'Gorman's retrospective question – why did we spend so much energy on those early years of George III's reign? – comes into better focus against this background. The history was never really about George III and Lord Bute and the Duke of Newcastle and the Elder Pitt; it was not even about that bounder Fox. At issue was the identity of the British state and an undertow of discussion among historians about what its defining characteristics and virtues should be taken to comprise. At stake, when not at issue, was political history itself and a series of values about what the task of the historian should be amid the swirling ideological currents of the twentieth century.

7 Ideological environments

All ages are ideological whether they admit it or not, all historians are political whether they feel committed or not, all cultural environments fashion their participants whether they know it or not. That said and acknowledgement made, is there not something specific in time and space about the political engagement of western intellectuals through the era of two world wars, the menace of totalitarian movements and the coming of the Cold War? One need not have in mind the agonies of a Heidegger or a Sartre; the conjecture might have importance at a much lower level of daily activity, even within so firmly an anti-intellectual group as English historians. It need not take the form of treatises. It might be a history textbook whose story screams political presupposition. It might be an historical monograph stained more subtly with its particular present in an observable way. It might be a notice on a faculty notice-board, like the following pinned up by one *Führer*, George Richard Potter of the University of Sheffield, while a better-known one entertained Neville Chamberlain at Berchtesgaden, Bad Godesberg and Munich. It runs thus:

Our historical class on INTERNATIONAL RELATIONS will be resumed at the University next Thursday, September 22nd, at 7.30pm prompt. During the coming weeks we shall consider together the relations of the Great Powers since 1919 . . . In addition to describing the course of world events since 1919, the rise of the totalitarian states, the failure of the League of Nations in the Far East, Africa and Europe, we shall try to analyse the diplomatic relations of the countries of the world with one another, the cause of the wars in China and Spain, the nature of the conflict in central Europe and the origins and implications of the present situation.

. . . It is my personal conviction that if there is any real meaning in, or adequate control of foreign powers by democratic countries, each of us must try to understand the course of events and contribute our instructed judgment to a solution of the problems that vitally concern us all.[1]

---

[1] Notice by Potter, undated but either 1938 or 1937, Potter MSS, Box 22.

The question that this document puts in my mind is simple. Can we imagine, making all allowances for context, a similar effusion from Freeman or Seeley? 'Only in our day', said Maurice Powicke in that tremulous year of 1938, 'has liberty been derided as an absurdity, and justice formally identified with the expression of political expediency, and reason made the tool of racial instinct.'[2] His despair leads to a larger question. Are there elements within this charged atmosphere of challenge to democracy by communism, fascism and the threat of atomic destruction that help explain why parts of the whig condition lapsed and why modernism found its mission so urgent in a battle against 'bias'?

This chapter will ruminate on that possibility by considering the political ambience within which English history became envisaged by Powicke's generation. The point does not lie in claiming that all whigs had one politics and all modernists another, or that the nineteenth century had no ideologies and the twentieth nothing but ideologies. The argument begins from three more reasonable contentions that have some *a priori* force. First, it assumes that writing history against a background of ideological heat will have deepened the modernist conviction that historical duty will lie in the direction of protecting the modernized past from prejudice (modernists, it will be recalled, do not believe themselves to have presuppositions; everyone *else* does) and raising the tone of historical argument to make sure that 'the facts' lead. Second, it is likely that the increasing assimilation of 'ideological' views within the academy after the Second World War will have posed a threat to the modernists' sense of themselves. More obviously, and finally, the presence of so much controversy about totalitarianism and the conflicts it placed in public imagination must have had its impact on the topics that historians wanted to write about and helped define what counted as relevance when 'we are in an age of ideologies & there are so-called loyalties above those of countries'.[3]

---

[2] F. M. Powicke, *History, Freedom and Religion* (1938), 36–7. These Riddell Memorial Lectures do not dwell on totalitarianism, all the same: to the extent that eternal verities intrude, they do so via quotations from Kant and Kierkegaard. As if to confirm the specificity of that year, David Chambers recalled in 1961 that 'my studies [of modern politics] stopped in 1938'. J. D. Chambers to George Bilainkin (copy), 9 Oct. 1961, Chambers MSS C1.

[3] J. E. Neale to Wallace Notestein, 30 Nov. 1956, Notestein MSS 544/1/6/536. As one example, consider the revival of 'authoritarian' figures in the British past during the era of the dictators, especially Laud, Strafford and Cromwell. I owe this last point to my research student, Paul Churchill.

Liberalism, socialism, Toryism

When H. A. L. Fisher looked back on whig historians in his Raleigh Lecture of 1928 he took the view that the whigs really had been Whigs: political progressives animated not by radical distempers but by what he called 'golden mediocrity', a commitment to a centrist understanding of political life which enabled them to write good history despite their enthusiasm for Gladstonian or Liberal Unionist causes.[4] The problem with that view is that it not only portrays the contemporaries of Stubbs and J. R. Green as more dispassionate than their works suggest is plausible, but that it also makes it impossible to see Stubbs, a lifelong Tory, as a whig at all when John Burrow has given us excellent reasons for counting the bishop as a central figure in whig historical thought.[5] So it makes sense to begin instead with the assumption that the story of historical whiggery escapes any over-determination by the history of the Liberal party. On the other hand, it seems hard to dodge the implications of two other contentions about that assumed relationship. It is indeed undeniable that the whig historians enjoyed their greatest moments among a clerisy dominated by Liberal values. It is no less obvious that Liberal politics suffered asphyxiation after 1918 at the hands of a newly powerful Conservative party and an urgent Labour movement. By 1939 many of the ground-assumptions made by Victorian historians about their own polity found little fit with a National Government responding, or failing to respond, to the challenge of Hitler and the threat to western civilization, as they often saw it, from Moscow. Even the most liberal among them had to retune their strings to find the correct register in which to consider the lessons of history. Butterfield was not alone in drawing parallels between Hitler and Napoleon – a favourite pastime of his in the 1930s – and his little biography of Napoleon published in 1939 drew from the self-proclaimed Whig, G. M. Trevelyan, the far-from-golden thought as war broke out across Europe that 'the Jacobins did much to originate the Fascist-Bolshie-Nazi form of govt and Napoleon much to confirm it . . .'[6] Even with its changes of key, however, liberalism

---

[4] H. A. L. Fisher, 'The Whig Historians', *PBA*, 14 (1928), 297–339 at 326–7. There is little of Butterfield's animus here. 'We know whence we have come and we are made to feel whither the forces of the time are taking us,' he writes of Macaulay. 'Macaulay revels in exhibiting the significance of the transitions which he recounts, as his wide knowledge of the later history of England enables him to do in an instructive and illuminating way' (314).

[5] John Burrow, *A Liberal Descent: Victorian Historians and the English Past* (Cambridge, 1981), 126–51.

[6] G. M. Trevelyan to Herbert Butterfield, 5 Dec. 1939, Butterfield MSS BUTT 531/ T126.

by no means exhausted the possibilities for twentieth-century historians, and for every Trevelyan or Pollard or Fisher or Gilbert Murray who cleaved to liberalism, one can cite a Tawney or Cole[7] or Clapham or Helen Cam, whose inspiration came from the world of labour and socialism, or 'social democrats'[8] who drew inspiration from an intellectual radicalism that found its best historical embodiments in Lawrence and Barbara Hammond and H. N. Brailsford, or a group of more elusive Tories who sometimes look like bad-tempered whigs from a distance but who wanted to say something rather different about society, the state and national destiny.

Whatever its discordant tunes, this generation took its libretto from war and its evils: not the Second World War but the First, for it was there that liberalism ran into crisis and dissolution. Part of the difficulty for English intellectual Liberals in 1914 lay in their loathing for Tsarist Russia as an embodiment of autocracy, their suspicion of 'secret diplomacy' about which E. D. Morel and others had educated them, and a widespread admiration for Germany which the next few years would throw into confusion. A few weeks after the beginning of hostilities, Albert Pollard, a party Liberal of the clearest stamp, tried to hold onto the faith about a Germany which this war would not touch, despite the efforts of that 'unspeakable ruffian' Bernhardi and the historical school of Heinrich von Treitschke. 'A great defeat for them', he trusted, 'would mean a revival of the older Germany of Schiller, Goethe, von Ranke etc and also a proper Parliamentary and responsible government.'[9] The young Butterfield, at grammar school throughout the war, imbibed the same lesson. He recalled in 1947 his feelings about Germany in those days.

Perhaps because I studied in the outlandish north, perhaps because I read historians who were out of date, perhaps because one tends to be fed at school with the historical teaching of an earlier generation, I was brought up on the view that Germany was the home of liberty & that the freedom of Englishmen was the effect of the German side of our heritage. All our liberty and democracy went back to primitive Teutonic freedom. Our very parliament was the product of the Germanic elements in our history.[10]

---

[7] G. D. H. Cole (1889–1959), son of Cambridge jeweller. St Paul's and Balliol College, Oxford; Prize Fellow at Magdalen College from 1912. Fabian, Gild Socialist and theorist of modern socialism. Reader in Economics, Oxford, from 1925. *A History of Socialist Thought* (5 vols., 1953–60); Cole and R. W. Postgate, *The Common People* (1938).

[8] See Peter Clarke, *Liberals and Social Democrats* (Cambridge, 1978). The Hammonds and H. N. Brailsford fall most obviously into this category among historians.

[9] Albert Pollard to his parents, 13 Sep. 1914, Pollard MSS Box 4.

[10] Herbert Butterfield, 'I suppose it is true to say . . .' (1947), Early Writing, Miscellany.

It was hard, having been taught that Germany was the home of true civilization, to be made to turn round and regard the Germans as monsters, and Butterfield for his part, never did turn – a decision that held major consequences for his understanding of and reaction to Nazism. As with so many of his generation, the First World War worked as a crux in his imagination so that, as we turn the pages of his highly original book on *The Statecraft of Machiavelli*, published in 1940, we sense two time-frames operating side by side: 1494 sits next to 1914 and brings similar thoughts to mind. 'The consciousness that the year 1494 had opened the gates to disasters which had tormented Italy ever since was a great incentive to historical inquiry and political analysis in other people beside Machiavelli; and the country seemed moved, as we were moved after the war of 1914 to enter upon a more intensive self-examination.'[11] Unlike most of his Liberal contemporaries, however, Butterfield resisted the call to express that self-examination though a commitment to the League of Nations.

Liberal opinion among historians and students of the international system bifurcated sharply about the future after Versailles and the establishment of the League. One fragment employed a new form of whiggery to underpin the old: it invented its own *Zeitgeschichte* with the intention of displaying German guilt for starting the war and showing how the Peace Conference had to be seen in a European focus that itself was the outcome of an evolving history of enlightenment since the Congress of Vienna. George Peabody Gooch and Harold Temperley (both impeccable Liberals), whose *British Documents on the Origins of the War* began to appear from 1927, confirmed the high-mindedness of the British. The second project, a history of the Peace Conference, rested on a need to silhouette the League as a great – indeed the only – resource against another decline into Great Power diplomacy and arms races. Its editor felt the weight of the moment, but when he looked back to Acton's famous letter to contributors to the *Cambridge Modern History*, he felt that the world no longer allowed the luxury of even-handedness.

In his instructions to the Cambridge Modern History Lord Acton suggested that the account of Waterloo should be such as to satisfy Belgians, French, British and Prussians . . . Such impartiality, if possible in the past, is impossible in the present. But contributors should aim at the international point of view and regard the Conference not from Washington or London but from Geneva – where for the first time in world history a permanent world organization will be established.[12]

---

[11] Herbert Butterfield, *The Statecraft of Machiavelli* (1940), 27.
[12] Harold Temperley, 'Suggestions to Contributors', n.d. (1919), copy in Webster MSS 1/ 3 f.30. The work appeared as Temperley (ed.), *The History of the Peace Conference of Paris*

Here was the milk of the gospel. Historians had been part of the international experiment from the start – 'thick as bees' at Versailles, in Webster's evocative phrase – with Wilson, Foch and Masaryk, all members of the professoriate,[13] representing the primacy of academic judgement as much as their national governments. The task lay in lifting minds above the common hatreds of the moment and in pointing the way to a fresh future. In doing so they invigorated a familiar past with the new lessons, making the settlement of 1814–15 look like a failed attempt at Wilsonianism with only Canning, as usual, absorbing the right lessons, and Wellington, as usual, behaving like a 'born fool'.[14] At home the same impulse enhanced Trevelyan's admiration for Grey of the Reform Bill for his wisdom, his balance, his prudence, his being so very unlike Lloyd George, and reinforced E. D. Simon's conviction that 'the story of 1830 to 1930 in England is a magnificent and heartening example of successful democracy'.[15]

Yet some Liberal historians showed a more sceptical cast of mind in the changed political conditions of the 1920s (and not only in the

(6 vols., 1920). It identified the origins of the war in 1688, as though to salute the whig gods, and proclaimed the new peace 'a great constructive experiment . . . Guilty nations have been punished, and war, which was previously regarded as justifiable, is henceforward looked on as a crime.' Vol. I, xxiii, xxx. Cf. Charles Webster and Harold Temperley, *The Congress of Vienna, 1814–15 and the Conference of Paris, 1919* (1923). By 1923 Webster's tone had changed in his inaugural lecture on taking the Wilson Chair at Aberystwyth, whose audience learned that 'the Historian must cultivate a far more impartial attitude towards events than he has hitherto managed to achieve'. *The Study of International Politics* (Cardiff, 1923), 21. This involved ridding international history of 'national bias' as he believed Adolphus Ward and George Gooch had succeeded in doing (21–2).

[13] Woodrow Wilson had been Professor of Jurisprudence and Political Economy at Princeton and President of the University from 1902 to 1910. Foch held the Chair of Military History at the *Ecole supérieure de guerre* for four years before the turn of the century. Masaryk had been a professor of philosophy at Prague between 1882 and 1914. American historians beyond Wilson embodied this mood, with Jameson urging inclusion of Germans in the International Congress of Historical Sciences and Charles Haskins complaining about Keynes's *Economic Consequences of the Peace*, which was only read in the USA, he said, 'because of the non-economic chapters, which are misleading if not dishonest'. J. Franklin Jameson to Webster et al., 8 Jan. 1923, Webster MSS 1/6 f.2; Charles Haskins to Webster, 5 Oct. 1920, ibid., 1/4 f.61.

[14] Temperley to Webster, 6 Apr. n.y. [1924], Webster MSS 1/7/25. Webster, no less an expert on the period, assured the League's British champion, Lord Robert Cecil, that parallels of failure should not be employed now when conditions were so different. '[T]he experience of 1815–22 demonstrates clearly to my mind that an association which depends merely on the personal connections of one or two men is doomed from the outset. The inevitable reaction against their personalities would be in itself sufficient to destroy any chances of success. *And now it is possible to go further.*' Webster to Cecil (draft), n.d. [?Aug. 1921], Webster MSS 1/5 f.18 (emphasis added).

[15] G. M. Trevelyan, *Lord Grey of the Reform Bill: being the Life of Charles, Second Earl Grey* (1920), vii–viii; E. D. Simon to R. C. K. Ensor, 2 Feb. 1938, Ensor MSS box 48.

emblematic texts of *Eminent Victorians* and *The Economic Consequences of the Peace*), over that 'celebrated mare League of Nations by Uncle Sam out of Holy Alliance', as C. H. Firth described it.[16] Butterfield strove harder than most, albeit privately, to contest a comfortable whig smugness that turned all modern history into a linear trajectory leading inexorably towards the League and post-war internationalism.[17] We find the same effort in his monograph on Napoleonic diplomacy wherein the Great Powers have personalities of their own whose interactions prove as troublesome, contingent and as vulnerable to misperception as do human ones.[18] As for Namier, his cosmopolitan liberalism, if he ever had any, did not blind him to the realities of world politics and there is a grim pleasure in his contempt for all that the League stood for. The pleasure had a self-conscious Jewish tinge in one who knew perfectly well that his Jewishness was an issue in the minds of his contemporaries. Anti-Semitism in English academic life had told against him in Oxford where he had been denied a Fellowship. Left to Pollard, it would have told against him again when the Manchester Chair became available in 1931.[19] Though he professed never to have been a Zionist in an ideological sense, his connexion with Chaim Weizmann during the 1930s,[20] after he had been London political secretary to the Jewish Agency for Palestine between 1929 and 1931, inevitably placed his thinking about international politics within that frame. Writing against this background and the trauma of the Blitz in 1940, he simultaneously distanced himself from Anglo-Saxon stupidities about the League and saw them as redolent of Jewish ones:

The League was to cure humanity and lead it into better ways. It was an expression of the morality and idealism of the Anglo-Saxons and of what it

---

[16] C. M. Firth to Webster, 2 May 1921, Webster MSS 1/5 f.13.

[17] Butterfield, ' . . . not have taken a shorter cut' (1930), in Early Writing, Miscellany.

[18] Herbert Butterfield, *The Peace Tactics of Napoleon* (1929), 47. '[F]our powers arise, like four shapes looming through a mist. Each has its peculiar countenance as it sets itself to meet France, for each is a personality. So everything is ready for the next scene . . . and we have all the elements of what the novelist would call a "situation".'

[19] 'Namier is a brazen pot, a Jew of the Jews, and the worst bore I know.' Pollard to E. F. Jacob, 25 Nov. 1930, reviewing possible candidates for the Chair, Pollard MSS, box 6b. I owe this citation to Professor David Hayton who most generously shared with me his work on Pollard.

[20] He acted as political adviser to Weizmann and became close to him. The relationship stopped dead when Namier was baptized into the Church of England after the war: he found himself cut outrageously by Weizmann in a chance meeting at the Athenaeum. Weizmann told Isaiah Berlin that he took Namier's 'conversion' as 'some form of public renegadehood' and they never spoke again. Material from a dictated note by Namier, *c*. 1930, on his connexion with Zionism; Berlin's account of the rift in Berlin to Lucy Sutherland, 18 Sep. 1961 and Julia Namier's memory of the Athenaeum incident in a letter to Sutherland, 7 Oct. 1961: all in Sutherland MSS, box 9.

means to suffer of neighbours and disputed borderlands. (Ulster alone knows it). [T]here was shrewdness and self-deception, the will to do good and the wish to have it cheap; a vast amount of humane feeling, confused thinking, and doctrinaire impatience.
The Anglo-Saxon mind, like the Jewish, is inclined to legalism.[21]

The blurredness identified by Namier appeared the more fuzzy for most historians in a decade afflicted by new certainties, moreover. The time when the English intelligentsia was monolithically Liberal or Liberal Unionist had passed; and the custody of whig or counter-whig views of English history now rested as much in the hands of socialists and visionaries, on one side, and hard-bitten Tory cynics, on the other. A Liberal historian such as Ramsay Muir might protest that Liberalism was surviving in a new form as the third point of a political triangle, with its own space and status and a distinctive high-mindedness in face of fascism.[22] They might put their faith in the clean politics of Viscount Grey and the uplift of the League of Nations Union, as with Gilbert Murray. But there was no disguising the degree to which the two decades after 1919 brought a stratified class society, industrial dislocation and demands for a politics of action along a line of impatience from Oswald Mosley to John Strachey and whose tendency would far outrun the capacity of Liberals to follow.

Assuredly, that intellectual and political environment did not have its origins in the war. Ever since the appearance of translations of the more fundamental elements of Marx's thought in the 1880s, and in particular through the development in Germany of a new school of economic history with Gustav Schmoller at its head,[23] the pioneers of an analytical history resting on an examination of economic conditions and the fate of all sections of society, not just elites, made themselves felt in Britain.

---

[21] Lewis Namier, 'After Vienna and Versailles', in Namier, *Conflicts: Studies in Contemporary History* (1942), 28–9.
[22] Ramsay Muir (1872–1941), Professor of Modern History at Liverpool University, had a dual career as academic and political activist for the Liberal party. His political side can be followed in Michael Bentley, *The Liberal Mind 1914–1929* (Cambridge, 1977), 177–9, and Michael Freeden, *Liberalism Divided: a Study in British Political Thought 1914–1939* (Oxford, 1986), 131–7. Evocative among his historical works is his *Brief History of Our Own Times* (1934; 3rd edn, 1940) and especially its epilogue on the period after 1933: 'the sanctity of treaties and agreements between nations, which is the only foundation of security in international relations, was cynically disregarded by the totalitarian States. If this ugly reaction towards mere barbarism were allowed to triumph, the essentials of a civilized way of life would be destroyed; the slow advance of centuries would be undone; and the world would relapse into the conditions of the jungle.' Muir, *Brief History*, 299.
[23] For the impact of these developments in England, see Alon Kadish, *Historians, Economists and Economic History* (1989).

Paralleling the emergence of now-familiar political organizations such as the Social Democratic Federation, the Fabian Society and the Independent Labour Party, the rise of a thoughtful critique of contemporary historical preoccupations by the elder Toynbee, the Webbs, the Hammonds, William Cunningham, R. H. Tawney, G. D. H. Cole and a younger generation including J. H. Clapham, R. C. K. Ensor and his friend Richard Pares[24] had already made available an alternative approach to the history of British society and politics long before the war impinged. Much of that writing sat fairly comfortably with the whig interpretation of history. It shared the mood of progressivism that had always infused radical Liberals; its concern for the underprivileged in society did not conflict with Whig compassion; its willingness to think in long chains of development provided explanations that have a whig feel for all their difference of terminology and range of subject matter.

Tawney's picture of the agrarian problem in the sixteenth century, published in 1912, might stand as exemplar. If its content contained much to irritate whigs, its fundamental shaping of the narrative derided the 'shallow view which has no interest to spare for the rivulet because it is not yet a river. Though many tributaries must converge before economic society assumes a shape that is recognizable as modern, it is none the less true that in the sixteenth century we are among the hills from which great waters descend.'[25] Here was Freeman in a motor car. The universe inhabited by liberals did require, however, that sections and strata within society should find their place in a history that displayed structure only as an adjunct to story, and that those sections should understand that the past and future improvement of English society would have its roots in an acceptance of the social organism and the interdependence of its various parts. By no means all socialist history met this requirement over the decades to come. It wanted to fasten on subaltern social groups, as Tawney fastened on the English peasantry, and to read their miseries or triumphs as owing something to social misalignments and human evil, replacing organicism with a language of exploitation, on the one side, and rebellion on the other. Tawney could lyricize as much as any nineteenth-century whig about 'the crude barbarities of tramp ward and workhouse'; but he wanted also to insist that 'those who tramped and toiled, who sat in stocks and were whipped from town to town, were not the victims of trade depression or casual unemployment, but peasants thrown onto the labour market by the

---

[24] The young Pares ran a Workers' Educational Association class on Thursday evenings in Oxford: Richard Pares to R. C. K. Ensor, 14 Feb. 1936, Ensor MSS box 46.
[25] R. H. Tawney, *The Agrarian Problem in the Sixteenth Century* (1912), 403.

agrarian revolution'.[26] That view could not readily adjust to the curved but continuous narratives emanating from a Freeman or J. R. Green. Above all, these socialist or *ouvieriste* histories implied the presence of theory as an inevitable device, not only in the author but in the choice and treatment of the subject being studied, throwing light where whigs had left shadow by going beyond a reiteration of what contemporaries said to an analysis of the context and framework of assumption in which they said it. 'The supreme interest of economic history lies', according to Tawney, 'in the clue which it offers to the development of those dimly conceived presuppositions as to social expediency which influence the actions not only of statesmen, but of humble individuals and classes, and influence, perhaps, most decisively those who are least conscious of theoretical bias.'[27] That is the sharp end of the critique: theoretical bias of which its practitioners remain oblivious. Whig history – with its overt-nesses and givens, its willingness to take the world as it found it and lack of curiosity over whether its found world were a real one – had no room for a view of the past that seemingly wanted to look for seamy sides in the history of England and redescribe its uplift in ways that made great men appear unconsciously complicit in social injustice.

For all these important pre-war intimations, the war, when it came, threw them into starker relief for those on the Left, at least in retrospect when it marked a threshold for the British working class. Writing in 1937, A. L. Morton reflected in his popular *People's History of England* on the pointlessness of the conflict and its ominous message from St Petersburg. 'The War decided nothing,' he said, 'though it changed many things. It left unsolved all the major assumptions of Imperialism and added a quite new contagion, that between the world of capitalism and the world of socialism, in the form of the first workers' State . . .'[28] For those sympathetic to this view the police strike in the autumn of 1919 appeared more significant than the proceedings at Versailles. In the wake of Lenin's inspirational movement in Soviet Russia, the tone of English socialist historians hardened as history showed, to their satisfaction, the truth of what socialists had been saying for fifty years: capitalism was an eradicable disease; left unchecked it produced war and fascism; the past pointed the way to working-class power quite as surely as liberals thought it pointed to the League of Nations.

Among the young of the 1930s this message obtained maximum impact in a world now seemingly driven by ideological division. 'Everybody going

[26] Ibid.
[27] Ibid., vii.
[28] A. L. Morton, *A People's History of England* (1938), 521.

in academic circles is becoming either a Fascist or a Communist,' it seemed to Richard Pares, the socialist of 1930.[29] Thinking back on Pares's career – the distinguished imperial historian, professor and Ford Lecturer – these early enthusiasms seem the product of a foreign age; and that is a phenomenon readily replicable. So Nottingham's Professor of Economic History, J. D. Chambers, a ferocious critic of Marxism, recalled the 1930s in some embarrassment as the period when his sister Jessie (of D. H. Lawrence fame) would drag him out on demonstrations against the iniquities of capitalism. Better still, consider this moment of historical communion between two fellow-travellers in a private correspondence of 1936:

I think there is basic struggle between feudality & the emergent bourgeoisie underlying the Wars of the Roses, tho' most of the actual fighting was done by baronial factions (broadly – Yorkist = bourgeoisie; Lancastrian = feudality) . . . and I disagree with MacFarlane [sic] in regarding the political role of the bourgeoisie as being of far greater importance between 1450 and 1470 than in the reign of Henry IV when, in my opinion, the dominant issue is the struggle of the baronage against the Crown supported only by a very small section of the bourgeoisie, tho' the period of equilibrium at the end of the reign is the product of the gradual rallying of the bourgeoisie to the side of the Crown after the chaos created by the baronial struggles of 1403–1408.

This is Rodney Hilton writing to Christopher Hill? Not at all. It is the newly graduated Edward Miller sharing insights with his friend Jack Plumb.[30] Both of them in later life would have wanted to forget such an exchange, but it deserves its place as a marker in 1930s' assumptions that were very common and need to to be held in the mind if so ideological a decade is to make sense.

Yet, beyond the excesses of youth and a core of individuals associated with the new Communist Party of Great Britain, founded in 1920, how many mature historians in inter-war Britain went down this road? We readily overstress the permeability of the English intelligentsia in general and historians in particular to ideas from outside the culture in which they had been brought up. Basil Willey recalled this period in his autobiography and knew that he ought to make it sound a cauldron of ideological issues.

But of the major corrosives of the century, of Marx and Freud for example, hardly more than a *soupçon* had as yet trickled through into our fool's paradise . . . We none of us looked instinctively, and primarily, for Freudian or sociological explanations of writers or their works; ideas, theories, and works of art, were

---

[29] Pares to Wallace Notestein, 2 Feb. 1930, Notestein MSS 544/1/6/581.
[30] Edward Miller to J. H. Plumb, 17 Sep. 1936, Plumb MSS.

supposed to live and move and have their being in a world of their own. They influenced each other but it was not taken for granted that all were epiphenomena, derived from and determined by underlying psychological, historical and social forces.[31]

Thus unaware, Willey could cheerfully write about the relationship between literature and what he called 'the background' to a century's literature[32] without any constipation over the meaning of a 'background' and the relationship it bore to its foreground. It turned out that he did not need to frame his discussion in a whig way. But *any* whig way would need that same breeziness. If things were not as they seemed but rather something else entirely into whose terms they required translation before they could be understood, then how could one be expected to do history at all? The whig's horse ran lame at precisely the point that the socialist's broke into a canter.

For much of the inter-war period neither horse showed much promise. Labour history often proclaimed nothing more radical than a wish to see ordinary people brought back into the narrative of English experience. Max Beer's history of British socialism brought a continental enthusiasm to Britain's post-war situation in which Beer saw 'social difficulties and weltering movements which are visibly coming to a head'; but most indigenous labour history talked in a more relaxed way about the need to educate the working man into looking back as well as forward as he prepared himself and his class for the responsibilities of government – the more so after Ramsay MacDonald's ill-fated administration in 1924.[33] Hints sometimes worked their way into the serious historical work of the period. It is hard, for example, to read Helen Cam's essays dating from this time without becoming aware of a well-tempered sympathy for democratic advance resting on economic change, whether in her celebration of how much the 'balance of economic and political power' had been taken out of the hands of the landed aristocracy, or in her deciding how soon it is reasonable to begin discussing the rise of

[31] Basil Willey, *Cambridge and Other Memories* (1968), 23.
[32] Basil Willey, *The Seventeenth Century Background: Studies in the Thought of the Age in Relation to Poetry and Religion* (1934); *The Eighteenth Century Background: Studies on the Idea of Nature in the Thought of the Period* (1940).
[33] Max Beer, *A History of British Socialism* (1919), ix; G. D. H. Cole, *A Short History of the British Working Class Movement 1789–1925* (2 vols., 1925), vol. I, v: 'Nothing seems to me more important than this – that, as the working class grows towards the assumption of power, it should look back as well as forward, and shape its policy in the light of its own historic experience.' The proofs of Beer's volume were corrected by the Oxford Fabian socialist R. C. K. Ensor, who produced his own volume for the *Oxford History of England* fifteen years later: R. C. K. Ensor, *England 1870–1914* (Oxford, 1936).

capitalist modes of production.[34] But despite the immensity of 1931 as an economic threshold and its suggestion that the end of capitalism beckoned, even a *parti pris* witness such as Christopher Hill[35] testifies that no compelling historical work containing Marxist analysis appeared before 1938 – again the fateful year – when his own reporting of the work of Soviet historians began to appear in the *Economic History Review*[36] and when Morton's *People's History* enjoyed wide distribution under the aegis of Victor Gollancz's Left Book Club. Morton's book, designed for working-class pockets and vocabulary, achieved its impact through its structure which left little to the reader in the shaping of the narrative. The first eight sections had the following titles: Tribes and Legions; The Growth of Feudalism; Feudal England; The Decline of Feudalism; The End of the Middle Ages; The New Monarchy and the Bourgeoisie; Origin of the English Revolution; The English Revolution. This catalogue of rigidity did not prevent Hill from describing the 150 pages on the sixteenth and seventeenth centuries as the best introduction available to the period.[37]

It was the anniversary of what Marxists called 'the English revolution' in 1940 that brought the most direct statements of Marxist intent and the crudest distillation of the Marxist message for English historians.[38] To quote the extravagances of those texts would raise a smile, for their coarseness and naivety now seem astonishing. But that is not the point. A seismic shift had taken place, not so much in the generation of Butterfield and Namier as in the next one, the cohort of Hill, Hobsbawm and Hilton. Though these became loyal to Marxism until at least 1956, others drifted in their wake persuaded of at least the need to present something that constitutional history did not offer: an approach to social history that would mean more than Trevelyan's now-clichéd definition and embrace all those people that history had heretofore left out, or so it was alleged. In fact the allegation brought with it its own cliché. Whig

---

[34] Cam in her collection of papers, *Liberties and Communities in Medieval England: Collected Studies in Local Administration and Topography* (Cambridge, 1944), 61, 222.

[35] J. E. Christopher Hill (1912–2003). Balliol College, Oxford and All Souls. Fellow and Tutor at Balliol from 1938; Master 1965–78.

[36] Christopher Hill, 'Soviet Interpretations of the English Interregnum', *EcHR*, 8 (1937–8), 159–67. He followed this with an article discussing the Soviet historian Arkangelsky, 'The Agrarian Legislation of the Interregnum', *EHR*, 218 (1940), 222–50. For his contentions about the late development of English Marxism as a vehicle of historical explanation, see his essay translated into French as 'L'oeuvre des historiens marxistes anglais sur l'histoire britannique du XVIe et du XVIIe siècles', *La Pensée*, 28 (1950), 51–62.

[37] Hill, 'L'oeuvre des historiens Marxistes', 56.

[38] See in particular Christoper Hill (ed.), *The English Revolution, 1640* (1940).

history had not excluded the people but instead had made them part of an imposing edifice of law within an evolving polity. Constitutional history at their hands turned into an indirect history of society rather than simply a history of government or the monarchy. What it did not include was, first, the spine of economy that Marxists wanted to stiffen in historical analysis; if whigs ever recognized sectionalism and a war of every man against every man in English history, they did not approve of it and turned history into a more uplifting story. Second, and above all, whig constitutionalism rejected the Marxist claim that the state itself must be regarded as a non-neutral and potentially baleful construction. Whigs wanted and needed to retain their conception of the state – that sublime connexion of people, governance and progress-in-ordered-civility – as a privileged sovereign, intrinsically benign. It had been many years since Bernard Bosanquet had argued in his *Philosophical Theory of the State* that the very idea of the state made it unthinkable that it could act badly.[39] Moscow, Berlin and Rome joined hands to show otherwise after 1918, and to that demonstration whig historians had little riposte other than nostalgia for better days and an Actonian instinct to avoid debasing the moral currency.

And what of Tories? They, too, had their nostalgias in this epoch of totalitarian tyranny, but often repined over different pasts from those celebrated by whigs or castigated by the Left. Their initial enemies after 1918 lurked within rather than without in all those forces of democratic destruction (what the liberals called democratic advance) that threatened civilization itself. A Tory view of the international system would remain hard to announce until Hitler made it respectable: one had to say something admiring about the League and collective security no matter how much cynicism was voiced privately.[40] But Tories felt relaxed in discussing socialism and the more damaging elements of liberalism at home, and they could see the various historical perversions on which they deemed these positions to rest. Their counter-whig tendencies had already come out strongly before the war in rubbishing a liberal historiography that saw progress in disintegration and enlightenment in degeneration.[41] Often the public attacks lost their edge in coded language and

[39] He had thought it 'barely conceivable', for example, that a state might 'actually order a theft, murder or the like'. Bernard Bosanquet, *The Philosophical Theory of the State* (1899), 300 and n.
[40] Algernon Cecil defended himself against an attack from Charles Webster thus: 'How happy they who see the world as a fertile field of progress! . . . God help the world if, as you say, the League of Nations is its only hope!' Cecil to Webster, 19 Oct. 1919, Webster MSS 1/3 f.52.
[41] The title of Lord Salisbury's celebrated attack on liberal social thought in 1883: see the *Quarterly Review*, 156 (Oct. 1883), 559–95; cf. Michael Bentley, *Lord Salisbury's World:*

the demands of Edwardian *politesse* between gentlemen. A wonderful private example survives among Pollard's papers. He had joined many other English commentators in writing a volume for the Home University Library – in his case an abbreviated history of England.[42] It fell into the hands of a close friend, the formidable Tory don C. R. L. Fletcher of Magdalen College, Oxford, and Fletcher's response to reading it produced the sort of letter that tests true friendship.

You have no-where faced the question of the possibility of educating the greater number of mankind up to any standard worth speaking of . . . And I suppose that you would rather that the old Europe went on, than that it were dominated by the present ideals of the Keir Hardie class – you would say 'better to have government by any amount of privilege than by the dead level of hopeless ignorance and stupidity.' That is the real answer which I, like all tories, have to give to all radicals; and it is Sir H[enry] Maine's answer[:] 'all real improvements, all knowledge, all reform, have originated with the few: the many are incapable of education & therefore of producing anything intellectual'. Democracy would be the most glorious thing in the world if it did not mean the dominion of ignorance over intellect; and that means pure materialism.

I should be altogether dishonest if I could pretend not to be sorry that the book was ever written; and what I regret most is that it came from All Souls. There is in it a sort of assumption that you have got your foot on the neck of *old* England . . . an almost Roman cocksureness of the future.[43]

In this remarkable letter of February 1913 so much of the Tory historical environment finds authentic expression and its visceral content held good until at least 1945.

It was around the same time that a less formidable scholar, the Tory buffoon Oscar Browning,[44] despaired of England altogether and left for

---

Conservative Environments in Late-Victorian England (Cambridge, 2001), 144–54. 'Degeneration' had become the theorists' buzz-word of the 1890s in the wake of hyper-Darwinist speculation and Max Nordau's much-discussed text, *Entartung* (Berlin, 1892), translated into English as *Degeneration* (1895).

[42] Albert Pollard, *The History of England: a Study in Political Evolution* (1912).

[43] C. R. L. Fletcher to Pollard, 5 Feb. n.y. [?1913], Pollard MSS, box 47. Fletcher (1857–1934) was connected through his mother, and his initials, with the artist C. R. Leslie. Eton, Magdalen College, Oxford and All Souls. Fellow and Tutor in Modern History, Magdalen College, 1889–1906. He had written his own *Introductory History of England* (5 vols., 1905–23) and later co-authored a *Short History of England* with Rudyard Kipling (1911).

[44] Oscar Browning (1837–1923). Suffered Cory's House at Eton; emerged emaciated, conceited and homosexual. Master at Eton and simultaneously Fellow of King's College, Cambridge. Dismissed from former in 1875 after relationship with George, later Viscount Curzon. University Lecturer in Cambridge from 1884. *Wars of the Nineteenth Century* (1899); *History of Europe, 1814–48* (1901), *History of the Modern World, 1815–1910* (1912). Forcibly retired in 1909.

Italy. While Mussolini's forces massed for their march on Rome in October 1922, Browning awaited them in the Palazzo Simonetti where he, too, caught sight of a Liberal friend's book – this time Charles Webster's history of the Congress of Vienna; and he, too, found in friendship the licence to exercise his views of true leadership and its relation to freedom:

> The great fault of your book is that you do not attempt to make or justify moral or political judgments which to me is the first duty of an Historian. To say that a man is a Tory or a Whig is to you a sufficient reason for praise or blame. You speak of liberating from Napoleon without an idea that his rule was the exercise of liberty and the breaking of it the imposition of a degrading servitude. To me Napoleon is not only the greatest man that ever lived except perhaps Julius Caesar but the BEST man that ever lived since Jesus Christ, an absolutely faultless character . . . It would have been a blessing for England and the world if N had won at Waterloo . . .
>
> I wish I could talk over these matters with you, do come to Rome for the purpose. Ever yours OB[45]

Of course these shrill pronouncements cover an extreme end of the Tory spectrum and one would read in vain respectable bastions of the Conservative party such as Sir Charles Petrie or Sir Keith Feiling or Sir John Marriott or Sir John Neale – those who simply 'look[ed] at everything . . . thro Ultra Conservative spectacles'[46] – if one looked for similar outbursts. They suggest some poles of the argument for all that: an anxiety about democracy (present and past) as a false god, a concern with effective and moralized leadership (present and past) and often a burning nationalism, a feeling about the English nation that inflamed their prose with genuine passion. 'Yes!' exclaimed Arthur Bryant, one of Toryism's most representative and significant authors, when Wallace Notestein accused him of nationalism. 'I am afraid I am an inveterate nationalist', he said; 'all Englishmen – whatever they say to the contrary! – are.'[47] That sense of nation in the Tory sensibility had a poetic character which no one announced as compellingly as Bryant in a vast array of publications that kept his views before the public. Purple his prose may have been, but Bryant was taken seriously by academics as well as the general reader – especially for his life of Charles II and the

---

[45] Oscar Browning to Webster, 12 July 1922, Webster MSS 1/5.
[46] Lord Sankey to Goronwy Edwards, referring to Marriott, 2 Sep. 1943, Edwards MSS 203 f.25.
[47] Wallace Notestein to Arthur Bryant and reply, 8 and 13 May 1954, Bryant MSS E2. Cf. Ernest Barker's *cri de coeur* during the war: 'I cannot help feeling the surge of

three volumes on Pepys[48] – and the undercurrent of his desperate love
for England is as inescapable as he believed England's history to be. 'We
cannot recreate the past,' he warned at the beginning of *English Saga*,
written through the depressing days at the beginning of the Second
World War, 'but we cannot escape it. It is our blood and bone. To
understand the temperament of a people, a man has first to know its
history.' In Bryant's hands that history then became a spun web of
England's associations, melting the abstract into the tangible, the constitutional into the visual. He continues in this way:

> The social conditions of that older England – Christian, rural, half-democratic
> and half-authoritarian – were the outcome of centuries of evolution. They
> combined diversity with great cohesion and strength. Within their strong but
> narrow confines the English had developed the capacity for compromise, ordered
> freedom and toleration which is the core of a modern democracy . . . They left
> posterity the English village and countryside, the parliamentary system, the
> genius of Shakespeare and Newton and the London of Wren.[49]

Now, seen from one point of view, these rhapsodies could appear
whiggish in their relentless mood of celebration, their triumphalism,
their Protestantism albeit of an Anglican and Erastian sort, and their
wish to educate the public in the greatness and singularity of the English
past. G. M. Trevelyan, no mean judge, certainly thought so and reserved
some of his warmest remarks for what Bryant was achieving in the
1930s. 'It is my hope and belief', he assured Bryant in 1935, 'that your
Toryism, without ceasing to be Toryism, is broadening into Englishry as
I hope my Whiggery has to some extent so broadened in the course of
years.'[50] When he worked out that Bryant was on Franco's side in Spain,
was a keen and sympathetic student of the Third Reich[51] and a by-no-
means enthusiastic convert to fighting Hitler in 1939, his ardour cooled
for a while until Bryant demonstrated his patriotism during the war; but

---

nationalism, and I am not ashamed of it – the surge of admiration for the people I have
been born among and lived with – a sense of gratitude for the way they behave and help
me to behave . . . I throw no stones at nationalism when I think of the nation I belong to.'
Barker to Michael Oakeshott, 29 Dec. 1940, Oakeshott MSS 10/3/1.
[48] Arthur Bryant, *King Charles II* (1931); *The England of Charles II* (1934); *Samuel Pepys*
(3 vols., 1933–49).
[49] Arthur Bryant, *English Saga* (1940), xi–xii.
[50] G. M. Trevelyan to Bryant, 1 Aug. 1935, Bryant MSS E3.
[51] In print this sympathy came out most clearly in *Unfinished Victory* (1940), whose earlier
drafts probably tended more obviously toward defending Nazism than the final version.
But Bryant used German examples to underline his anti-socialist message: 'Law-abiding
Britons who in the past have cast doubt on the genuineness of the popular German
dread of Bolshevism should try to conceive the effect on themselves if, in an hour of
famine and defeat, Manchester, Bradford, Hull, Birmingham, Nottingham, Plymouth,
West Ham and Bristol had in turn been sacked by the mob, and Buckingham Palace,

in fact Trevelyan's appreciation was in any case based on a category error. One man who saw the error was Butterfield's colleague in Peterhouse, the political theorist Ernest Barker, who found himself drifting away from what he called the 'abstract intellectualism' of the Liberals and towards Bryant's solution – 'the practical wisdom of the good, ordinary Englishman'. But when he read Bryant's account of 1688 with its illiberal suggestion that it was a disaster to have liberated the aristocracy from their duties to the state and the community, he saw readily enough in the month of *Kristallnacht* that Bryant's argument 'could be applied, in many ways, to the defence of Hitlerism and Italian Fascism'.[52] Quite so. The point is not that Tory historiography in these years amounted to conceding the claims of totalitarianism; it mostly did not. Rather it lies in the central difference between a Tory and Whig understanding of the English past. What Toryism commended was a particular relationship between individual, society and state and the strengthening of coherence within that relationship at the expense, if need be, of the individual's ability to choose his own destiny. For the whig historian the flowering of individual personality and genius stood at the centre of English history; it preceded and sometimes countermanded the claims of society. Clarifying the mind over this distinction helps formulate the very important point that it was possible to be an anti-whig historian without becoming a Tory one. It is a point of special moment, for example, in considering the place of, and the distance between, the two protagonists we saw battling over the eighteenth century and who so readily summarize the argument between modernism and its critics.

Modernist moments

Once again, Namier supplies the more straightforward case, partly because, as a Pole, he neither sought nor required the anchorage in British party politics or national ideologies to which most historians were prone. His Jewishness explains some of his urgency as a publicist for the Jewish case on behalf of a national home and it accounts for some of his aggression against Hitler's state, but that side of his mentality can be greatly over-worked. Namier was never a Zionist in his own estimation;

after the King's flight, tenanted for months by a gang of armed mutineers. That theoretical sympathy for Communism among the well-to-do and sheltered classes in this island . . . would have had little chance to grow under such circumstances.' Bryant, *Unfinished Victory*, 112.

[52] Ernest Barker to Bryant, 7 Oct. and 13 Nov. 1938, Bryant MSS E1.

he worked towards a limited end and, that end once achieved, he stopped. Even when we recall his Anglicanism in later life, moreover, we readily forget that both his parents were Catholics. His European vision was largely an eighteenth-century vision, as was Butterfield's. His nineteenth-century perceptions built on that base and saw the influence of intellectual elites more readily than pressure from below, producing along the way what Butterfield considered to be his, Namier's, best book on the revolutions of 1848.[53] Over one issue at least he approved of the exercise of modern public opinion and that was over Britain's entry into the war in 1939; it was 'the pressure of public opinion which prevented the miserable crew of Munichers from ratting a second time, as Bonnet would have wished to do', he thought, and he almost broke with Basil Liddell Hart after the war when the latter continued to insist that only German blunders had saved England from defeat, granted the relative strength of the two states in 1939/40.[54] His temperament took him closer to Toryism than Liberalism, aided by a passionate dislike of socialist politics, but his aversion to whig history, which was far more consistent than Butterfield's, stemmed more directly from questions of method than from the ideological content of any particular political doctrine. Namier distrusted all ideologies because he distrusted most ideas. Whiggery he thought a corrupt and silly collection of ideas because it produced a style of historical construction whose inadequacy he knew he could disprove from forensic evidence. He loathed whigs for the same reason that he loathed popular biography of the kind produced between the wars by Philip Guedalla, 'carriages clattering over cobbles & music drifting into the summer night'.[55] Namier was a Tory only in the sense that Cripps was a socialist, out of reaction against indulgence and in favour of austerity. How he would have been nauseated by Butterfield's broadcast obituary of him, congratulating the dead enemy

---

[53] Namier's '1848: the Revolution of the Intellectuals' had originally been printed as the Raleigh Lecture for 1944 in the *PBA*, 30 (1944), 161–282, though its length argues that it cannot have been delivered in that form. It was later reprinted as a free-standing volume with the same title. His point was that 1848 marked a '*révolution des clercs*' rather than of the masses, though he disarmingly conceded that '[t]here was undoubtedly also an economic and social background . . .' (162).

[54] In an angry exchange of letters in September 1949, on the anniversary of the beginning of hostilities, Namier had publicly expressed his 'awe' and 'gratitude' for the decision to fight: see his article, 'Ten Years Ago', *The Times*, 3 Sep. 1949. Liddell Hart retorted privately: 'I cannot see that there is any reason for "awe" about decisions taken in a state of illusion as well as hot-headedness by men who had got themselves into a hole by their persistent blindness. As for "gratitude", the outcome and the present state of the world make that term sound extremely ironical.' Basil Liddell Hart to Namier (copy), 3 Sep. 1949, Liddell Hart MSS 1/539.

[55] Namier to Liddell Hart, 19 Jan. 1952, Liddell Hart MSS 1/539.

on all the virtues Namier had striven to avoid, applauding his 'passionate depths, streaking his work with veins of poetry', condoling with him as 'a man whom many things in life had hurt' and – the last twist of the knife – upbraiding him for never having realized that he was 'master of all of us when he looked on the world with love'.[56]

Butterfield looked on the world with a love streaked with veins of cynicism, and what he made of the ideological world around him after 1919 poses more difficulty; it takes the argument about the nature of his mind deeper than can be dealt with here and diverts attention from the styles of modernism that he disliked. Fundamental to his case was the contention that liberalism was not the cure for western civilization but the disease, a contention that itself depended on a view of European history since the Renaissance and a conception of religion as the sole bulwark against barbarism. Properly understood, liberalism arose as a frame of mind within western Christianity and took its authentic meaning from that situation. But modernity had brought about a divorce between Christian liberalism and a new form whose stipulations became free-standing and a source of celebration in and for themselves. The result, for Butterfield, became the modern western state and the state carried in its bloodstream the bacilli of totalitarianism. 'I wish to show', he had reflected in an early private jotting, 'why I think that the mistakes of secular liberalism are themselves responsible for transitions that led to our present disasters; in other words, why, after liberalism had secularised itself out, the deified state and a modern totalitarian system were the inevitable next step in the process of paganisation.'[57] This original but perplexing hypothesis produced strange consequences in Butterfield's political thought which partly conditioned, partly stemmed from his historical work. Within the British political spectrum he remained a Liberal all his life: he voted Conservative only once, in 1945, when, finding himself with three votes, he voted for all the major parties simultaneously. Intellectually, however, he manifested a pervasive and sometimes aggressive anti-liberalism which undoubtedly played a role in his rejection of whig doctrines about how history should be understood. This anti-liberalism did not take him towards a Tory conception of the past of the kind discovered in Bryant because he remained committed to an ontology that contained only the individual personality, not 'society', not 'the state'. For Butterfield, collective representations produced communism and fascism and in order to protect the world from the latter he

[56] Butterfield, 'Sir Lewis Namier as an Historian', *The Listener*, 18 May 1961.
[57] Butterfield, 'Humanism, political liberalism, internationalism and humanitarianism . . .' n.d. [?early 1930s], 'Early Writing', Miscellany.

rejected the former. A little of this developing disposition flavours the *Whig Interpretation* of 1931 which undermines some of the secular gods he disbelieved in; it is more noticeable in his little book on *Napoleon* (1939), his analysis of *The Statecraft of Machiavelli* (1940) and the effusions of *The Englishman and his History* (1944), which later embarrassed Butterfield considerably, not because he did not believe them but because he thought that they made him sound like a Tory defending conservatism rather than whiggery.[58]

But then the Second World War shifted the life-experience of every mature historian working within its climate and made itself felt in texts from Frank Stenton's *Anglo-Saxon England* (1943) and Wilhelm Levison's Ford Lectures[59] (delivered in the same year but published after the war) to the post-war reconstructions of recent military and political history by John Wheeler-Bennett,[60] G. M. Young,[61] Keith Feiling[62] and Alan Bullock,[63] and the works of a younger generation who had had good wars and who would run the tape of those years forever in their historical minds – Philip Magnus,[64] M. R. D. Foot,[65] many more. What it did not do was produce a Treaty of Versailles or a League of Nations Union or Wilsonian uplift. Its concluding text was not *Eminent Victorians* but *Die deutsche Katastrophe* or *Nemesis of Power*.[66] And its *ideological* consequence in Britain became an argument with an excluded middle, that very centre of golden mediocrity previously occupied by whigs. This modernist generation quarrelled among itself, certainly, about the events of the past five years; it wrangled in particular

---

[58] 'When I re-read the work this week . . . the result was ludicrous . . . Even to me the work seemed to be a treatise in favour of conservatism rather than whiggism. And since I wished to show that a whig tradition had become a national one, I seemed to have written not only in praise of tradition as such, but in praise of England herself.' Journal, 1 Oct. 1969.

[59] Wilhelm Levison, *England and the Continent in the Eighth Century* (Oxford, 1946).

[60] John Wheeler-Bennett, *Disarmament and Security since Locarno, 1925–32* (1932); *Munich: Prologue to Tragedy* (1948); *The Nemesis of Power: the German Army in Politics* (1953).

[61] G. M. Young, *Early-Victorian England 1830–1865* (2 vols., 1934); *Mr Gladstone: the Romanes Lecture, 1944* (Oxford, 1944); *Stanley Baldwin* (1952).

[62] Keith Feiling, *The Life of Neville Chamberlain* (1946); *A History of England: from the Coming of the English to 1918* (1950).

[63] Alan Bullock, *Hitler: a Study in Tyranny* (1952); introduction to *The Ribbentrop Memoirs* (1954); *Hitler and Stalin: Parallel Lives* (1993).

[64] Philip Magnus, *Edmund Burke: a Life* (1939); *Gladstone: a Biography* (1954); *Kitchener: Portrait of an Imperialist* (1958).

[65] M. R. D. Foot, *British Foreign Policy since 1898* (1956); *Men in Uniform: Military Manpower in Modern Industrial Societies* (1961); *SOE in France* (1966); (ed.), *War and Society: Historical Essays in Honour and Memory of J. R. Western 1928–1971* (1973).

[66] Friedrich Meinecke, *Die deutsche Katastrophe: Betrachtungen und Erinnerungen* (Wiesbaden, 1946); Wheeler-Bennett, *Nemesis of Power*.

over the wisdom of unconditional surrender as a strategy and the ethics of dropping the atomic bomb. Larger forces, however, pulled the generation closer together into some of the assumptions claimed by Noel Annan as a cohering tendency.[67] Nothing lends coherence so effectively as an Other against which to rally; and while Hitler and Nazism were dead, Stalin and Soviet Communism were not. Nor did the division of world power into two super-powers help weaken the post-war law of the excluded middle. This was a bad time to be G. M. Trevelyan, as he was the first to recognize.

Until the eventual reaction of the late 1960s, the ideological future among historians lay with the Left, not least because the Left was young. The appearance in the same year, 1946, of the Communist Party Historians' Group and Maurice Dobb's *Studies in the Development of Capitalism*, the founding of *Past and Present* in 1952 and the orchestration of Marxist history from Hill, Hobsbawm, Hilton, Kiernan, E. P. Thompson and others through the 1950s and '60s,[68] shook the frame of historical analysis and eventually left historians who knew nothing else about the sixteenth and seventeenth centuries aware of the storm over the rising and falling gentry, or the most untheoretical generalist aware of names like Kojève and Althusser even when they were thought mad and foreign. The New Left despised the whigs for their lack of understanding about social structures, about economic dynamics and, not least, the historical relationship between those things that they thought they could scientifically demonstrate. Their opponents of the same generation, such as the émigré Geoffrey Elton, quietly pointed out that aristocrats may have oppressed people but revolutionaries killed them.[69] Yet neither Old nor New belonged to the circles of professional modernism, or so at least the latter hoped and believed, with their deplorable dress, their polemical journalism, their support for student activism and all those destabilising ructions that so perplex principals and vice-chancellors who emphatically now did belong to the age of modernism and sometimes counted historians among their ranks. After 1950 Stenton and Woodward, Namier and Butterfield had become rhetors of their generation, using

---

[67] Noel Annan, *Our Age: Portrait of a Generation* (1990) and *The Dons: Mentors, Eccentrics and Geniuses* (2000).

[68] For the Communist Party Historians' Group, see Harvey J. Kaye, *British Marxist Historians: an Introductory Analysis* (Cambridge, 1984), esp. 9–18; Eric Hobsbawm, *Interesting Times: a Twentieth-Century Life* (2003). Dobb's book struck Hill as seminal: 'L'oeuvre individue, la plus importante qui ait été produite jusqu'a ce jour par un marxiste anglais sur l'histoire britannique', *La Pensée* 28 (1950), 57.

[69] Elton ruminating on what he took to be the prejudices of George Rudé: Geoffrey Elton to Richard Ollard (copy), 6 Oct. 1964, Elton MSS.

public statement to attack unsavoury politics and bad history, whether it was Namier's rubbishing of ideas that revolutions are other than random events, like cyclones, or Butterfield's growing conviction that Britain could not be 'saved from Marxist history unless we show more self-discipline and greater integrity . . .'[70]

Seen from the angle, though, of serious historical monographs and professional reactions to them, this public argument amounted to little more than noise, at least until Thompson's *Making of the English Working Class* in 1963[71] and that took a beating from calmer minds convinced that Thompson had manipulated his evidence to fit a case – the reverse of what modernists thought a proper procedure. In doing so *The Making of the English Working Class* announced that it was 'slanted' and that would never do. 'He is, I suspect,' said one reviewer in private, 'a Trotskyite revolutionary who can see revolution round every corner . . .',[72] an allegation that would have crippled Thompson with laughter if he had seen it. Christopher Hill suffered far more, not only from J. H. Hexter's unforgettable evisceration of his method, but also from a sort of poisonous professionalism that wanted to nail what it thought of as 'bias' among those who did not achieve objective judgement as the profession thought they should. J. E. Neale, now an old man, deemed Hill 'incorrigibly twisted in his mind as an historian' by the malevolence of 'Marxist reasoning' that had become 'ingrained'. 'He's as biassed [*sic*] as Catholic historians used to be.' But this mood of dismissal was already proving harder to sustain than it used to be. Perhaps the real incursions against it came from scholars running with their heads down who, without reflecting on it, perhaps without knowing it, insinuated a form of structural analysis into history that carried all the stains of twentieth-century exposure to socialist or populist ideologies. It seems doubtful that the majestic medievalist Helen Cam would have described herself as the Marxist that Gavin Longmuir came to see in her.[73] Nor was so intelligent an author unaware of the dangers of importing twentieth-century supposition into historical argument.

---

[70] 'A gale blows down whatever it encounters, and does not distinguish. Revolutions are anonymous, undenominational and inarticulate . . . But revolutions are not made; they occur.' Lewis Namier, '1848: Seed-Plot of History', in Namier, *Vanished Supremacies* (1958), 21–30 at 21; Butterfield, *Christianity, Diplomacy and War* (1953), 39. In private, and in the same year, Butterfield preferred to talk about communism as 'the anti-Christ of our time . . . I think there is a myth of revolution as well as a myth of war.' Butterfield to Adam Watson, 25 Aug. 1953, Butterfield MSS 531/W30.

[71] E. P. Thompson, *The Making of the English Working Class* (1963). This extraordinary construction – brilliant, elegant and remarkably persuasive in the minds of young people – attained cult status for the best part of a decade and then, like so many cults, died.

[72] J. D. Chambers to Alfred Cobban, 31 Jan. 1964, Chambers MSS C3.

[73] Gavin Longmuir to Helen Cam, 7 Oct. 1954, Cam MSS 2/2/11.

The fact that little William Marshall played 'conkers' with King Stephen in 1141 as children play it today, or that he was a hostage, only differing from the hostages of the Gestapo in that his jailers had kind hearts . . . must not lead us to assume that . . . the twelfth century can be understood without . . . some detachment from the assumptions of the twentieth century.[74]

Yet throughout her collected papers and more starkly in her general history of medieval England, her language about incipient capitalism as early as the fourteenth century, about gilds functioning like modern trade unions, about the emergence of classes beyond Powicke's vision of the *communitas*,[75] there is the contagion that beat whiggery at its own game and infected professional modernism, not by denying a shape to history but by replacing it with a more plausible one relevant to the matters of the moment.

While Butterfield and Namier fiddled with George III, their England – present and historical – was quietly burning. Even the memories of once-held passions began to fade. When the Revd Charles Smyth wrote to Butterfield in 1971 recalling the mood after 1918 – Morel, Wilson, Mussolini's attack on Corfu – he wondered 'who remembers this now, but you and me'.[76] Manchuria, Spain, China, the Nazis – all those contemporary dreads that George Potter put on his notice-board – each had dwindled to a point of memory in the age of the Cold War whose terms and conditions were different. And Maurice Powicke, insisting on the uniqueness of his era in 1938, was an old man in 1954 concerned about far-away places of which he knew nothing.

I feel very overwhelmed by the thought that India and Africa now spell a 'multiplicity of wills' in political life. It was bad enough when Ireland was the outstanding example of this universal truth. No wonder the communists concentrate on killing it, and in scotching religion, so as to create a desert of quiet concurrence which they call the peace of democracy.[77]

That phrase, 'a desert of quiet concurrence', recalls Namier's startling description of modern dictatorship as 'the monolatry of the political desert'.[78] Communists or Nazis, they bequeathed deserts – sands in

---

[74] Helen Cam, *England before Elizabeth* (1950), x.
[75] See F. M. Powicke, *King Henry III and the Lord Edward: the Community of the Realm in the Thirteenth Century* (2 vols., Oxford, 1947); *The Thirteenth Century 1216–1307* (Oxford, 1953).
[76] Revd Charles Smyth to Butterfield, 16 Nov. 1971, Butterfield MSS 531/S114.
[77] F. M. Powicke to Helen Cam, 15 Jan. 1954, Cam MSS 2/2/14.
[78] Louis Namier, 'The First Mountebank Dictator', in Namier, *Vanished Supremacies*, 54–63 at 54. Whom he had in mind (beyond his subject, Napoleon III) soon becomes clear enough: 'the taciturn, shadowy, impassive figure of Napoleon III has puzzled the century which has gone by as the shrieking, convulsed, hysterical figure of Hitler will puzzle the one to come' (56).

which no whig optimism or rationalism would regain its root. One day that optimism about continuity and story, the possibility of fixing an epoch through its narrative, would return, though few of our modernists would live to see it. The precondition for that return was a revolution of another kind that would transform the basis of historical method and by so doing invite a reinvigorated conception of historical knowledge. That precondition tells us something indeed, about what made modernism work in the first place: a particular conception of historical knowledge with its basis in method.

8   Modernist method

Various aspects of a continuing whig history and an opposing series of modernist investments have preoccupied us: an uneasy tension between intimations of a changing discipline and persistent memories and re-enactments of a whig canon; the working out of that tension in the eighteenth-century world of Butterfield and Namier; the wider political and ideological setting against which all such substantive history fashioned itself. Each of those aspects has left an impression, I hope, of the content of those divergent histories and some explanation of why that content took the form that it did. Joining these and other streams of argument about post-whig history into some distilled meaning or conclusion invites us to think, however, beyond content and to consider in a more frontal way what it is about the truth-claims of this generation that defines their specificity; and doing that, in turn, requires an invigilation of the practice that they all shared. Several types of method come to mind but the most obvious characterization of history in the modernist persuasion – that it saw itself embodying an investigative science – merits immediate attention and would do so even if J. B. Bury had never uttered his sole famous phrase at the end of his only famous sentence. For if, in 1903 with Acton safely dead, it seemed plausible to insist on history's status as 'a science, no less and no more',[1] then it may seem equally plausible in retrospect to hypothesize that Bury's phrase amounted to a knife in the back for the whig tradition. An historian could, *pace* Trevelyan, be an unliterary whig, like Gardiner, as well as a literary one;

---

[1] J. B. Bury, *An Inaugural Lecture delivered in the Divinity School, Cambridge, on January 26, 1903* (Cambridge, 1903): 'if, year by year, history is to become a more and more powerful force for stripping the bandages of error from the eyes of men, for shaping public opinion and advancing the cause of intellectual and political liberty, she will best prepare her disciples for the performance of that task . . . by remembering always that, though she may supply material for literary art or philosophical speculation, she is herself simply a science, no less and no more' (41–2). Bury (1861–1927), Professor of Modern History at Trinity College, Dublin, then Regius Chair at Cambridge. *History of the Idea of Progress* (1920).

he could be an illiberal whig, like Stubbs, as well as a liberal one; he could even, acknowledging Freeman, try to become a European whig as well as an English one. But could he be a *systematic* whig? Perhaps H. G. Wells came closest in his outline of world history,[2] but then his method, as opposed to his conclusions, hardly followed laboratory procedure. Those who took Bury's prescription seriously felt the need to go beyond description of the past towards a form of analysis of its detritus that turned on a micro-examination of detail that threatened to subvert spacious narratives; and towards a view of historical knowledge that preferenced accretion above inspiration, one that saw its practitioners making bricks one by one, each a solid accumulation of what was known rather than supposed or conjectured. They saw science where others yearned for artistry, rejoiced in a new professional superstructure that embodied their assumptions, and contributed to a modernist mood about the nature of factuality that would dominate the writing of history for three-quarters of a century. In our final look at these people, each of these perceptions should detain us before the inevitable onset of the p-word compels us to speculate on the special place of the modernism they embody and the image of this period in the eyes of a postmodern age.

Science

No less than a science, but what kind of science? The word altered its frame of reference for historians through the twentieth century and one should recognize the complication of the story and its contestedness. What late Victorian historians meant by science was a version of comparative method across time and space, essentially the application of historical insight to all other disciplines. 'For what is the theory of evolution itself', Prothero wrote, 'but the achievement of the historical method?'[3] It could mean even less than that, a simple commitment to what Round predictably called accuracy.[4] Seen under this light, 'science' operated as a rhetorical device (outside Stenton's work on place-names or R. L. Poole's developing field of diplomatic and his aspirations for

---

[2] H. G. Wells, *The Outline of History: Being a Plain History of Life and Mankind* (1920). I have suggested elsewhere that Wells might be seen as a 'laboratory whig': see Michael Bentley, 'The Singularities of British *Weltgeschichte*', in Benedikt Stuchkey and Peter Wende (eds.), *Writing World History 1800–2000* (Oxford, 2003), 173–96 at 174–5.
[3] G. W. Prothero, *Why Should We Learn History?* (Edinburgh, 1894), 4.
[4] In *The Early Life of Anne Boleyn* (1886), for example, Round expressed his admiration for the German levels of accuracy, 'boast as we may of the achievements of our new scientific school'. Quoted in W. Raymond Powell, *John Horace Round: Historian and Gentleman of Essex* (Chelmsford, 2001), 57.

'a real Ecole des Chartes' in England[5]) rather than a self-conscious investigation of how historians went about their business and the procedures they followed in regard to relating evidence to argument. Seeley spotted this anomaly in an essay on methods of teaching history in 1885 in which he expressed himself with his normal vigour:

> We have given to history the conscientiousness of science, but we have not yet given it the arrangement of science. We still arrange historic phenomena under periods, centuries, reigns, dynasties, but what is wanted is a real rather than a temporal classification . . . Whereas the investigation of historical facts has lately been made honest and careful, the reasoning about historical facts is still, it seems to me, oracular and unsatisfactory; I wish to make this, too, honest, methodical, explicit.[6]

He never lived to see such a development. Indeed it is rare to find method the subject of study among historians until after the First World War and then patchily or defensively. Most forensic, as always, was Maitland, who brought a brilliant scientism to his legal studies, and of course Tout who was capable of writing a paper entitled 'An Historical Laboratory', which was presumably situated in the University of Manchester, and of recommending to historians that they employ 'the methods of the observational sciences'.[7] But these approaches sat more comfortably within the confined horizons of legal and administrative history than with narratives of long periods or the demands of biography.[8] It was all very well for Stenton to say in the inter-war period that history was now a branch of science and that 'no histories written on the great scale & inspired by the spirit of former days are being written now',[9] but his confidence, as we have seen, was misplaced.

---

[5] R. L. Poole to Sanday, 7 Feb.1896, quoted in P. B. M. Blaas, *Continuity and Anachronism* (The Hague, 1978), 61.

[6] Quoted in Roland G. Usher, *A Critical Study of the Historical Method of Samuel Rawson Gardiner* (Washington, 1915), 147–8. The brutality of Usher's treatment brought forth some responses defending Gardiner's achievement but the study remains one of the few seriously to attempt a critical account of historical method in this period. Cf. Hereford B. George, *Historical Evidence* (Oxford, 1909).

[7] Quoted in Kathleen Burk, *Troublemaker: The Life and History of A. J. P. Taylor* (New Haven, 2000), 104. Or perhaps one should read not Manchester but University College, London. Tout apparently told Pollard that he, Pollard, 'had developed the teaching of historical science further at Univ. College than in any other British university'. Alfred Pollard to parents, 2 June 1918, Pollard MSS, box 5.

[8] Ruville was particularly contemptuous of the latter. 'It is a prevalent custom in England to construct biographies of eminent personages in the following manner. Quantities of letters and extracts from letters or other documents are welded, with the assistance of a certain amount of connecting literary matter into a continuous narrative, frequently with very insufficient observance of the chronological order of events . . . It is a hybrid species, the cultivation of which is of no benefit to science . . .' Albert von Ruville, *Pitt, Earl of Chatham* (English trans., 3 vols., 1907), vol. II, 355.

[9] F. M. Stenton, MS of lecture, n.d. [?c. 1930], Stenton MSS 8/14.

The years between the wars sustained a different climate for all that. Einstein's two theories of relativity found their way by osmosis into a wider intellectual culture through the mediation of R. B. and J. B. S. Haldane, Bertrand Russell, A. N. Whitehead, Sir Arthur Eddington, Sir James Jeans and many others, joining the work of Rutherford and his team at the Cavendish Laboratory as the stuff of dinner conversation. In the humanities as in the visual arts, the result was a certain astringency: a rejection of all forms of metaphysics, a caustic view of religion, an insistence on hypothesis confirmed by proof. So pervasive did this mood become that it provoked its antithesis in the years of R. G. Collingwood's *Speculum Mentis* (1924) and Michael Oakeshott's *Experience and its Modes* (1933), both putting science in its place, a place far removed from where historians should be. Historians themselves tend to be too busy with their record-cards and folders to see the train before it hits them, but that lowering of the eyes should not blind us to ways in which a cultural milieu can affect a discipline – ways seen better retrospectively than at the time. Occasionally it happens *at* the time. So we have the pleasant picture of Basil Willey, as a junior appointment in English at Cambridge, sitting in Lyons coffee house in Petty Cury in July 1932 reading Whitehead on *Science and the Modern World*. 'There and then it dawned on me', he wrote in his autobiography, 'that "Truth" was not all of one kind: that "scientific truth" was not the whole truth . . . and that the seventeenth century could be seen as the struggle of scientific truth to emancipate itself from religion and poetry and to claim for itself unique validity.' A single meditation measured out in a coffee spoon thus originated his two volumes on the intellectual background to English poetry and religion in the seventeenth and eighteenth centuries.[10]

Far more general than explicit references was an awareness after 1918 that science had become the motif of historical study and that 'choosing problems of equal importance to those of the scientist, and treating them with equal accuracy'[11] would lead historians to command the same wide audience for their work. Another author preoccupied by the study of religion, from a very different standpoint, saw science as the true victor in the Great War and as the discipline pointing a way forward for all students:

---

[10] Basil Willey, *Cambridge and Other Memories, 1920–1953* (1968), 60–1. See Willey, *The Seventeenth Century Background: Studies of the Thought of the Age in Relation to Poetry and Religion* (1934); *The Eighteenth Century Background: Studies on the Idea of Nature in the Thought of the Period* (1940).

[11] G. G. Coulton, *Five Centuries of Religion* (4 vols., Cambridge, 1923–50), vol. III, v.

In the realm of intellect, as in that of manufacture and commerce, the world is worked by science; just as the recent war was waged and won in the laboratories and closets wherein the specialists in physics and chemistry and electricity and mathematics were silently and out of sight experimenting and perfecting the machinery of victory. Similarly is it in the realm of thought; patient workers . . . advancing scientific work . . . must lay the foundations . . . [12]

The objective in this work lay in the 'discovery' of 'facts' that were taken to exist in the past: certainties that could prove a bedrock on which the discipline could rise assured of its foundations. Single, crystalline, unchallengeable facts, what the first editor of the *English Historical Review* had called 'the indestructible atoms by the adding of which together true history could be composed',[13] had become the quarry for all serious historians. By compressing these atoms together one reached an almost literal hard-core that would only later become surrounded by the fleshy pulp of opinion – one of the most pervasive (and damaging) metaphors of the modernist persuasion. So for George Clark in the 1940s a certainty continued that '[a]ll our knowledge of the past has a hard core of facts, however much it may be concealed by the surrounding pulp of disputable interpretation'.[14] Within this world, the task facing scholarship consisted in making judgement so certain that it allowed of no criticism;[15] and it helped generate the notion that an ideal seminar paper would be the one that produced no questions whatsoever, so crushing and overwhelming would be the force of its demonstration. Above all a modernized past would contain no 'bias' and allow only judgements that aimed for 'objectivity'. For David Knowles this would become, indeed, the summation of method. He might compliment one author for her 'objective and scientific presentation of economic facts'. He might pay homage to another for his 'realization of the great advance towards objectivity, and therefore towards historical truth, that has been made by the best modern historical scholarship'.[16] Economic facts recall

---

[12] Cuthbert Butler, *Benedictine Monachism* (1919), 378 and 379n.

[13] Mandell Creighton, 'Introductory Note', *Cambridge Modern History* (Cambridge, 1902), xxiv.

[14] G. N. Clark, *Historical Scholarship and Historical Thought* (Cambridge, 1944), 20.

[15] E.g. Richard Lodge's commendation of Douglas Horn: 'you have been very fair and dispassionate; but give as few loopholes for controversial criticism as you can.' Lodge to Horn, 22 Jan. 1926, Horn MSS Gen 766/1. D. B. Horn (1901–69). Entire education and career at University of Edinburgh. Professor of Modern History from 1954. *A History of Europe* (1936); Horn and Mary Ransome (eds.), *English Historical Documents, 1714–83* (1957).

[16] David Knowles, review of Marjorie Morgan, *The English Lands of the Abbey of Bec* (Oxford, 1946), *EcHR*, 16 (1946), 147–9 at 149; Knowles to F. M. Stenton, 2 Feb. 1944, congratulating him on *Anglo-Saxon England* (Oxford, 1943), Stenton MSS 8/27/1.

J. H. Clapham: just look at the nouns and adjectives in which Munia Postan celebrated Clapham's achievement by 1939:

On the ground on which Dr Clapham has worked and still works he found a mass of half-knowledge, overgrown with picturesque and stubborn weeds. This ground he has not only cleared, but in his own inimitable, lapidary way, has covered with a structure of facts as hard and certain as granite. On his ground in his manner nothing else remains to be done.[17]

It is the finality that becomes breath-taking, together with an optimistic sense that a closure of this kind is open to anyone possessed of a determination to seek the truth. Cervantes was not much of a modernist but the economic historian T. S. Ashton was; and he thought that what Cervantes had to say about history remained after several centuries good enough for modern students making their way in the subject. In recommending him he spoke for his own generation. 'An historian', Cervantes had written, '. . .ought to be exact, sincere and impartial; free from passion, and not to be biased either by interest, fear, resentment, or affection to deviate from the truth, which is the mother of history . . .'[18]

Embedded in 'the facts' lay 'evidence' which, in this disposition, often lost itself in a language about 'the sources'. Five minutes with Collingwood would have cured anyone of this confusion: 'sources' comprise all surviving relics of a period (documentary or otherwise); 'evidence' should be understood as a subset of such sources selected for the purposes of framing an argument or making a case. But the modernist case could easily conflate into an account of what existed in the documentary record; and virtue lay with the historian who could find new bits of the record to present. Method in this respect turned into a hunt for 'new material', unearthing that unseen letter or an unnoticed section of a charter, and the subject thus became 'source-led', rather than following a range of questions or hypotheses in the mind of the historian as Collingwood would have urged. Here is a typical example of the resulting mentality, from a private letter in 1933:

I spent a few weeks last year at the British Museum. My aim then was to see what I could fill up on Hainault. I got a lot of stuff but nothing very exciting. In fact, there seemed to be very little [sic] new things available, I mean that have not been used up in books on Jacqueline of Hainault.[19]

---

[17] M. M. Postan, 'The Historical Method and Social Science', in N. B. Harte (ed.), *The Study of Economic History: Collected Inaugural Lectures 1893–1970* (1971), 129–41 at 129.
[18] T. S. Ashton, message sent to the Student Economic History Society at Exeter University, n.d., Ashton MSS 457/18.
[19] L. V. D. Owen to Stenton, 7 Mar.1933, Stenton MSS 8/16/2. Hainaut, in its modern spelling, is a province of south-west Belgium.

The assumptions here could not be more suggestive: one has to 'fill up' a subject by searching for 'a lot of stuff'; it is damaging to find no 'new things' on offer that have not already been 'used up' by other historians. A corollary is that history has set its course towards the ever more minute as its practitioners desperately search for an unused piece of the past – the bane of a hundred periodical articles and a thousand doctoral dissertations.

Namier and Butterfield, our constant spectators and critics, avoided this confusion and science played a more ambiguous role in the thought of both of them, reinforcing the one from a distance, causing the other perpetual anxiety. Namier had little demonstrable interest in scientific procedure itself, yet his drive to bring off a kind of *archéologie du savoir* and reveal strata of truth previously buried in rhetoric and propaganda turned him into an analyst more naturally than a narrator. When the young Keith Feiling reviewed *The Structure of Politics* in the *Observer* in 1929 he talked about the author's success in rescuing the past from oblivion and commended Namier's 'dovetailed innumerable facts which distinguish history from historical legend and, if men will have patience, make the past live again as it was'.[20] Namier did indeed face Ranke's perplexities over restoring a past society *wie es eigentlich gewesen* but the problem lay not in essence – far too foggy an idea for Namier – but in balance, bringing individual and collective agency, atom and molecule, into harmony. Lucy Sutherland saw something of the sort in Namier's later years as he struggled with 'aggregates otherwise than in vague generalizations' and tried to make a history in which individuals somehow retained their distinctive individuality.[21] He could only do it, granted the ferocity of his individualism, by making society precisely that: an aggregation, a bag of ball-bearings. Like Lady Thatcher, Namier disbelieved in the idea of society as an entity and all his powers of analysis tended towards its resolution into discrete biographies. Prosopography therefore functioned for Namier not merely as a method but as a window on how the world was.

Curious, then, that Butterfield, whose interest in science was far more direct and long-standing, should have gone in so different a direction. When he began his wide-ranging lectures on modern history in 1931 he

[20] *Observer*, 20 Jan. 1929. Keith Feiling (1884–1977). Mother related to novelists Anthony Hope and Kenneth Grahame, father a stockbroker. Marlborough, Balliol College, Oxford, and All Souls. Student of Christ Church for thirty-five years from 1912. *A History of the Tory Party, 1640–1714* (Oxford, 1924); *England under the Tudors and Stuarts* (1927); *The Second Tory Party* (1938); *A History of England* (1950).
[21] Lucy Sutherland, 'Sir Lewis Namier', *PBA*, 48 (1962), 371–85 at 382.

included six performances on the rise of modern science – an interest that brought him into contact with Joseph Needham in particular but also the people at the Cavendish.[22] That tendency ultimately gave rise after the war to an invitation to lecture on the history of science to the scientists, which in turn produced an important book in Butterfield's intellectual development, *The Origins of Modern Science*, in 1949. The problems that science puts in the way of history make up a large theme in Butterfield, to which I shall turn later, but in an early meditation on 'technical history' one can almost hear Namier's contention and Butterfield's critique:

> The new technique of history concentrates almost entirely upon the delivery of what really happened in the past rather than upon the method of presenting and unfolding the story . . . It is the technique not of a man painting a picture on a blank canvas, but of a man correcting a picture already painted . . . The modern technique of history is essentially a negative thing, not only failing to create in the larger sense but actually being a method of preventing oneself from being creative at all . . . It is a gigantic science of caution, a colossal elimination of one's self [*sic*].[23]

No one understood better than Butterfield the power of this new dispensation, 'the temptation', as he called it, 'to catch habits of mind from the scientists or the scientific temper of the present age' which brought 'fallacy and menace' by persuading historians that abstraction would work for them and that they could use, like the scientists, tools such as classification, inference and hypothesis.[24] He hated it and by reacting against it he preserved society and *Zeitgeist* as explanatory forces and threw a lifeline to the beleaguered whig sensibility. G. M. Trevelyan, embodying that sensibility, looked back on the last half-century from 1945 and shared Butterfield's unease. He saw three things behind the scientific method: the prestige of the physical sciences in late Victorian England; the dereliction of the Germans with their 'crabbed German

---

[22] Kenneth W. Thompson, *Masters of International Thought: Major Twentieth-Century Theorists and the World Crisis* (Baton Rouge, 1980), 9.

[23] Untitled, undated [?1930s], 'Early Writing', Butterfield Miscellany.

[24] 'There can be nothing more just . . .', [?late-1930s], ibid. Cf. his published reconsideration of the place of society many years later: 'It is an active collaborator in the work of history-making . . . [H]istory is no longer merely a line or stream of story, but has to be conceived at the same time in terms of the underlying structure. The result is more like a glacier moving along a path but also possessing depth.' Herbert Butterfield, *George III and the Historians* (1957), 195. His remark that 'one can be too scientific, or rather one can be so mechanically scientific as to defeat the purposes of science itself' (ibid., 198) brought amused incredulity from his friend Dudley Edwards. 'Can History be too mechanically scientific? . . . Would the Oakeshotts hold with this use of the world scientific?' Edwards to Butterfield, 9 Jan. 1958, Butterfield MSS 531/E9.

ideal of the learned man who has nothing to do with literature'; and the professionalizing universities, places where the felt need to make history a more rigorous discipline had advanced unwelcome tendencies.[25] 'We Englishmen shall be amateurs to the end,' Maitland had once reassured a correspondent,[26] but his confidence, for such it was, seemed more hollow as the century progressed.

Professionalization and truth

By 1945 Namier and Stenton, Trevelyan and Butterfield were all professors, caught in a system with its own dynamics. The process of professionalization of the discipline was distinctive in England seen against the experience of Germany, France and America for a variety of reasons, among which the most central lies in the peculiar relation between a post-formative state, a distinctive nationalism and the particular nature of what Noel Annan called 'the intellectual aristocracy'.[27] It is possible to read this trajectory, as Reba Soffer reads it, as a coalescence of state and clerisy in which professors construct the idea of history as a discipline serving the burgeoning state and make it the operative instrument of their own and their students' status within English society.[28] My concern with it is different and turns on the degree to which a professional ethos and organization militated against whig conceptions of the past by imposing a method of historical practice that became inimical to it. We have already seen how attempts to keep whig history alive in the inter-war period depended heavily on those outside the university system who wanted to communicate with a broader audience. Those inside it felt the weight, certainly, of a more powerful hierarchy but also of that hierarchy's intellectual motif, a bastard term that had been brought into historical studies through a category error from which the profession still suffers today, one which may yet kill the subject its admirers believe it to be furthering. It is not certain when English professional historians began to deploy the word 'research' as a global

---

[25] G. M. Trevelyan, *History and the Reader* (1945), 12.

[26] Maitland to Hubert Hall in 1901, recalled in Hall to Pollard, 28 Jun. 1939, Pollard MSS 860 box 47.

[27] Noel Annan, 'The Intellectual Aristocracy', in J. H. Plumb (ed.), *Studies in Social History: a Tribute to G. M. Trevelyan* (1955), 241–87. For a more general treatment of this relationship, see Michael Bentley, 'The Organization and Dissemination of Historical Knowledge', in Martin Daunton (ed.), *The Organization of Victorian Knowledge* (Oxford, 2005), 173–97.

[28] Reba Soffer, *Discipline and Power: the University, History, and the Making of an English Elite, 1870–1930* (Stanford, CA, 1994), *passim*.

description of their enterprise rather than as a precise term for the systematic analysis of, say, place-names or bibliography.[29] It is completely certain that doing so brought consequences for the thought-world of historians trained under its sway; and one of them implied a collection of procedures for the generation of historical texts. Just as the scientist who is properly and legitimately engaged in *Naturwissenschaft* fills files with headings such as laws, apparatus, method, control, result (and looks forward to 'writing up' his research), so historians began the journey – in their case often a hopeless and damaging journey – to fill notebooks with the same language and with the same objective of making the text impregnable,[30] confirmed and encouraged in their practices by a professional superstructure that made their doing so the test of intellectual credibility[31] and the criterion for a successful career in academic life.

This emphasis followed from an unspoken commitment to the past's visitability and the idea that a living pastness still existed in its various deposits in the present. Because the deposits were often large and various, it made sense to study short periods as historians had been trained to do in their 'special subject' classes when they were undergraduates, for then one might garner more of the past by embracing more of its deposits. This is the argument of A. S. Turberville of Leeds, writing in 1933.

It is when we are reading the manuscripts which our forefathers wrote, listening to the music and poetry which they made, exploring the houses in which they lived, the castles and churches which they built, that we are learning what they are really like. For they are speaking to us directly, and the gulf of the centuries has been bridged.[32]

---

[29] Dr Johnson spoke of research only as enquiry into any field, with no scientific resonance, as in 'the researches of human wisdom' (*A Dictionary of the English Language*, etc. (1755)). Isaac Disraeli has 'the researches of the historian' in 1830 but nineteenth-century examples of the word come preponderantly from scientific discourse. The *OED* conflates 'careful consideration or study of a subject' and 'a course of critical or scientific enquiry' (2nd edn (Oxford, 1989), XIII, 692).

[30] '. . . an article has damn well got to leave [its readers] with no alternative [to agreement]': K. B. McFarlane to Norman Scarfe, 5 Sep. 1949, in McFarlane, *Letters to Friends 1940–1966* (Magdalen College, Oxford, 1997), 68.

[31] 'There is', Galbraith wrote in the 1960s, '. . . a large output of "research", which is frankly unreadable; on the other hand, an ever-growing number of popular syntheses . . . win little or no acceptance.' *An Introduction to the Study of History* (1964), 76.

[32] A. S. Turberville, 'History Objective and Subjective', *H*, 17 (1932–3), 289–302 at 296. Turberville (1888–1945) was the son of the vicar of Stansted. Cheltenham College and New College, Oxford. Went to Liverpool, Bangor and Manchester before, in 1927, arriving in Leeds where he remained. Professor of Modern History, 1929–45. *English Men and Manners in the Eighteenth Century* (Oxford, 1926); *The House of Lords in the Eighteenth Century* (Oxford, 1927); *To Perish Never* (1941).

Looking back on assumptions such as these half a century later, the sociologist A. H. Halsey found throughout the humanities 'the voice of the elitist researcher' which, he thought, had 'probably been the most effective force for change in the twentieth-century English universities'.[33] That is undoubtedly correct and the transformation has often proved a positive one. But in historical work it could also occur at a price and those sensitive spirits who found the trend depressing stand as a reminder of how high the modernist price might rise. 'They make a darkness, and call it research,' wrote Tawney in one of his most human moments, 'while shrinking from the light of general ideas which alone can illuminate it.'[34] His profound insight, uttered at the high-point of modernist enthusiasm, shows both an awareness of danger and the possibility of avoiding it if only question and answer could be got the right way round.

The First World War had supplied a crucial environment for this new mood in presenting research as a way to govern the new world that must follow, and among historians the period from Versailles to Britain's economic crash of 1931 marks a high point in its urgency. No small part in fomenting the new mood was played by University College, London and its historical organizer and presiding force, Albert Pollard. Pollard came genuinely to believe that he could construct a new profession with new criteria. When a research student came to him from the University of Bristol during the war, he made sure that his message travelled back to the river Severn. 'None of the Bristol people', he wrote to his parents, 'have the ghost of a notion of historical research, and Miss Hodnett's presence for two years at my seminar [note the word, 1918] has been useful in setting a standard for Bristol University.'[35] Today Bristol, tomorrow the world. By the end of 1919 an Oxford correspondent could hope 'that some good soul would start a similar institution [to the Thursday conferences] here . . . I think there is great hope for us . . . so long as men like yourself throughout England are ready to fight and work for the establishment of adequate research schools', complementing Goronwy Edwards's disgust at discovering that 'there isn't enough organization of research here' in post-war Oxford.[36] Of course Pollard had every intention of fighting and working for more than his Thursday evening meetings of historians, though they were still going as late as

---

[33] A. H. Halsey, *Decline of Donnish Dominion: the British Academic Professions in the Twentieth Century* (Oxford, 1992), 38.
[34] R. H. Tawney, 'The Study of Economic History', *Econ.*, 13 (1933), 1–21 at 19.
[35] Pollard to parents, 4 Aug. 1918, Pollard MSS, box 5.
[36] E. A. Lowe to Pollard, 30 Dec. 1919, Pollard MSS 860 box 47; J. G. Edwards to Tout, 26 Jan. 1925, Edwards MSS 219.

1954;[37] and the result – a brilliant achievement and testimony to Pollard's extraordinary energy – emerged in his Institute of Historical Research (IHR), founded perilously in 1921, which would absorb his energies until he passed the directorship to Vivian Galbraith in 1944.[38] Its success proved remarkable. Coinciding with the first Anglo-American Conference, the establishment of the IHR made possible in its first year the creation of four preliminary courses in history and the establishment of eight historical seminars; by the end of session 1925–6, it offered six courses and seventeen seminars.[39] There were, of course, setbacks. Tout's attempt to replicate it in Manchester failed. Nicholas Murray Butler of Columbia refused even to permit an institutional subscription.[40] Oxford never found its good soul, beyond Poole, because the one it had already, Firth, retired sick at heart.[41] But the ripples ultimately ran far wider than matters of organization. Positive evaluations of Pollard's new institution far outweighed the criticism, and gratitude deepened with the years. Wallace Notestein, then at Cornell, sent his approval of Pollard's 'splendid dreams for history'.[42] George Sayles recalled a quarter of a century later that he was the first Scot to join it, in 1923.[43] Galbraith, returning from Edinburgh to take over during the war, wrote in terms that transcended piety:

the Institute is you & you are the Institute. Your weekly Conferences there after the last war were the most vivid & living meetings of historians in my life-time and (for example) helped me to keep alive an interest in research when my official superiors in another place were doing their best to kill it . . . If you look around you will find that nearly every one of my generation who values History today is a pupil of one of two men – Tout & Pollard.[44]

---

[37] They had diminished to two per term by then: Edwards to Helen Cam, 8 Sep. 1954, Cam MSS 2/2/5.
[38] It is rarely recognized how very close the Institute came to closing in 1926 when the University of London allowed the Grosvenor estate to return to charging an economic rent for the Gower Street site occupied by the building that housed Pollard's brain-child. See Pollard's memorandum on 'The Critical Position of the Institute of Historical Research', 14 May 1926, Pollard MSS 860 box 27. Though the university later took responsibility for the Institute, Pollard never forgave its treatment of his work in 1926.
[39] Pollard, 'Critical Position', 3.
[40] Carlton Hayes had pressed for one: correspondence in Hayes MSS 1.1.46.
[41] 'I am very sick of my job, and should be glad to stop the futile attempt to lead here.' C. H. Firth to Charles Webster, ?11 June 1924, Webster MSS 1/7/63. He retired in 1925. When he died in 1936 his widow found Godfrey Davies's obituary 'offensive': Frances Firth to G. R. Potter, 24 Feb. [1936], Potter MSS, box 21.
[42] Wallace Notestein to Mrs Pollard, 20 Oct. n.y. [?1926], Pollard MSS 860 box 48.
[43] George Sayles to J. G. Edwards, 13 Mar. 1948, Edwards MSS 204. Edwards succeeded Galbraith as Director.
[44] Galbraith to Pollard, 2 Mar. 1944, Pollard MSS 860 box 47.

In the generation after Tout and Pollard, scholars made their way in the environment of research that these men had done much to construct, and whiggery, to the extent that it survived, had to learn survival within it. With research came papers, with papers periodicals. *History*, the periodical, first appeared in 1912, describing itself as 'A Quarterly Magazine and Review for the Teacher, the Student and the Expert' and carrying on its title page a ghostly woodcut of Thomas Carlyle. Once the Historical Association took it over during the First World War, its objectives became less Carlylean and caught the new professional sensibility. When Ernest Barker attempted in its pages a very restrained defence of the Italian philosopher of history, Benedetto Croce, some of whose vast output had begun to make its way into English by 1922, Pollard fell on him like an avenging Hun with a polemic whose title, 'An Apology for Historical Research', said as much as its text.[45] Pollard's own journal had always occupied a place in the Institute idea, and the *Bulletin of the Institute of Historical Research* began from 1923 its celebration of Pollard's mission to make historians deploy a systematic research method to produce results and then 'to make common to the world of historical research a knowledge of these results and of the ways and means by which truth in history is to be ascertained'.[46] Further forensic excitement came from the *Cambridge Historical Journal*, also in 1923, and the *Economic History Review* in 1927, offering the fruits of research in political and economic history respectively. By the side of these the *Transactions of the Royal Historical Society* and the *Proceedings of the British Academy* seemed behind the pace. Even the *English Historical Review* had its ghostly moments in the 1920s, as when its former editor, R. L. Poole, sent a postcard from Grindelwald to the current incumbent in 1925: 'Dear Clark: This day being the feast of St Swithin, forty years ago the English Historical Review was founded at Bryce's house in Bryanston Square. Of the party assembled there I am now the only survivor.' And then he trundled through the dead: Acton, Creighton, Church, Ward, York Powell . . .[47] A glance at *EHR* through the 1920s and '30s confirms by contrast an entrenched professionalism, albeit one exercised under the continuing pressure to correct and extend parliamentary and constitutional history. The momentum reached Ireland in Moody's *Irish*

---

[45] Ernest Barker, 'History and Philosophy', *H*, 7 (1922–3), 81–91 and Pollard's reply, ibid., 161–77.

[46] 'Introductory', *Bulletin of the Institute of Historical Research*, 1 (1923), 1–5 at 5.

[47] R. L. Poole to G. N. Clark, 15 July 1925, Clark MSS 159. His full list ran James and J. Annan Bryce, Lord Acton, Creighton, [Dean] Church, R. Garnett, A. W. Ward, Robertson Smith and York Powell.

Historical Studies in 1937 and found its ultimate destination in 1952 with *Past and Present*, the journal of scientific history whose mood was not at all constitutional, but whose scientization of the research project reached new heights in its various manifestos for social science, and new levels of depression in Keith Thomas's celebrated conclusion in 1963 that the only important difference between history and anthropology was that you visited your subject in the one case and not in the other.[48]

These two initiatives – the burgeoning of the learned journal and a later imperative to take to heart what historians tend in their unself-conscious way to call ancillary subjects – made their presence felt increasingly between 1920 and 1970 and helped impose a view of correct method in the historical discipline. What was that view? It envisaged, as we have seen, that periods of study would be short so that primary evidence could be mastered. H. A. L. Fisher's remark as early as 1928 that the anticipated hundred and fifty years of Macaulay's unfinished history could not have been produced from a modern university chair[49] perhaps reflected just this view. Second, it demanded documentary verification for each proposition and documentary contextualization for each description: it invited and required the hundred-footnote article narrating events over a minute compass or analysing a particular problem or text in micro-detail. Trained by a supervisor in the methods of doctoral research (or those needed for the B.Litt at Oxford where gentlemen tended not to bother with the D.Phil. introduced there in 1917), candidates for entry into academic life learned the importance of scientific method. They could also apply that method in more places than national libraries. Until 1930 or so there was only one decently appointed County Record Office; eleven new ones appeared in the 1930s and another thirteen in the immediate post-war years.[50] Probably much of the impetus (national and regional) came originally out of medieval history – a distinguished cohort in Britain between 1890 and 1910; it is noticeable that Stenton later thought that Round was the instigator of much in the genealogy and prosopography that would later preoccupy figures as diverse as Lewis Namier, Bruce McFarlane (who bought Namier's two great books on the eighteenth century) and in particular Ronald Syme.[51] Indeed an English medievalist perhaps

[48] Keith Thomas, 'History and Anthropology', *P&P*, 24 (1963), 3–24 at 4.
[49] H. A. L. Fisher, 'The Whig Historians', *PBA*, 14 (1928), 297–339.
[50] Data from Christopher Haigh, 'A. G. Dickens and the English Reformation', *HR*, 77 (2004), 24–38 at 29.
[51] (Sir) Ronald Syme (1903–89). New Zealander; Oxford from 1925, Camden Professor of Ancient History from 1949. His use of prosopographical techniques is illustrated in *The Roman Revolution* (Oxford, 1939) where he acknowledged that 'exhaustive detail

marked the apogee of the entire movement in the twentieth century. C. R. Cheney[52] enforced the virtue of precision in historical studies, but at a level of resolution that sometimes left him looking as though he could not see the trees for the branches. He recurred to a whig theme, for example, when he took up in 1950 a document referred to by Stubbs, the so-called 'paper constitution' inserted by Matthew Paris into his chronicle, 'a series of startling radical provisions', according to Cheney, 'for the control of executive and judicature'. Rather than concern himself with the meaning and significance of these provisions, however, he devoted an entire article in *EHR* to arguing with Denholm-Young over whether they were written in 1238 or 1244.[53] There is nothing intrinsically wrong with seeing history in this way, but recognizing its omnipresence as a method among modernists helps fix the preoccupations of the persuasion.

Unlike in France or Germany or America, meanwhile, the claims of sister disciplines made comparatively little impact on English historians in the first half of the twentieth century. The degree to which English historians escaped a *Methodenstreit* or a proto-*Annaliste* movement or the currents of opinion that would produce James Harvey Robinson's New History seems more worthy of emphasis. Lone voices did urge the assimilation of, first, archaeology – 'an exact science', in the opinion of Alan Mawer, with 'a vast body of concrete fact' to its credit[54] – and then later of geography, not so much in the wake of *Annales*, which took many years to impinge except in the new economic history, but probably out of a concern with the empire and the need to educate citizens to its demands.[55] Nevertheless, when one compares, say, a pre-war history syllabus drafted by Carlton Hayes at Columbia University in New York as early as 1913, one insisting on provision for political economy,

---

cannot be provided about every family or individual', but produced nevertheless a mine of information and an index 'mainly prosopographical in character' (vii). He quoted Namier's opinion that history is an 'intelligible disorder' (*Fictional History: Old and New Hadrian* (Oxford, 1986), 23n), but placed some confidence in this 'new technique' for helping resolve it (*Classical Elites: Rome, Spain and the Americas* (1958), 14).

[52] C. R. Cheney, (1906–87). Professor of Medieval History, Manchester, 1945–55 and Cambridge 1955–72.

[53] C. R. Cheney, 'The "Paper Constitution" Preserved by Matthew Paris', *EHR*, 65 (1950), 213–21.

[54] Alan Mawer, 'The Viking Age', *H*, 1 (1912), 94–107 at 95. Sir Alan Mawer (1879–1942) specialized in Anglo-Saxon and Scandinavian studies. Director of the *Survey of English Place-Names* and Provost of UCL, 1930–42.

[55] Ramsay Muir had this intellectual background and his paper to the annual meeting of the Historical Association in 1912 may have drawn from it; see 'The Relations of History and Geography', *H*, 1 (1912), 41–54; cf. the evangelism of C. R. Crutwell, 'A Plea for the Teaching of Historical Geography', ibid., 9 (1924–5), 213–17.

anthropology, philology, sociology and current philosophical trends,[56] the moves towards width seem tentative at best. From 1945 the mood began to alter, however, and quickened in the 1960s. An image of structural analysis imported from sociology and anthropology sharpened, as we have seen, in a socialist reading of political history and played an increasing role in stimulating 'analysis' – the refrain of the period – which joined with forensic method to produce varieties of history-from-below articulated in that vocabulary of scientific recon-struction that we have been reviewing.

One does not need great imagination to see ways in which this lan-guage of method undermined the claims of whig historiography to represent serious historical work. The latter might be acknowledged as having literary grace and cultural importance, but for those hard-bitten with modernist assumptions – none more so than Geoffrey Elton – there could be no point in returning to ways long superseded. '[I]n truth these men wrote in the pre-historical age,' wrote Elton in the *Times Literary Supplement* in 1956, 'and if we do not read them to-day we are not much to blame.'[57] A sympathizer might urge in defence of Elton's opinion that critics such as he wanted merely to disparage outmoded forms of schol-arship and not the insights that lay behind it. Perhaps method should be seen, therefore, as a purely instrumental thing, following from deeper matters concerning the limits of historical knowledge and the nature of truth? In fact, it worked the other way round. English historians of this period received no teaching in conceptual issues beyond a recommenda-tion to treat them sceptically: everyone had to cut his or her own path through the material, equipped with the tools that their education had supplied and, happily, a prose crafted more in the manner of Evelyn Waugh than Karl Popper. Rather than find itself attracted to the idealism of Collingwood or Oakeshott, as Christopher Parker seems to believe,[58] the profession largely ignored them *et hoc genus omne* and forged a common-sense notion of truth and factuality out of a daily engagement with historical sources. Epistemology, a theoretical enquiry into the nature and limits of historical truth, collapsed among the modernists into a practice for seeking and confirming it. Method mattered so much to them, therefore, because it generated the world that should have generated method. History expanded its sense of itself as a disciplinary

---

[56] 'A Syllabus of Modern History', copy in Hayes MSS. The 'newer social sciences' were to form part of the section on 'Contemporary Civilization'.

[57] G. R. Elton, 'Fifty Years of Tudor Studies at London University', *TLS*, 6 Jan. 1956.

[58] Christopher Parker, *The English Historical Tradition since 1850* (Edinburgh, 1990); *The English Idea of History from Coleridge to Collingwood* (Aldershot, 2000).

practice rather than a style of meditation and Clio was to be seen, as Galbraith famously said, checking her references in the Public Record Office.[59]

Between the wars, then, at precisely the moment when American facts were losing their crystalline quality at the hands of Carl Becker and Charles Beard and when American objectivity had begun its deliquescence into 'that noble dream' of which Beard spoke,[60] *English* facts hardened into the building bricks of historical reasoning, the components of the platform on which the past rested. It was no good just knowing where to look for facts – A. C. Benson proposed that in a loose moment in 1912 and disappeared under the usual ton of bricks from University College;[61] one had rather to carry them by their thousand in the head to count as an historian. In their natural state they lay around like rubble, waiting to be gathered; and, once acquired, they gave one the power of judgement against extremes of mere opinion for they contained within them truth itself, the point of historical enquiry. That Cassandra of international history, Charles Webster, despaired even in the 1920s of 'progress being made in establishing historical truth in this country'.[62] But setbacks did not dissuade him from establishing it and punishing those who distrusted what he had built. Even on the Left, where more sophisticated epistemologies had been available for years, an author like Douglas Cole could share the sense of factuality as a domain constructed by the world rather than one formed by historians deploying competing images of it. 'Writers may differ in the interpretation of . . . facts,' he said in the binary opposition that stamped itself on these decades. 'The facts themselves are not disputed.'[63] Note the definite article, the article of definiteness. One had to know 'the' facts because facts were finite and identifiable. How reassuring, too, that they supplied their own implicit cards to trump opinion. If historians differed in their 'interpretations', the best thing to do was to find a point in the centre of their wayward

---

[59] V. H. Galbraith, *Introduction to the Study of History* (1964), 4; cf. his *Introduction to the Use of the Public Records* (Oxford, 1934).

[60] See in particular Beard's celebrated addresses to the American Historical Association: 'Written History as an Act of Faith', *AHR*, 39 (1934), 219–29; and 'That Noble Dream', *AHR*, 41 (1935), 74–87. Cf. Peter Novick's very able discussion of this period in American historiography in Novick, *'That Noble Dream': the 'Objectivity' Question and the American Historical Profession* (Cambridge, 1988), esp. 250–78.

[61] See Pollard's denunciation of Benson's idea – 'little more than a fallacy' – in 'Our Point of View', *History*, 1 (1912), 128.

[62] Webster to Algernon Cecil (copy), 26 Jan. 1924, Webster MSS 1/7f.6.

[63] G. D. H. Cole, *A Short History of the British Working Class Movement, 1789–1925* (3 vols. (1925–7), vol. I, 179.

opinions, as Carless Davis always recommended,[64] for there 'the' truth resided. Contributors to the new series of the Oxford History of England planned in 1929 received an injunction from the editor, G. N. Clark, to use footnotes sparely and deploy them only for 'exceptionally doubtful points': the text itself should be bricks, what one historian called 'a clear summary of ascertained facts'.[65] This cumulative activity, 'knowing and registering the facts',[66] became still more cherished through the era of ideological embitterment that we have discussed: it offered an anchor against whig 'bias'[67] and held out the hope that opinion would never triumph over reality. For George Kitson Clark, composing his manual for the critical historian in the 1960s, the problem remained bias; the solution lay in controlling its distortions through an effort of will. Know thyself, the message ran, and by a Rankian process of self-dissolution an historian would see the truth rising from his documents like steam after rain.[68]

The fly-bottle

Now this world of academic historical method had, of course, its critics and modulations. It amounted less to a formalized doctrine than to an environment like Wittgenstein's famous fly-bottle out of whose glass walls all can see but from whose incarceration none ever escapes. Even those who, like Pollard, became avatars of modernist thinking understood that there existed 'no absolute canon of truth', that facts could be manipulated 'like the letters of the alphabet', enabling one to spell words

---

[64] 'He taught one that truth could be found and that it lay in sort of mean between extreme views.' Reported by a 'distinguished Oxford tutor of today' and quoted in J. R. H. Weaver, 'Memoir', in Weaver and A. L. Poole, *Henry William Carless Davis 1874–1928* (1933), 26.

[65] Memo by Clark, n.d. [Dec. 1929]; copy in Stenton MSS 8/12. A. Hamilton Thompson to Stenton, 4 June 1926, Stenton MSS 8/9.

[66] Basil Liddell Hart to Namier (copy), 18 June 1936, Liddell Hart MSS 1/539. David Douglas had emphasized a few years before that '[h]istory is not merely the expression of opinion any more than it is merely the art of telling a story. It is also an attempt to rediscover truths hitherto unappreciated'. 'John Richard Green' in Douglas, *Time and the Hour: Some Collected Papers of David C. Douglas* (1977), 41–49 at 47.

[67] '. . .bias seems almost of the essence of English history as written in the traditional great style . . .' J. L. Morison of Armstrong College, Newcastle, 'Bias in History Writing', *H*, 11 (1926–7), 193–203 at 201.

[68] G. Kitson Clark, *The Critical Historian* (1967), 3. Cf. Powicke's warning thirty years earlier that the historian must isolate his own thought-world from that conveyed in his sources: 'he is not expected, as an historian, to permit philosophical or theological considerations to intervene between him and his treatment of the evidence'. Powicke, *History, Freedom and Religion* (Durham, 1938), 5.

of one's choosing – 'League of Nations, conservatism, communism or anything else'. But then into the glass wall he crashes. 'History should therefore be taught without specific reference to any ulterior object,' as though that would remove the difficulty.[69] There were always scholars whose sheer intelligence broke bounds, who knew, like Vivian Fisher, how 'a few facts frequently repeated soon begins to look like truth'.[70] Or one might observe the fly-bottle on its side rolling around the bench with a buzzing A. J. P. Taylor[71] inside. His method followed a Namierite modernism – composing diaries, as Kathy Burk shows us, of the actions of his participants in order to make a tight chronology of intersections[72] – but his temperament constantly took him beyond method to command an audience. 'If he goes on like this', Bruce McFarlane observed in 1950, 'working himself up and dancing like mad, he'll burst.'[73] Who else would have electrified readers by declaring, on the basis of nothing whatsoever, that Armistice night in 1918 witnessed total strangers copulating in doorways?[74] Who else could render Henry Pelling apoplectic by confessing that he relied more on feel than on figures?[75] And yet . . . Taylor in his dismissal of self-consciousness as a hindrance to creativity was too busy to find his way out of that enclosing glass: it was one struggle for mastery that he lost. His gifted generation did often see beyond whatever enclosed them and kicked at their boundaries as strongly as any generation before or since. Few kicked harder than our two protagonists in their very different ways – in Namier's case to disarm mechanical method and whiggery by applying mischievous intelligence; in Butterfield's to offer, eventually, the most telling critique of modernist method made in England before 1970 and to revive by doing so the

---

[69] Albert Pollard, 'Froude', *TLS*, 18 Apr. 1918, 177–8 at 178; Pollard to Ivan Power (copy), 21 May 1929, Pollard MSS 860 box 48.

[70] D. J. V. Fisher to Helen Cam, n.d. [postmarked 3 Mar. 1951], Cam MSS 2/2/6.

[71] A. J. P. Taylor (1906–90). Son of Lancashire cotton merchant and schoolmistress. Bootham School, York, and Oriel College, Oxford. Research student in Vienna, 1928–30. Manchester University, 1930–8. Magdalen College, Oxford, 1938 until retirement from Oxford. Beaten by Trevor-Roper to Regius Chair in 1957. Directed Beaverbrook library in late 1960s and early 1970s. Scandalized public with *The Origins of the Second World War* (1961). More than thirty books, including *English History 1914–45* (Oxford, 1965), but mostly with a European focus.

[72] Kathleen Burk, *Troublemaker: the Life and History of A. J. P. Taylor* (New Haven, 2000), 268, 288.

[73] McFarlane to Norman Scarfe, 16 May 1950, in *Letters to Friends*, 76.

[74] A. J. P. Taylor, *English History 1914–45* (Oxford, 1965): 'Total strangers copulated in doorways and on the pavements. They were asserting the triumph of life over death' (114).

[75] See Pelling's famous review, 'Taylor's England', *P&P*, 33 (1966), 149–58 in which he alleged that Taylor also relied more on memory than on documentation.

aspirations of what William Dray would later call a 'humanistically oriented historiography'.[76]

Lewis Namier disclosed many examples of his commitment to an austere methodology, particularly in his studies of eighteenth century England. The dismissal of badly edited texts, the constant search for *echt* material in unpublished archives, the focusing on a tiny section of chronology, the density of referencing in the *Structure of Politics* and his absorption in the vast History of Parliament project – all these facets imply a clear sense of procedure, just as his violence against those who sinned against procedure confirm the impression. But we have already seen another side of Namier's academic personality in his friendship with Arthur Bryant and can see it again in his regard for Winston Churchill as a writer of history. He admired *Marlborough* and when Churchill's biography began to appear in 1933[77] he wrote to the author to congratulate him on having avoided the frigidities of 'don-bred dons'. 'Too much history', he said, 'is written by . . . dons with no knowledge or understanding of the practical problems of statecraft.'[78] This aversion to the intellectualist fallacy among university teachers informed one mood that interfered with Namier as a simple representative of professionalization and perhaps made him half-sympathetic to those who, like Gibbon or Macaulay, at least knew about politics from the inside. It informed his approval of a close friend of the 1930s, Basil Liddell Hart, who brought to history an expertise based on practical knowledge without the trammels of academic schooling. Namier's own sense of the trammels impinged, at least theoretically, on method itself. Everyone knew, not least Namier's students, how wedded he was to supporting contentions about the eighteenth century with quotations from contemporaries. When one of his Manchester students tried to impress a class by doing precisely that, Namier played devil's advocate and told the class, as he reported with satisfaction to Liddell Hart himself, 'that I would undertake to write a most thoroughly documented history in which every single statement would be wrong. People will say, or even write, the most fantastic nonsense about their own thoughts or intentions, to say nothing of deliberate lies about their actions'.[79] Here is the Viennese side of Namier's temperament: intentionality is a waste of time as an objective because the participants literally do not know their own mind and

---

[76] William Dray, 'The Historical Explanation of Actions Reconsidered', in Patrick Gardiner (ed.), *The Philosophy of History* (Oxford, 1974), 66–89 at 89.
[77] Winston Churchill, *Marlborough: his Life and Times* (4 vols., 1933–8).
[78] Quoted in Julia Namier, *Lewis Namier: a Biography* (1971), 230.
[79] Namier to Liddell Hart, 12 Sep. 1949, Liddell Hart MSS 1/539.

therefore mislead posterity. Whig history could not cope with that thought because it claimed to evoke states of mind and purposive behaviour that, according to Namier, had vanished beyond historical retrieval.

In Butterfield's earlier years, say before 1945, he shared this need to imply the failure of whig history by commenting on the failure of all patterns and systems. Weber's perceived link between capitalism and Protestantism could have been demolished, he thought, by an intelligent undergraduate sitting in an armchair and thinking about the difficulties it raised.[80] Similarly he found a serious 'optical illusion' in types of linear history which threw together quotations from authors in a chronological series, 'an overwhelming chain of story', as though they had all been tending in a similar direction when read in their original context. Such a series could only become 'valid' if the individuals who made it up had all been 'driven by the same logic' or if 'they had been directly inspired by one another, each man taking the torch from the last, and so handing down from age to age one developing line of thought, as might happen in science or political theory . . .' Otherwise, 'the grouping that we have made in our minds,' he warns, 'though it may be an arbitrary grouping, we take to represent real connections between things. The historian becomes the victim of his own processes.'[81] Yet even amid these austerities in the 1930s an undertone of doubt about the hardness of facts – atypical, as we have noticed – and the role of historian in merely reporting them strikes up from Butterfield's writing. He may have seen a striking short essay in one of the early volumes of *History* that pictured historical facts in two dimensions – one travelling along the flow of time, the other working vertically, 'in the same way that a piece of music may be at once part of an air and part of a chord'.[82] Certainly he used the same image. 'A true historian', Butterfield wrote in a private meditation, 'is one in whose mind a thousand chords may vibrate at a touch of one piece of generalization, a man who after the bell has struck catches undertones and secret amplifications of the sound; till the one fact is magnified in the stimulus which it has given . . .' As always with Butterfield the intensity of his thought catches the prose with flame and conviction:

[80] Herbert Butterfield, *The Study of Modern History* (Cambridge, 1944), 25.
[81] Butterfield, Untitled draft, 'There is a foreign book . . .', Early Writing, Miscellany. The remark about science would not have survived his later scepticism about scientific continuities in *The Origins of Modern Science* (1949). His dislike of and contempt for 'political theory' never changed.
[82] Preston Weir, 'Modes of History', *H*, 3 (1914), 48–53 at 51.

The autumn leaf that flutters into the market square is moved by a complexity of forces and is entangled in a whole web of time and circumstance. Each historic event is the precipitate of a number of movements that come to a point, it is really a knot of historical happening; and if the knot is untied we are left by no means with one thread that has been unravelled but with a whole handful of threads that had come together there . . . So [the author's] history must appear to him as a web, not as a line or a linear series.[83]

This is a long way from Tout and Pollard, but it tends in the same direction away from a whig history that sought horizontal linearity at the expense of factuality's complication and its capacity for sending out bewildering filiations.

In his later thought, not least in his controversy with Namier, Butterfield brought narrative back to the centre of his historical preoccupation, but also integrated it with structure to produce an argument on separate levels in which structure must 'not merely serve as a picturesque background . . . [but] . . . a constituent of the episode itself, an actual partner in the story'.[84] Linear teleologies he never brought back, but he became more open to what he called 'patterns' in the historian's design, the dialectical unfoldings of Marxists, for example, or the antinomies of Arnold Toynbee.[85] The more extreme claims made on behalf of structural explanation after 1960 called some of this optimism into question, and his language became more insistent on the damage done to history when the individual becomes submerged in process or becomes an anonymous datum to be counted in a computer as the cliometric fashion of those years took root.[86] As I argued in reviewing Butterfield's life in 1999, none of these reservations about the direction of historical culture made Butterfield a postmodernist *avant la lettre*. Rather they display the degree to which he was simultaneously a penetrating critic of modernist method and, in his commitment to 'technical history', its ultimate prisoner.

---

[83] Untitled ?recension of essay, 'There can be nothing more just . . .', Early Writing, Miscellany.

[84] Butterfield, *Study of Modern History*, 21.

[85] Herbert Butterfield, *Christianity and History* (1949), 81–2. Such shapes make 'a better myth or pattern to have by us than the generally accepted view of a linear development, an ascending course of progress in history' (82). It is interesting to find Arnold Toynbee himself reflecting, after the appearance of his first volumes of *The Study of History*, that 'pattern history' was a 'dangerous game'. 'The pattern becomes clear in one's own head, without any guarantee that it isn't nonsense.' Toynbee to H. A. L. Fisher, 4 Dec. 1934, Fisher MSS 70 ff.53–4.

[86] See Butterfield on 'The Role of the Individual in History', *H*, 40 (1955), 1–17 and concerns about a new generation that recognized only the history of social classes and 's[aw] the individual as the victim of historical processes rather than as an agency'. Journal, 2 Jan. 1963.

Noel Annan wrote about his generation as people who were '*our* age', but in doing so he wrote at the same time about those contemporaries who made up 'our *age*'.[87] We could see the modernist generations in the same way as a long moment of historical practice in England running from 1920 to 1970. The age, like all ages, spoke multiply: its constituents wrote about very different subjects and often argued incompatible theses about their subjects. They engaged in robust, sometimes violent debate and their disagreements must not lose their intensity in the perspective of those who have come after them. It has been the argument here, notwithstanding those disagreements and debates, that one can speak about the two or three academic generations who came after the whigs as making up a frame of mind about the English past and how it should be studied. And it has been the burden of this exposition that, of all those parallel trains we observed sliding forwards and backwards in relative motion, it was the one carrying whig method that ran into the buffers. Others continued and sometimes even accelerated. Yet losing that engine of method would always lessen progress and perhaps lead to changes of destination. The method and outlook that replaced a whig outlook – what I have called modernism – became central to the post-whig enterprise of making truth-claims and certifying facts from within a professionalizing discipline; an enterprise that brought together historians who wrote on subjects a thousand years apart and from points of view they took to be radically disparate. But we must distinguish between perception and deeper reality, and to do so let me abandon trains and take to the road. Each of us drives along the motorway in his or her own capsule of space, conscious of what is in front and what follows and perhaps of occasional vehicles going the other way. Our consciousness – that part of it we use in noticing other road-users – suggests that the incidence of cars is random and determined by the purposes – individual, private purposes – of each driver. Traffic censuses show that this is an illusion. Beyond the consciousness of drivers, vehicles travel, not as a steady or random stream, but in clumps and clusters. History books and their authors travel through time in precisely the same way. At the level of consciousness it seems as though a writer's individual intention focuses on specific problems that present themselves to awareness. But looking at historians' output systematically from a period that is not theirs, we discover clumps and clusters. Modernism now takes the shape of a cluster where once it seemed no more than random traffic. Recall

---

[87] Noel Annan, *Our Age: Portrait of a Generation* (1990) and *The Dons: Mentors, Eccentrics and Geniuses* (1999), in which many historians considered here make an appearance. Cf. Ved Mehta, *Fly and the Fly Bottle: Encounters with British Intellectuals* (1962).

the very considerable man who in many ways became the summation of modernism at the end of our period. G. R. Elton was born during Butterfield's second year at Peterhouse and he just lived to see the threats to his world-view as postmodern language encroached on it. He spent his later years volubly despising his former teacher, Sir John Neale, without ever seeing that they had embraced the same intellectual schemata. He so disagreed with his American cliometric friend, Robert Fogel, that he agreed to publish one of their discussions under the title *Which Road to the Past?*[88] It was in fact the *same* road because they were talking about scientific reconstructions of the same imagined past. He resisted abstract words for their lack of content – when semiotics was first mentioned to him, he preferred 'semi-idiotics'[89] – and with every reason, granted the world – his world – in which conceptualization had played so small a part and in which the concrete meant everything.

What happened in western culture from the mid-1970s remains unclear: the jury is still out. Indeed it seems probable that postmodern susceptibilities played a far smaller role in English historiography in the last quarter of the twentieth century than they did in French, Italian or American writing. Many historians only became aware of it twenty years later when polemical attacks on postmodernism appeared from the pens of main-line historical figures such as Richard Evans and John Vincent.[90] All the same, we can see in the intellectual environment of these later years a cluster of concerns and perceptions that had been foreign to modernist assumptions about what historians were trying to do and what they should be writing about; and it is hard to miss the strengthening of a certain self-consciousness (what the jargon wants to call reflexivity) over the problems involved in doing it. The new ideas to which this mood gave rise impinge on our discussion here in helping to identify the special nature of modernist assumption and practice by presenting a contrasting account. Had these new ideas not appeared, the age of the modernists would not have appeared either, but rather have remained below the horizon of our awareness as simply a period of historical development or transition. Its historians deserve better; and the vaguely postmodern condition that is our lot enables at least a preliminary assessment of that age and of the whig interpretation

---

[88] G. R. Elton and R. W. Fogel, *Which Road to the Past? Two Views of History* (New Haven, 1983).

[89] Private knowledge and Elton to Richard Ollard, 6 Oct. 1954: 'too often an abstract word is used without content'. Elton MSS.

[90] John Vincent, *An Intelligent Person's Guide to History* (1995); Richard J. Evans, *In Defence of History* (1997).

of history that it believed itself to be overcoming. What then, thirty years on, should our preliminary assessment suggest? My concluding impressions are three.

First, one stands in necessary awe of what many of these men and women accomplished in their bids to turn history into a technical subject that could take its place in the highest levels of academia and command the respect of a scientific intellectual community. The skill and assiduity that they brought to their monographs meant that their writing will never be superseded in any simple sense, because new reckonings must engage with their work and transcend it only by entering into conversation with it. Second, the quality of their minds and the coherence of their methods should not obscure the impossibility of their project as they conceived it. What Butterfield called 'technical history' is ultimately, as I suspect he knew in his more sceptical moments, an illusion and the post-whig sensibility, in trying to crush the tradition of writing great narratives for a wide audience, merely drove that tradition outside academia to the loss of both university and public. Peter Mandler's recent representation of these years as a 'drifting away' of history from the centre of English national life[91] comes into sharper focus as a deliberate jettisoning, achieved at a price, which only the rediscovery of an audience by professional historians in the past twenty years has begun to recoup. Finally, I think the task of subjecting this post-whig historiography to scrutiny, by bringing relativities and deep structures to the consideration of a generation too confined, too immersed, to see them, benefits our own age and throws light on an otherwise murky present.

Modernism may be half-dead but it has not gone away.

---

[91] Peter Mandler, *History and National Life* (2002), 47–92.

Coda: after the modernists

There is a 'One in History' as a One in Nature, but it is not shown to
the man whose idea of science is confined to making his inventory or
ticketing compartments of his cabinet . . .

William Stubbs (1877)[1]

All we know is that fifty years hence men will wonder how we could
have been so lacking in imagination; and – if they have compassion –
will say that in part our blindness can be historically explained.

Herbert Butterfield (1944)[2]

Such are the turns of the wheel of historiography . . . But when it comes
to saying why, things get much more complicated . . .

David Landes (1972)[3]

The modernists are always with us, if by the term one intends those who
anticipate the limits of the current discipline and rattle its bars. Even in
the narrower sense deployed in this book, there is no single collection of
unchanging attributes in which to make 'modernism' crystalline because
it never became so solid an entity as this might imply. Rather, it presented an historical language that underwent subtle modifications –
naively realist in its earlier days, more complicated in its later moments
of quantification and model-building. It survives today in the unspoken
assumptions that lie behind much formal training in historical work or in
the broad 'common-sense' position that many historians will always take
about the possibility of 'reconstructing' the past and acquiring historical
truth. Assimilating some of these assumptions, mastering the methods
that they validate and employing a decent literary agent will still take you
to the top of the profession in the twenty-first century if you can learn
some flexibility about topic and audience appeal; and whilst history

---

[1] William Stubbs, 'On the Purposes and Methods of Historical Study', *Seventeen Lectures
on the Study of Medieval and Modern History and kindred subjects delivered at Oxford . . .
1867–1884* (Oxford, 1886), 71–92 at 92.
[2] Hebert Butterfield, *The Study of Modern History* (Cambridge, 1944), 33.
[3] David Landes to Munia Postan, 22 Mar. 1973, CUL Add MS 8961/I/55.

enjoys its new-found position today as the 'new gardening', few busy practitioners will want to divert their energies by reflecting on what theorists of the subject say about the intelligibility of truth-claims or the omnipresence of narrative. So long as historians take particular pride in their resistance to theoretical issues, the sheer practicality of the modernist outlook will continue its appeal and to that extent a revised version of modernism still thrives. But *our* modernists are gone. The first generation began to fade away in the inter-war years – Davis (1928), Tout (1929), Firth (1936). Pollard and, tragically, Power went in the 1940s. The 1960s swept Namier, Powicke and Stenton and Cam towards their British Academy obituaries; and then one by one the long-lived succumbed – Woodward, Galbraith, Butterfield. Elton, in a different generation lived on until 1991 and Southern made the millennium. And what they believed – the persuasion from which their understanding of history derived its assumptions and character – did not survive as a complete *Weltanschauung* any more than they themselves survived as a coherent cohort. It always competed with alternative visions of the world, as we have seen, and the environmental elements that made it plausible lost some of their force after 1970. No date will suffice as a terminus because the history of ideas and culture disobeys imposed categories. We can say, all the same, that in 1960 most elements of modernism enjoyed predominance in English historiography, that by 1970 some of them had come under challenge and that by 1980 the climate no longer supported the modernist enterprise in the form we have been considering. Something had changed and changed utterly. It was nothing so trite (and often meaningless) as the arrival of 'postmodernism'. Nor did it affect all modernists in the same way or to the same degree. Somehow, in a mostly unremarked osmosis, English history changed in its focus, aspiration and method. We none of us can expect to see these things at the time of their happening. 'O how hard it is to understand what we are and why!' lamented Roger Mynors after the Second World War. 'If one were Wilamowitz and Mommsen and Powicke rolled into one, one w[oul]d hardly get started.'[4] But some generalizations become apparent in retrospect. Historians began to seek new audiences – the ones that modernism had so signally failed to touch.[5] It involved historians from a widening background of experience who worked in institutions quite different from the ones modernists had known. It gave rise to new journals and popular magazines and television

---

[4] Roger Mynors to Helen Cam, 16 Apr. 1949, Cam MSS 2/2/12.
[5] See Peter Mandler, *History and National Life* (1982).

programmes: an arena in which only one failed modernist – A. J. P Taylor – succeeded to the extent and for the reasons that he was rejected by the modernists themselves. Among the younger historians now known to the public for their skills in communication we detect nothing so much as a new whiggery. Stories have returned, footnotes have thinned or disappeared, history has relocated itself as a literary and visual medium. The very idea of a Stenton or a Tout, a Namier or a Woodward coming back to haunt the airwaves and bookshops seems farcical. They did things differently and their moment has passed.

What they did required specific preconditions in both intellectual ambience and life-style. They breathed the atmosphere of the past – or thought that they did; they 'steeped themselves' in a period – or imagined that they could; they railed against history as a series of skills or aptitudes or approaches and defined it, aggressively, as '*knowledge of the past*'.[6] Yet in all their violence about the importance of knowledge, modernists not only missed important constituents of meaning and understanding in their history but, more tellingly, in all their seeking for knowledge they forgot to look for ignorance and failed to see what an interesting history it has. One of the major implications of any conception of what it is important to know lies, after all, in what it is acceptable not to know; and as an historical culture the English have rarely posed to themselves the questions raised by acceptable ignorance.[7] Once raised, these questions focus attention on many facets of the historical enterprise. We have seen how brilliant young scholars after the First World War ran up against the frontiers of knowledge drawn by the previous generations. They saw their own frontiers in their demands for the resuscitation of a particular past verified by identifiable procedures. We are on safe ground in suspecting that none of them read a word of what was coming out of Vienna and that they could not have written two lines about logical positivism. Yet, implicitly and approximately, their history carried the imprimatur of an austere verification principle that tested what was true, rejected what was false and implied what

---

[6] I owe 'steeping' and the stress on factual knowledge to K. H. D Haley (b. 1920), pupil of Christopher Hill at Balliol College, Oxford, and an early modern historian specializing in the second half of the seventeenth century. Professor of Modern History, University of Sheffield, 1962–82. *William of Orange and the English Opposition 1672–1674* (Oxford, 1953); *The First Earl of Shaftesbury* (Oxford, 1968); *The Dutch in the Seventeenth Century* (1972), etc. Steeping is what one does in Yorkshire with peas: it involves the idea of total immersion over a protracted length of time and proclaims with unconscious eloquence exactly what modernists thought possible and necessary.

[7] For a development of this point in the context of Victorian historiography, see Michael Bentley, 'The Evolution and Dissemination of Historical Knowledge', in Martin Daunton (ed.). *The Organization of Victorian Knowledge* (Oxford, 2005), 174–97.

didn't matter. Their work clustered quite as unconsciously around particular nodes in its subject matter and mode of recounting. It could be exciting, rigorous, admirable. It could not disavow its foundations and went out of its way to squash those who tried.

Professionalization helped the process because it gave authority to those senior enough to squash conclusively, but it was a special sort of professional who could do it and we should recall the circumstances in which modernist professors had their being. Their institutions required them to teach and examine on a scale unthinkable today and across vast chronologies that made them busy but powerful since they could comment on everything. From Tout to Taylor, Manchester's lecturing treadmill ensured that if one did not have much knowledge when one arrived, a couple of years' experience would prove transformative. But their student numbers, bane of the twenty-first century, remained small; and the prevailing understanding of knowledge meant that one could cull its essentials from a textbook, at least until after the Second World War. They did not normally have to run their institutions, though some, such as Stenton and Butterfield, found themselves eventually slaves to administration. They found it helpful to write out their lectures, apart from Taylor, which had the advantage that when they had to see the dentist or visit an archive, a junior lecturer could be made to read them out. They owed explanation, and their salary, solely to a vice-chancellor or principal. They owed little else unless moved by conscience or human sympathy. When they went home, or were taken home, they moved without friction from one position of authority to another. They were mostly men, a very good thing to be among the professional classes in the first half of the twentieth century. They washed no socks and ironed no shirts because they had wives, saw little of their children because they had nannies and cooked none of their dinners because they had cooks.[8] They lived in large villas whose gardens they were not required to tend and from whose capacious studies all others were barred; they could afford a motor car or the consequences of not having one and could send their children to one of the better public schools without financial privation. They knew themselves to be significant local figures who might be called upon to provide lectures and talks beyond the academy as well as within. This agreeable universe of public and private recognition confirmed certainties in the minds of this privileged cohort and encouraged versions of 'research' that might take thirty years to

---

[8] A thought that rekindles admiration for Joan Thirsk who carried family responsibilities on top of her academic work.

accomplish, with no government-enforced 'targets' or public audit of published work and no one to gainsay its practitioners in their oracular statements about the purpose and nature of historical work. A hundred inaugural lectures underline their speakers' sententiousness, self-confidence and occasional moments of insouciance. C. H. Firth, the one exception in 1904, was made to apologise to his colleagues for having let the side down.

If these caricatures have their point in helping explain the scale of achievement of our modernists, they do nothing to explain them away. One may as well try to make Gladstone sound as though he were built on a human scale as to suggest that a Stenton or Tout or Namier owed everything to the advantages of his environment. These individuals brought their individual energy and genius to what they conceived as the historical task and their nature gives as strong an account of their careers as their nurture. Where discussion of ambient elements does have its place, rather, is in allowing some judgements to be made about when and why the ambience changed and pressed historians into a different mould. If old modernists never die, when did this particular modernism undergo transformation and expire?

Many of today's observers (most of them currently in middle age) will want to say that the 1960s marks the break. A culture in manifest quarrel with itself through the youth movement with its music, self-conscious dress and mood of rebellion; the largest expansion of university building and student numbers in the history of education in England; the rise of female emancipation as a powerful political movement; the prominence of a powerful Marxist school in history: there are many environmental reasons for seeing the writing of history taking place in a new situation. The historiography corroborates this to a degree. These are the years of E. H. Carr and his widely read *What is History?* (1961), of the new messiah of the left in E. P. Thompson and his acolytes, the birth of history-from-below as a self-conscious rejection of elitism, the time when *Past and Present* became the journal on everyone's table. Merely to take a clutch of history books published in the mid-1950s and compare them with a run selected from a decade later would suffice to suggest important change in the presence of an urgent social history undertaken in a fiercely structuralist spirit and a determination to *épater les bourgeois* or, failing that, at least to *épater les américains* whose adventures in Vietnam formed the subtext of so many seminars in modern history. History had taken a turn outwards, moreover, and now looked towards the anthropologists and sociologists in closer keeping with another French symbol, the *Ecole des Hautes Etudes* in Paris, than the Public Record Office in Chancery Lane. These years *felt* new and anyone who lived through them as a sentient adult carries still the force of that feeling. Senior historians now – I am writing in 2004 – are often products in a sense of that decade's power to hypnotize and beguile. They believe that the mood of the 1960s changed the nature of history because they believe that they are the contention's best proof – avatars of a culture that let air and light into the discipline through the window of a new, analytical intelligence. The 1960s have become a professional folk-memory.

Perhaps the structure of this book will have helped form a different sensibility. My rather artificial device of breaking the subject into two parts allows at least a crisper conclusion than would otherwise have been possible when facing the task of explaining and dating the modernists' demise. It allows us to see that what expired in the 1960s was a collection of whig legacies. What continued virtually unchallenged were the modernist investments that had given the persuasion its essential meaning.

One has only to relocate the first three chapters of this book in the 1960s to sense a termination. Constitutional history and the skills required to prosecute it at a high level, especially competence in Latin, died in that decade. The new political history dominated discussion and a mood of resistance to what now seemed a mood of weak legalism spread to most parts of the history of Britain. Having begun its twentieth-century career in the United States, so it now continued there as the old country looked elsewhere.[9] Nor did that old country feel the confidence of nationhood that it had known in the days of the whigs. The comfortable assurance that England was the 'predominant partner' in discussions with the Irish or the Welsh or the Scots no longer held good in years of a nationalist sentiment that found their ultimate reflection in the 'troubles' of Northern Ireland from 1969. It was a perception that led, many years later, to a strand of public discussion among historians that insisted on a need to think about British history as a whole and transcend the narrower nationalism that some of the whigs had projected.[10] Looking beyond the boundaries of Britain, meanwhile, the empire had

---

[9] Corinne Comstock Weston and John D. Fair are examples of this continuing tradition in the United States. See Weston, 'The Royal Mediation in 1884', *EHR*, 82 (1962), 296–322; *The House of Lords and Ideological Politics: Lord Salisbury's Referendal Theory and the Conservative Party 1846–1922* (Philadelphia, 1995); Fair, *British Inter-party Conferences: a Study of the Procedure of Conciliation in British Politics* (Oxford, 1980) and 'The Carnarvon Diaries and Royal Mediation in 1884', *EHR*, 106 (1991), 97–116.

[10] There may be no clear origin of this mood but J. G. A. Pocock's article on 'The Limits and Divisions of British History: in Search of the Unknown Subject', *AHR*, 87 (1982), 311–36 undoubtedly attracted attention, as did Conrad Russell's insistence on a British standpoint in thinking about the years before the English Civil War: see his 'The British

its own wind of change in the 1960s. If any decade marks the end of Britain's nineteenth-century empire, this one has many credentials as a candidate because of its numerous examples of decolonization and retreat from a world-mission. Wars became limited conflicts in the shadow of a dominant United States and if Britain could once have described itself as a 'warfare state', that moment, too, had gone.[11] As for the church, our evidence here has suggested a severe collapse in religious enthusiasm during the 1960s and a new mood of aggression against non-material explanation of historical events. The conclusion is clear. Most of the themes and pillars of a whig historiography underwent crisis during the 1960s. This did not spell the end of a whig tradition because parts of it proved capable of resurrection in the later years of the century. But it looked stale and unprofitable in 1970. Trevelyan had almost reached that 'nadir of his reputation' on which J. H. Plumb commented some years later.

Turn, however, to the second half of this book and consider its arguments in the light of the 1960s. Many of those lines of argument not only held their force but did so with a particular assurance. If a defining feature of modernism lay in a certain attitude to social and economic history together with a commitment to new forms of non-constitutional political history, then the 1960s marks a signal triumph rather than a defeat. These were the years of rampant self-confidence in quantificatory social science, and the structuralism on which it rested, as a fundamental form of historical enquiry and the eroding of that base still lay ahead. Namier was dead and Butterfield had ceased to publish on the eighteenth century, but their concerns continued to animate both those who wrote on that century and also a style of history that announced the importance of 'high politics' and argued an abrasive form of structural political analysis that dominated English political history for another decade. Or turn, again, to ideology as a component of the modernist environment. Despite the certainties of the American sociologist Daniel Bell, the 'end of ideology'[12] certainly did not appear in English historiography; indeed in many ways the 1960s resembled the 1930s in the depth of its political commitments. It was not only *The Making of the English Working Class* that epitomized that commitment:

Problem and the English Civil War', *H*, 72 (1987), 395–415, Both authors developed this thinking further in the 1990s. Cf. Keith Robbins, 'Core and Periphery in Modern British History', *PBA*, 70 (1984), 275–97.

[11] The subject of David Edgerton's forthcoming book on the relationship between military power and the British state (Cambridge, 2005).

[12] Daniel Bell, *The End of Ideology* (New York, 1960).

it appeared in the ideological discussions of Perry Anderson's *New Left Review*, in Taylor's provocations in his best-selling *Origins of the Second World War*, in a student body consumed by the ideals of the LSE in fostering dissent and seeking a new social history that embraced those ideals. The modernist engagement with ideology entered a higher, not lower, gear during these years. Above all, turn to method. The retrospective eye is dazzled by new historical *topics* in the 1960s. It ought not to remain blind, however, to the ways in which the historical enterprise as an intellectual activity replicated and enhanced the methods of modernism. An investment in refined truth-claims, the need for late modernist model-building and Weberian conceptual equipment to order to help that investment appreciate, did not lose its market position in the 1960s: it became, on the contrary, the mark of the true professional to buy into this stock in order to maintain his or her own position. Never had the loose amateur seemed so *déclassé*. Nor had Carr's raising the issue of history as a practice altered as much as he or his readers believed. If the earth moved in the after-shock of *What is History?*, with its tolerance of relativism and its attacks on naive 'objectivity', the earthquake sent tremors no further than the floorboards of the discipline. It did not bring the roof down because Carr sought to teach only that objectivity was multi-faceted, elusive and disfigured by the bias of historians, not that it rested on confusions about the enterprise itself.

For the situation to change, nothing less would be necessary than the internal collapse of the epistemology to which so much of this intellectual structure and claims to professional expertise referred themselves. It would need a world in which truth-claims became regarded as at best trivial forms of consensus and at worst a category-error. It would have to wait for a moment when language and representation shouldered out of the way naive realism in historical thought, and in which structures themselves became the disease rather than the cure. All of this came about only in mild and oblique ways in England; but it did not happen at all before the second half of the 1970s and it is there that we should look for graves.

There was no single epiphany. In the light of retrospect one might select a particular text or manifesto but for most historians hunched over their new toy, the word-processor, the period might have seemed no more than a widening of the subject into new domains and a proliferation of neologisms in which to talk about them. Text begat 'textuality', narrative 'narratology'. The historical world became so obsessed with 'discourse' that every conference and colloquium seemed to want to discuss nothing else. The distinguished American historian David Landes thought that everyone was now living through a time of 'synthesis rather than analysis', width rather than depth. 'There was a time we could all put the accent on one or another factor if only for heuristic purposes,' he wrote, 'but that's behind us.'[13] It was as though everything had entered flux rather than some limited feature of the situation having undergone transformation. In the same year as Landes's reflection, 1973, a keynote book appeared in America to a wave of hostility from beleaguered English modernists. Herbert Butterfield remained open to argument in these years of his retirement and it redounds to his credit that he wrote the single word 'Metahistory' into his appointment diary for that year. He probably got no further and most of the English profession did not get that far. But Hayden White's book[14] had done something astonishing and upsetting. He had taken the imperatives of structuralism as a way of thinking about the world and transferred them to a way of thinking about texts as representations of the world, leaving historical ontology itself – the *Ding an sich* which modernists had spent their lives studying – beyond construction except as a product of imagination and sympathetic projection. White chose to treat those texts as the sole reality available to the historian and turned history into a form of literary discourse whose stories – he could see nothing but stories – had their own structures and forms which prefigured how a particular account would turn out. The content of history, sacred to modernists, thus became the *consequence* of the form that an historian imposed rather than the other way round; and the form derived not from 'the facts' or 'the sources' but from the historian's own inner ear and an aesthetic vision of a past world.[15] Of course, White's own vision was radical and subversive. Members of a deeply conservative culture had no difficulty in dismissing it as fanciful.[16] The book was not 'influential' among English historians in the narrow sense of sales or even the wider one of immediate public awareness. Bit by bit, however, as the sun of Marxism slid below the horizon in the 1980s, this style of argument acquired weight and force within academic historical writing – in Italy, France and North America far more than in England, to be sure – and its unnerving refusal to die caused consternation in history departments where the entire approach had been held to

[13] David Landes to Postan, 22 Mar. 1973, CUL Add MS 8961/I/55.
[14] Hayden V. White, *Metahistory: the Historical Imagination in Nineteenth-Century Europe* (Baltimore, 1973).
[15] See Hayden V. White, *The Content of the Form: Narrative Discourse and Historical Representation* (Baltimore, 1987) and *Figural Realism: Studies in the Mimesis Effect* (Baltimore, 1997).
[16] For some comment on the receptions of White, see Richard T. Vann, 'The Reception of Hayden White', *H&T*, 37 (1998), 143–61.

be a deviation arising from departments of English Literature that had always been unbalanced and prey to foreign fads. Yet the argument did not have to be right or popular in order to be destructive of cherished assumptions. Because it subverted not one or two pillars but the central edifice of professional history as it had been practised in England since 1918, the historical thought now labelled 'postmodernism' produced a sense of disorientation, dismay and sheer *anger* over the questioning of an entire epistemology that had yielded such apparent triumphs as those great works now canonical in the English tradition.

It would be a mistake, all the same, to believe that 'modernism' had been succeeded by 'postmodernism' in the way that postmodernists want to declare. Most English historians had no idea whatever of what these new ideas were about, an ignorance hardly helped by the incomprehensible jargon in which much postmodern thinking announced itself, and the efforts of an isolated voice such as that of Patrick Joyce[17] to change the situation gained only a tiny audience. 'I'm a simple man,' groaned one of modernism's most distinguished scholars[18] and he spoke for a generation of elder statesmen within the profession who declared themselves appalled by the new language of history. Postmodern ideas remained an intimation and an unwelcome one. Like the complex relationship between whig history and its *soi-disant* replacements, a dialogue between modernism and various postmodern currents bounced between parallel tracks that ran alongside one another. The effect of postmodern intrusion lay less in superseding modernist history than in pulling it towards a revival of narrative as a principal mode of representation[19] and indicating subjects of study in cultural and intellectual history which traditional modernism had done differently or not considered subjects at all.[20] In the last thirty years of the century that undertow strengthened and became more respectable in a stream of publications that it would take another book to describe. Stuart Clark's brilliant attempt at *Thinking with Demons* in 1997 brought this movement to a head in English historiography as a top-flight professional historian found it necessary

---

[17] Patrick Joyce, Professor of Modern History, University of Manchester. *Work, Society and Politics: the Culture of the Factory in Later-Nineteenth-Century England* (Hassocks, 1980); *The Historical Meanings of Work* (Cambridge, 1987); *Visions of the People: Industrial England and the Question of Class 1840–1914* (Cambridge, 1991); *Democratic Subjects: the Self and the Social in Nineteenth-Century England* (Cambridge, 1994), etc.

[18] Professor R. B. Wernham in conversation towards the end of his life. Private knowledge.

[19] Lawrence Stone, 'The Revival of Narrative: Reflections on a New Old History', *P&P*, 85 (1979), 3–24.

[20] On the history of ideas, Quentin Skinner's well-known article on 'Meaning and Understanding in the History of Ideas', *H&T*, 1 (1969), 3–53 now seems seminal in date as well as content.

both to build the world of witchcraft from its own language and thought-patterns and to supply a theoretical introduction to show the reader why nothing else would do.[21]

Exactly as in the case of the post-whigs, however, the width of the argument becomes distorted when sight is lost of how the past directs the future, as well as vice versa, and that historians look behind them far more than they peer towards the unknown. Meditative minds did not need postmodern theory to tell them that history needed to relocate itself and move beyond the achievement of modernist writing. Historians in England already had a tradition running back to Macaulay that conceived accounts of the past as a form of imaginative literature – a tradition that Trevelyan, Butterfield, Powicke and Plumb among others had tried to keep alive, for all their becoming caught up in the filaments of modernist method. True, that tradition had largely suffered oblivion in the universities by the 1960s, but it flourished in the bookshops in the hands of authors who sold far more copies and who held modernist scholarship at arm's length for its inability to recognize the importance of audience. A. L. Rowse, Arthur Bryant or C. V. Wedgwood might be derided as mere polemicists or popularizers, but they had the ear of the publishers and took a certain pride in their lack of academic recognition. At the end of a long life of suffering patronage from academics who had never contrived an elegant sentence, Bryant felt greatly touched when Veronica Wedgwood wrote to congratulate him on his *Elizabethan Deliverance* in 1980. 'Being a profound admirer of your work,' he replied, 'I feel deeply honoured by what you write. That and dear Leslie Rowse's approval is the greatest honour I could ask.'[22] The attitudes of such people had been heard through the century as a perpetual dissonance. What changed from the 1980s was the willingness of ambitious young historians to pick up their themes and attempt a fusion of professionalism with the wider project of reaching the public. When David Cannadine brought G. M. Trevelyan back to the centre of academic history in his biography of 1992 he commented on a new mood that would infect tele-dons from Simon Schama to David Starkey – historians who, in an earlier incarnation, would have been trying to find a corner of unturned soil for dispatch to the *English Historical Review* or the *Historical Journal*. Television, a revolution in publishing and a shift in popular culture all made a huge impact in bringing this about. But dwelling on 'pull' factors leaves out of account the significant 'push'

---

[21] Stuart Clark, *Thinking with Demons: the Idea of Witchcraft in Early-Modern Europe* (Oxford, 1997), esp. 3–10.
[22] Bryant to C. V. Wedgwood, 11 Dec. 1980, Bodleian Library MS Eng.c.6829 f.52.

elements in the situation that made modernists prepared to change their habits – sometimes the habits of a lifetime.

A deeper process had been at work for some time within the modernist camp itself. The methods, ambitions, competitiveness and occasional ruthlessness of its thought-world had already become rebarbative to some of their own kind. Geoffrey Elton's rise to success as the role model had its price, for example, in the reputation he had developed for rubbishing all who had come before. His feud with his former supervisor, J. E. Neale, is too well known to need further rehearsal but we rarely see that controversy from the other direction. Resentment came to the surface at the end of Neale's life when Elton turned on Pollard whom Neale greatly admired.

Elton attacks Pollard as a historian who didn't use Manuscripts & didn't appreciate their importance. It is sheer nonsense. AFP taught us all to appreciate MSS . . . Elton was a student of mine, but he is shocking and annoying me with his lack of generosity of spirit.[23]

The substitution of hard science for a certain conception of humanity had begun to affect not only personal relations – fragile in any profession – but also the scope and potential of the subject itself. One expects to see an awareness of that in a thinker such as Butterfield who had voiced doubts about the direction of modernism even in the inter-war period. Hugh Trevor-Roper looks less likely as a critic in the wake of his trashing of Tawney and Stone and his well-known severity of mind when faced by sloppy scholarship or emotional ranting. But he read European literature which both gave him a perspective on the provincialism of English history and further reinforced a gent's dislike of provincial England itself. He also wanted an Oxford Chair rather badly which meant that he had to deprecate the institution he intended to reform. These contexts inform a letter to Wallace Notestein in 1957 which is at once quintessential Trevor-Roper and a devastating critique of half a century's historiography.

I quite agree with you about Firth. What a great man; but he was ostracized in Oxford, which, I'm afraid, still runs true to form. I despair of seeing good work born there now. *Manchesterismus* has killed it: the Manchester medievalism of Tout & Tait, Davis and Powicke, Jacob and Galbraith and that brood of clerically-minded hacks . . . The Manchester School, in my opinion, stand condemned by their record in this respect. They have dominated English historical work for a generation and they have ended by making it mere boring antiquarianism. Now what is the use of merely switching the narrow specialist

---

[23] J. E. Neale to Wallace Notestein (1965), Notestein MSS 544/1/6/536.

beam from the reign of Richard II to the reign of George III, from the Exchequer to the East India Company Board? What we need is a new spirit – the spirit of Pirenne or Bloch, Febvre or Braudel – if these dry bones are ever to live again. But where can we find it? The Manchester School have killed it and now Namierism has degenerated, in the hands of his disciples, into the cult of *minutiae*.[24]

Superb as a manifesto, the letter selects only a part of the target in blaming Manchester for the ills of English historiography. Those maladies infected most academic institutions in 1957 and a vague gesture in the direction of Paris brought little hope of curing them.

Together, however, internal anxieties about the nature of modernist history in the second half of the century and the presence after 1970 of a penetrating theoretical revision helped turn the wheel of historiography and open the way for a more humane and open form of scholarship, one concerned more with *mentalités* and cultural forms than structures. By sitting self-consciously in a present and *composing* a past from its particular (and limited) vantage point, English historians have learned to move away from an illusory transparency and bring back to the subject some of the conceptual distance, pluralism and artistry that it enjoyed before modernism threw its blanket and professionals came to believe that 'historian's history' is 'the only history that matters'.[25] The transformation may be judged a gain but with every gain comes loss. Gone is a certain clinical precision of which the modernists made themselves master. Absent, too, for a foreseeable future, are those rows of deeply impressive collaborative works along whose spines the finger can still run, stimulating amazement at their volume, range and knowledge. Audience has expanded in importance, to be sure, since the days of the *Cambridge Modern History*; but to see that development as universally beneficial would fly in the face of much current concern over its impact on the subject. Academic publishers now lead historians with a chequebook towards the banality of the television script or door-stop biography – the sort of history that Namier at the end of his life used to call 'flabby stuff'.[26] Professional historians at the height of their powers, who ought to be settling to a masterwork that might be read for a generation, become ensnared by the demand for narratives about one of the very few issues in which 'the public' has an interest. These things should warn

---

[24] Hugh Trevor-Roper to Notestein, 2 May 1957, Notestein MSS 544/1/8/747.
[25] From the inaugural lecture of the legendary H. S. Offler at the University of Durham (1958), quoted in David Rollason, *Northumbria 500–1100: Creation and Destruction of a Kingdom* (Cambridge, 2003), xviii.
[26] Namier to Lucy Sutherland, 30 Oct. 1959, Sutherland MSS box 9.

against an easy (and prevalent) sense of new enlightenment in the postmodern age. Critical historiography helps keep the guard high by reminding younger generations of what they owe to those who, like the men and women discussed in this book, made their way possible if only by following a different path.

'Why should I care about these people?' asked a young member of the Wiles seminar from which this study began. It is a real question that deserves to be asked. One answer points in the direction of a massive historical achievement that a civilized intellectual society should recognize and honour. To discard a century's authors and thinkers in a bin labelled 'empiricists' or 'positivists' encourages a trashy laziness of mind among young people all too ready to believe that history was born when they were. No culture can afford the loss of so much dedication and scholarship, even when their terms and procedures no longer seem applicable. But there is a more pressing answer. Historiography works as a constant conversation between past and future. Whigs and modernists shared a conversation in the century after Stubbs and the reality of this dialogue shows itself in the historical thought and practice of both persuasions – now pulling in one direction, now pulling in an opposite one. Working historians obscure the predicament of their own day when particular traditions and styles of thought – all of them provisional and subject to flux – become reified into a univocal statement of truth. The modernists, for all their successes, made that mistake and it is urgent that later generations do not condemn themselves to repeating it. We impoverish ourselves when we assume that our own condition timelessly raises English history as it is now fashionable to write it above the dialectical engagements with which this book has been concerned. The precipitates of professional memory and the anxieties of an unknown future are recasting England's past in the twenty-first century quite as powerfully as they did in the days when whigs supposedly expired and modernism beckoned. For we, too, have our ghosts; we, too, our intimations.

Bibliographical note

If historiography is not the same thing as bibliography, as this book has argued, it undoubtedly concerns itself with hundreds, sometimes thousands, of publications. To that extent and for that reason it seems disproportionate to present once more books contained in the footnote references, which are the best places to look for the primary printed sources taken to be significant here. Index entries in bold type indicate where the best starting points are to be found in those references in relation to any particular historian, both for biography and bibliography. But it will not have escaped readers that many of the references here have been taken from collections of unprinted archives and it may be helpful to compile an alphabetical list of the more relevant ones with their current locations:

Baxter MSS	Papers of J. H. Baxter, St Andrews University Library, Scotland
Browning MSS	Papers of Oscar Browning, Library of King's College, Cambridge
Bryant MSS	Papers of Sir Arthur Bryant, Library of the Centre for War Studies, King's College, London
Butler MSS	Papers of J. R. M. Butler, Trinity College, Cambridge
Butterfield MSS	Papers of Sir Herbert Butterfield, Cambridge University Library
Cam MSS	Papers of Helen Cam, Library of Girton College, Cambridge
Cambridge University Library Add MSS	Papers of Lord Acton, M. M. Postan, Eileen Power
Chambers MSS	Papers of J. D. Chambers, Nottingham University Library

Clark MSS	Papers of G. N. Clark, Bodleian Library, Oxford
Coulton MSS	Papers of G. G. Coulton, Library of St John's College, Cambridge
Edwards MSS	Papers of Sir Goronwy Edwards, National Library of Wales, Aberystwyth
Elton MSS	Papers of G. R. Elton, Royal Historical Society, University College, London
Ensor MSS	Papers of Sir Robert Ensor, Bodleian Library, Oxford
Finberg MSS	Papers of H. P. R. Finberg, Department of Local History, University of Leicester
Fisher MSS	Papers of H. A. L. Fisher, Bodleian Library, Oxford
Grant MSS	Papers of A. J. Grant, Brotherton Library, Leeds
Hayes MSS	Papers of Carlton Hayes, Columbia University Library, New York
Horn MSS	Papers of D. B. Horn, Edinburgh University Library
Hoskins MSS	Papers of W. G. Hoskins, Department of Local History, University of Leicester
Jenkins MSS	Papers of Claude Jenkins, Lambeth Palace Library, London
Liddell Hart MSS	Papers of Basil Liddell Hart, Library of the Centre for War Studies, King's College, London
Namier MSS	Papers of Sir Lewis Namier, John Rylands Library, Manchester
Notestein MSS	Papers of Wallace Notestein, Yale University Library, New Haven, CT
Oakeshott MSS	Papers of Michael Oakeshott, BLPES, London School of Economics and Political Science
Plumb MSS	Selection from the uncatalogued papers of J. H. Plumb, Cambridge University Library
Pollard MSS	Papers of Albert Pollard, London University Library
Potter MSS	Papers of G. R. Potter, Sheffield University Library
Round MSS	Papers of J. H. Round, London University Library

Stenton MSS	Papers of F. M. and Doris Stenton, Reading University Library
Sutherland MSS	Papers of Dame Lucy Sutherland, Bodleian Library, Oxford
Sykes MSS	Papers of Norman Sykes, Library of Emmanuel College, Cambridge
Tanner MSS	Papers of J. R. Tanner, Library of St John's College, Cambridge
Tawney MSS	Papers of R. H. Tawney, BLPES, London School of Economics and Political Science
Tout MSS	Papers of T. F. Tout, John Rylands Library, Manchester
Webster MSS	Papers of Sir Charles Webster, BLPES, London School of Economics and Political Science

Secondary accounts of English historiography for this period take far less time to compose; indeed, this book has partly been written to satisfy a manifest need in this area. The now-dated study by J. R. Hale, *The Evolution of British Historiography from Bacon to Namier* (London: Macmillan, 1967), still provides good background. Christopher Parker's two volumes on English historiography (*The English Historical Tradition since 1850* (Edinburgh: John Donald, 1990) and *The English Idea of History from Coleridge to Collingwood* (Aldershot: Ashgate, 2000)) give an overview, though one with which this book has taken issue. For the whigs themselves the most penetrating study is P. B. M. Blaas, *Continuity and Anachronism: Parliamentary and Constitutional Development in Whig Historiography and in the Anti-Whig Reaction between 1890 and 1930* (The Hague: Nijhof, 1978), which is critically reviewed here in chapter 4 (pp. 95–6). Particular strands of the argument offered in *Modernizing England's Past* have their historians. For the economic side, the work of N. B. Harte offers signposts, especially his *The Study of Economic History: Collected Inaugural Lectures 1893–1970* (London: Frank Cass, 1971). Imperial historiography has benefited from the concluding volume of the *Oxford History of the British Empire, vol. v: Historiography*, edited by Robin W. Winks (Oxford: Oxford University Press, 1999). The university context of historical work is introduced from different directions in Peter R. H. Slee, *Learning and a Liberal Education: the Study of Modern History in the Universities of Oxford, Cambridge and Manchester, 1800–1914* (Manchester: Manchester University Press, 1986) and Reba Soffer, *Discipline and Power: the University, History, and the Making of an English*

Elite (Stanford, CA: Stanford University Press, 1994). Comparative insights abound in volume III of *The History of the University in Europe*, edited by Walter Rüegg (Cambridge: Cambridge University Press, 2004) and in studies of individual institutions in England. For American perspectives the well-known account of Peter Novick, *That Noble Dream: the 'Objectivity Question' and the American Historical Profession* (Cambridge: Cambridge University Press, 1988), remains invaluable. William Palmer also offers transatlantic insights in his *Engagement with the Past: the Lives and Works of the World War II Generation of Historians* (Lexington: University Press of Kentucky, 2001).

Very often, however, one has to rely on biographical approaches in the absence of synthetic studies. Among recent biographies of the historians covered here one should certainly mention G. R. Elton on *F. W. Maitland* (London: Weidenfeld, 1986), David Cannadine on *G. M. Trevelyan: a Life in History* (London: Fontana, 1993), Maxine Berg on *A Woman in History: Eileen Power 1889–1940* (Cambridge: Cambridge University Press, 1996), Linda Colley on *Lewis Namier* (London: Weidenfeld, 1989) and C. T. McIntire, *Herbert Butterfield: Historian as Dissenter* (New Haven, CT: Yale University Press, 2004). Obituaries in the *Proceedings of the British Academy* sometimes throw light, albeit a roseate one, and in the late 1990s two biographical encyclopaedias provided a range of coverage previously unobtainable: D. R. Woolf (ed.), *A Global Encyclopaedia of World History* (2 vols., New York: Garland, 1998) and Kelly Boyd (ed.), *Encyclopaedia of Historians and Historical Writing* (2 vols., Chicago: Fitzroy Dearborn, 1999). Three resources available on-line also deserve inclusion. The new *Oxford Dictionary of National Biography* provides both a biographical account of a major historian and also a guide to primary and secondary bibliography in respect of many of the leading names mentioned in this book. The *Times Literary Supplement*'s on-line archive allows searching for and retrieval of reviews and articles, often with a helpful *curriculum vitae* of the reviewer, and provides a second line of attack. *Historical Abstracts* on-line, finally, permits sophisticated searching for recent secondary material and is especially valuable in tracing periodical articles.

Index

Entries containing biographical or bibliographical information have been printed in bold type to help readers find their way among the many names listed here. In order to make the length manageable, entries for persons other than English historians have been kept to a minimum. The central themes of the book may be tracked through the entries for 'whig interpretation of history' and 'Modernism'.